THE
WOLVES
AT THE DOOR

THE
WOLVES
AT THE DOOR
THE TRUE STORY OF AMERICA'S GREATEST FEMALE SPY

JUDITH L. PEARSON

THE LYONS PRESS
Guilford, Connecticut
An imprint of The Globe Pequot Press

The Lyons Press is an imprint of The Globe Pequot Press.

Printed in the United States of America

10 9 8 7 6 5 4 3 2 1

Library of Congress Cataloging-in-Publication Data

Pearson, Judith, 1953–
    Wolves at the door : the true story of America's greatest female spy / Judith L. Pearson.
    p. cm.
    Includes bibliographical references and index.
    ISBN 1-59228-762-X (trade cloth)
    1. Goillot, Virginia, 1906-1982.   2. Spies—United States—Biography.   3. Intelligence officers—United States—Biography.   4. World War, 1939–1945—Secret service—United States.   5. World War, 1939–1945—Underground movements—France.   I. Title.
UB271.U52G6 2005
940.54'8673'092—dc22

                                                                    2005020783

*This book is dedicated to the men and women
whose bravery, sacrifices, and vision in the little-known world of espionage
turned the course of a world war.*

This is no time for ease and comfort.
It is the time to dare and endure.

—*Winston Churchill*

CONTENTS

ACKNOWLEDGMENTS

VIRGINIA HALL WAS ONCE ASKED why she never told her story. Her reply was that she was never asked. Unfortunately she died before I had the chance to ask her. But there were a great many individuals who were available to ask questions of, and whose knowledge and memories made this book all the richer. This is but a brief token of my appreciation.

In the United States, my thanks to Virginia Hall's niece, Lorna Catling; at the National Archives in College Park, MD, Larry McDonald and John Taylor; at the CIA Museum, Toni Highly; at the International Spy Museum, Amanda Abrell; at the Chambon Foundation, Pierre Sauvage; former OSS members Réné Défourneaux, Fisher Howe, Geoffry Jones, Robert Kehoe, Tom McGuire, Elizabeth McIntosh, and General Jack Singlaub, as well as the members of the OSS Society; also Professor Arthur Layton Funk and Maia Wechsler.

In Great Britain, a tip of the hat to Clive and Mary Bassett, Leslie Fernandez, John Harding, Delphine Isaman, Steven Kippax, and M.R.D. Foot.

In France, my appreciation to Serge and Michelle Blandin, Gérard Bollon, Gabriel Eyraud, Serge Fayol, Annik Flaud, Jean Lebrat, Jacqueline Pery d'Alincourt, and Germaine Tillion.

No book would be possible without a dedicated agent and a hardworking editor and I'm fortunate to have both. Thanks to Peter Rubie, who is not only my agent, but my friend. And many thanks to my highly knowledgeable editor, Jay McCullough.

This book's shape was aided by my dear and patient writing pals: Cindy Goyette, Wanda McLaughlin, Val Neiman, Gary Ponzo, and Rich Schooler. Your attention to detail is always a marvel to me.

And finally, a great big thank you is due my husband, who patiently endured dozens of history programs and movies, my middle-of-the-night brainstorms, and frequent dinner conversations that centered solely on World War II. He still manages to be my biggest fan and I love him for it.

—JUDITH L. PEARSON

TEMPE, ARIZONA

JULY 2005

MARCH 1944

THE OLD WOMAN BENT HER GRAY HEAD against the frigid wind blowing in from the English Channel as she struggled along the rocky Brittany seaboard. The French province had 750 miles of coastline, all of it inclement during the month of March. And on this particular March day in 1944, the wind seemed set on toppling her over. She was determined to stay her course, however, and shuffled on.

The old man traveling with her also struggled. He appeared less steady than she was and occasionally took her arm to regain his footing. It was obvious from his gait, even to the most casual observer, that his left leg caused him pain. To make matters worse, the wooden sabots they wore were not suitable shoes for hiking along such a rutted road.

Each carrying a battered suitcase, they struggled against the cold wind for a little more than five miles before they finally arrived at their destination: the city of Morlaix. There, the elderly couple made their way to the railroad station and purchased two second-class tickets for Paris. When the time came to depart, they sat in adjacent seats, her bulky woolen skirts taking up a great deal of room on both sides. The train ride took nearly six hours, and it was late when they arrived at the Montparnasse station in the southwestern part of the city.

Paris looked nothing like it did when the old woman had been there on a previous visit. That had been in the spring of 1940 when national spirit ran high and the *tricolore* flew proudly from many buildings. Then, even the spring sun had made an effort at encouragement, shining through the smoke

1

of burning structures and exploding shells. The French army was fighting furiously to repel the powerful advancing Nazi forces. Under the leadership of seventy-two-year-old General Maxime Weygand, the French had hastily prepared defenses. The old woman had done her part for the war effort too, transporting wounded French soldiers as an ambulance driver.

The German onslaught continued, and just before the invaders dealt their sledgehammer blow on June 5, the old woman had left the city. The French line soon crumbled and by June 14, Paris was declared an "open city," a request to the enemy to cease firing upon it. On the twenty-first, Hitler himself was at Compiègne, 80 kilometers outside the capital and the precise spot where the Germans had been forced to surrender to the French at the close of World War I. The Führer had malevolently chosen the same location to dictate his harsh terms for this surrender.

It was now almost four years later. Blackout curtains kept the "City of Lights" in the dark. Signs of war were everywhere—burned-out buildings, abandoned military vehicles, looted shops. But nowhere was the war more apparent than on the faces of the passersby the old couple encountered on the streets. Fear and mistrust, borne out of the hell of brutal control under the Nazis, was common among French citizens.

A few among them were oblivious to the condition of their beautiful city. They pranced by, dressed in furs, their pampered poodles on satin leashes. They were the collaborators—the kept women of the Nazi officers.

The old woman did not feel fear. Rather, the ravages of war that had destroyed the city repulsed her. The farther she and the old man trudged, the more that repulsion festered into anger and determination. She drew her shabby valise closer in an unconscious effort to guard its precious contents.

Despite their appearances, the feeble, elderly couple's true identities couldn't have been further removed from their current personae. He was Henry Laussucq, code-named Aramis, a sixty-two-year-old American agent of the Office of Strategic Services (OSS). She was Virginia Hall, code-named Diane, the accomplished, thirty-eight-year-old spy who had built a reputation among colleagues and enemies alike while working with the British Special Operations Executive (SOE). Now also a member of the OSS, Hall was returning to France despite a price on her head and a Nazi pledge to "find and destroy her." Together with other OSS agents, they were to assist the newly formed French Forces of the Interior in coordinating Resistance efforts.

The couple's elaborate disguises had been created out of a necessity to camouflage Hall's more recognizable features. She had dyed her soft brown hair a shade of dirty gray and pulled it into a tight bun, giving her young face a severe appearance. Then she hid it all under a frayed babushka. She disguised her slender figure under peplums and full skirts, topped with large woolen blouses and a shabby oversized sweater, to give her a look of stoutness. Her most identifiable feature, however, the limp caused by her artificial left leg, couldn't be eliminated. But it could be altered. An accomplished actress, Hall taught herself to walk with a shuffle, a gait suitable for a woman of her assumed age.

The couple spent the night at a safe house, resting and enjoying a fairly substantial meal, considering the scarcity of food in Paris. The next morning, they made their way to the Saint-Lazare train station, passing numerous Nazi soldiers who paid them little, if any, attention. What, after all, would be the purpose of harassing an impoverished, elderly French couple? Still, Hall's heart skipped a beat at each encounter; a combination of trepidation, knowing the fate awaiting her should she be caught, and anticipation, knowing the damage her work would wreak on the Nazi war machine.

Their train journey southward to the city of Crozant took a little over two hours. After walking another mile to a nearby village, they located a farmhouse belonging to Eugène Lopinat. M. Lopinat was not a declared member of the growing French Resistance, but neither was he a Nazi sympathizer. The Resistance had chosen him for his reputation of being short on conversation and asked him to find the old woman lodging. He had chosen a one-room cottage he owned at the opposite end of the village from his farmhouse, a shack with no running water or electricity.

Aramis had orders to install himself in Paris and departed soon after Hall settled into her cottage. She was glad to be free of him. She thought he talked too much and was somewhat indiscreet, two qualities that could bring a quick and painful end to an OSS agent.

In exchange for rent, Hall was to work at Lopinat's farmhouse cooking meals for the farmer's family, taking their cows to pasture in the morning, and retrieving them each evening. It was then that Hall's real work began. The suitcase she had carried since landing in Brittany contained a Type 3 Mark II transceiver. Hall used the set to transmit messages to the London OSS office, giving coordinates of large fields she had located during the day while moving Lopinat's cows to and from pasture. The fields were to serve as parachute drops for agents and supplies in support of the French Resistance. The work carried high risks. Hall had to be vigilant of Nazi direction finders, instruments used to zero in on radio transmissions. She would need to relocate quickly if it became apparent that the Gestapo was moving in.

During the day, Hall kept the worn suitcase and its valuable contents hidden in the loft of her cottage. Its location would be imperceptible to a casual observer, but she didn't expect visitors. Trained Gestapo agents, however, would tear the cottage apart for even the slightest suspicion of collaboration with the Resistance. Each time Hall returned from her day with the Lopinats and their cows, she carefully surveyed all sides of the cottage from a distance to make certain she would not be walking into a trap. For several weeks, all seemed secure.

Hall's feeling of security came to an abrupt end. Making her way through town to the Lopinat farmhouse one morning, she saw a small crowd gathered. Curious, she shuffled toward them until an appalling tableau came into view. Three men and a woman, all dead, hung from iron fence posts, spiked through the neck. The Nazi soldiers who stood guard over the grisly scene held the villagers at bay with their rifles, insisting that the bodies remain as a reminder to all who dared resist the Führer.

That night, Hall sent her last message to London from the little cottage. Its meaning would be understood by the few with a need to know: "THE WOLVES ARE AT THE DOOR."

4

1

ALTERED COURSE

TO WALK THE STREETS OF SMYRNA was to exploit all of the senses. The ears were assaulted with the whine of *kemence* violins, the shouts of children at play, the horns of impatient motorists, the muezzin calling the faithful to prayer. The pungent odor of roasting lamb filled every breath, while dust from the narrow streets parched the throat. Strings of drying laundry waved from buildings like semaphore signals and colorful rugs brightened even the darkest thresholds. This was Turkey—a paradise of sun, sea, mountains, and lakes; a land of historic treasures and mystery.

On this day, Friday, December 8, 1933, a crisp winter sun reigned high in the sky, with temperatures pleasant in the midfifties. The weather reminded twenty-seven-year-old Virginia Hall of an early fall day in her native state of Maryland. And in Turkey, as it would have been in Maryland, it was a perfect day for a hunt. While most of Virginia's days were consumed with clerking duties at the American Consulate in the coastal city of Smyrna, her spare time allowed her to pursue her passions, which included horseback riding and hunting.

Virginia had learned to handle firearms at an early age from her father and had spent many summer days hunting birds and small animals on the family's 110-acre Maryland estate, Box Horn Farm. Never one to shy away from the slightest challenge, Virginia grew up a tomboy in every sense of the word. At five foot seven, she was taller than most of the other girls in her class at school. She was slender and pretty, with high cheekbones and a determined chin highlighting her face. Her soft, brown hair fell in natural

5

waves, and her eyes, clear, bright and deep brown, never caused anyone she encountered to think twice about where she stood on an issue.

W. Perry George, the American consul in Smyrna and Virginia's boss, considered the consulate lucky to have her on staff. In his 1933 annual efficiency report, he described Virginia as "absolutely reliable as to honesty and truthfulness" and having a "good sense of responsibility." And while he said her typing was not always accurate and she was somewhat absentminded, he reported that she was "very conscientious and helpful with a charming personality." For her part, Virginia considered her position at the consulate in Smyrna one step closer to her dream, that of becoming a Foreign Service officer.

Plus, the city of Smyrna rendered many of the facets that had always been important in Virginia's life. She was an avid reader. Smyrna was the birthplace of Homer, the father of dramatic literature. She greatly appreciated nature, and the city's mild climate made flora and fauna plentiful. The constant, refreshing sea breezes tempered the summer sun's heat and kept the winters mild. Virginia loved any kind of outdoor activities, and she was in her element in Smyrna. The city was situated at the head of a long, narrow gulf dotted with ships and yachts. Fishing and hunting were readily available to anyone willing to devote a few hours of leisure time.

Virginia arrived in Turkey in April 1933. Her job at the consulate gave her the opportunity to brush shoulders with Turkish diplomats and statesmen. Although the post had no great importance other than for goodwill purposes in view of the political and business calm of the time, Americans had heavily invested in business and education in Turkey. If anything was to disrupt this element of calm, the consulate would be extremely active helping to protect those interests.

Smyrna was in remarkable contrast to the atmosphere Virginia had left in the United States. The Great Depression was raging and had been the topic of the newly elected president's inaugural address the month before her departure. Virginia had listened on the radio, along with some sixty million other Americans, as Franklin Delano Roosevelt spoke to the rain-soaked crowd at the Capitol.

> So, first of all, let me assert my firm belief that the only thing we
> have to fear is fear itself—nameless, unreasoning, unjustified

terror which paralyzes needed efforts to convert retreat into advance. In every dark hour of our national life a leadership of frankness and vigor has met with that understanding and support of the people themselves which is essential to victory.

They had been grim days. One of every four American workers was unemployed, thirteen million in all, and almost every bank was closed. And since the United States had never before faced such a disaster, there were no federal programs to address the needs of the populace.

Roosevelt intrigued Virginia. He had been raised in a world of privilege and wealth, with the patina and optimism of his class. It was a world not unlike the one Edwin Hall had provided for his family. Yet Roosevelt was able to sympathize with the downtrodden and meant to put the full force of his executive powers into smashing their economic despair. He gave Virginia the impression that he would be a man of action, something his predecessor, Herbert Hoover, had not been.

Nor was Roosevelt a stranger to suffering, though of a different kind from what now gripped the United States. And it was this fact that most fascinated Virginia about the man. In the summer of 1921, at the age of thirty-nine, Franklin Roosevelt had been stricken with poliomyelitis. Polio had left him partially paralyzed, able to stand only with the aid of heavy metal braces locked around his legs. Virginia found his indomitable courage remarkable; he refused to be held back by his disability. Rather, he was intent upon carrying on his life and achieving his goals.

BUT THE AMERICAN ECONOMY was a world away in Virginia's thoughts on this particular day in December. She and the four other members of her hunting party were going after snipe in a bog about fifteen miles from the city. The group consisted of two fellow consulate workers, Maria and Todd; Todd's wife, Elaine; and Murat, a Turkish man from Virginia's neighborhood. The five met at Todd and Elaine's house around noon, each bringing a contribution for their picnic lunch. The day had been carefully planned. Snipe are more prevalent during the late afternoon hours, so the party had decided to begin their excursion with lunch and then hike through the wet meadow in the afternoon in search of their prey. In truth, their camaraderie was far more important than whether they actually shot any birds.

Their mood was lighthearted all the way into the country. They had their picnic and packed the remains in the trunk of Todd's car, then donned their hunting clothes and took their firearms out of cases. Virginia was using her favorite gun, a twelve-gauge shotgun that had once been part of her father's collection. Todd complimented her on it.

At this point, Maria begged Virginia to tell the others about her family. The Halls, Maria exaggerated, were practically the most fascinating clan on America's entire eastern seaboard. Virginia didn't think her family history was that spellbinding, but the group pleaded and Virginia obliged with tales of her legendary grandfather, Captain John Wesley Hall. At the age of nine, Hall had stowed away on one of his father's clipper ships. After a multiyear adventure at sea, he had saved enough money to buy his own ship and ultimately became very successful in the shipping industry and as an importer of Chinese goods.

Her father, taking a lesson from his own father, had built a successful business in real estate and movie houses. Virginia and her friends went to any movie they wanted to, absolutely free. She told her friends that although he had died very suddenly two years earlier and she missed him very much, she and her brother and mother still laughed about all the good times they'd had.

Virginia paused in her storytelling when they came to a wire fence, obviously constructed years before, as its condition now would neither keep anything in or out. One by one, Todd, Elaine, and Maria made their way over the fence until only Virginia and Murat were left. Virginia tucked her shotgun under her arm, leaving her hands free to negotiate the relatively slack top wire of the fence.

She would relive the next ten seconds many times in the coming months. As she lifted her right leg to climb over the fence, her left foot skidded slightly in the damp earth. The gun slipped from under her arm, its trigger catching on a fold of her hunting coat. The sound of her shotgun discharging started flocks of birds from the nearby trees. But no one in the hunting party noticed the feathered flurry. They were fixed in horror on Virginia's mangled left foot, her blood staining the tawny field grass beneath where she lay.

The ensuing ten minutes seemed to Virginia as though she were not part of the drama, but rather watching the scene unfold before her. She was quite certain she was conscious—and was later able to describe her friends'

8

actions, though their voices sounded to her as if someone had turned down the volume control on a radio. She wasn't really in pain at that point, rather her body felt wooden.

Marie, Todd, Elaine, and Murat had not had any formal first-aid training, but their quick actions most probably saved Virginia's life. They determined that a tourniquet was needed to halt the bleeding, so they tore off articles of their clothing to make one. They made a pillow for her head out of someone's hunting vest and covered her with a coat when she had begun to tremble from shock. A discussion ensued among them on the best way to get her to the car. In the end, they fashioned a stretcher with the remaining hunting coats and their now unloaded guns to carry her. Virginia was aware of arriving at the car before everything faded to black.

AMPUTATION OF LIMBS was a form of surgery that had been performed routinely on the battlefields of World War I. With no means for reconstruction and only sulfa drugs available as an antibiotic (penicillin was not put into general use until 1941), amputation was frequently a doctor's only choice to save his patient. Military medical books at the time state that although immediate amputation is not indicated in traumas caused by bullets, it is certainly necessary in cases of confirmed gangrene. It is also necessary when a limb is completely smashed or torn off by a large projectile or fragment. Virginia's injuries included both of these dim scenarios.

Because of the gun's proximity to her body, the shotgun pellets destroyed Virginia's foot. It caused extensive soft-tissue and bone damage. In addition, the wound had been badly contaminated by environmental material—fragments from her boot, the grass she fell on, the clothing her friends had used to cover her. By the time the very shaken group arrived at the hospital in Smyrna, more than an hour had passed since the accident, and infection had already begun to set in.

Although the utmost was done to treat Virginia's wound, there was no way to adequately manage the infection. Evidence of gangrene appeared and Dr. Lorrin Shepard, head of the Istanbul American Hospital, was rushed to Smyrna. He determined that a BK amputation, the removal of her leg below the knee, was the only course of action possible to save Virginia's life. As she was unconscious, Dr. Shepard was unable to discuss the situation with her. Nor was he willing to risk waiting for her to come to.

Even before word of the accident had reached her mother in Baltimore, Virginia Hall was being taken into the hospital's surgical ward, where her life would be changed forever. The surgeons waiting there would have been astounded had they known the patient lying before them would soon play an integral part in the greatest war the world has ever known.

2

FIRST STEPS

VIRGINIA FLOATED IN AND OUT of consciousness following her surgery. During her conscious moments, which early on were accompanied by nausea from the ether she'd been given during the amputation, she attempted to recreate the events that had brought her to the hospital. She remembered the hunting expedition and the fact that she'd been injured, but nearly everything after leaving the field was a blur. During a brief segment of consciousness she had asked about her leg and was told that it had been amputated as a result of the injury.

However, thinking about the drastic life changes that would now occur was not what consumed the hours. It was her torturous pain, a red-hot burning that spread from her left hip to the tips of her now absent left toes. A different position in the bed might have alleviated the torment, but her body was so weakened from the surgery she was unable to gather the strength to move. Dr. Shepard was attempting to manage Virginia's pain with a steady dose of morphine and this brought another complication: the vivid dreams and delusions common to those on the powerful drug. The combination of excruciating agony and morphine-induced hallucinations even led Virginia to absurd thoughts of freedom from the misery through death.

From behind her mental haze, Virginia was completely unaware of the outstanding care she was receiving. Dr. Shepard and two American nurses watched her closely the first twenty-four hours to be sure that there was no more evidence of gangrene. Additional infection would mean further surgery and an above-the-knee amputation, which would leave a far less desirable result. The shorter leg stump would be more difficult to fit with a workable prosthesis.

On the second night after surgery, a most unusual event unfolded in Virginia's hospital room. She lay alone in a semiconscious state, when she had the sense that someone had approached the side of her bed. Standing there was her father, Edwin Hall. Virginia was flabbergasted. Her father had died in Baltimore two years earlier. She had watched the coffin containing his body being lowered into the ground. Yet there he was, smiling down at her, wearing a dapper gray business suit just as he had done almost every day of his life.

The next thing Virginia was aware of was her father lifting her out of the hospital bed. She floated in his arms to a nearby chair where they sat down together, with her on his lap as if she were a small child.

"I know you're in a great deal of pain, Dindy," Edwin Hall said. The nickname brought a faint smile to Virginia's lips. When she was born, her brother, John, two years older, had been unable to say Virginia. The closest he could come was "Dindy" and the name had stuck.

"And I know that it seems as though your pain is endless," her father continued, rocking her gently as he spoke. "Can you be strong, Dindy? Your mother needs you very much. She's terribly upset by the news of your accident. If you don't survive, dear little Dindy, she'll be heartbroken.

"But if, Dindy, it's more than you can bear, I'll return for you tomorrow night to take you away from the pain."

Virginia felt herself floating in her father's arms again back to her bed. She remembered nothing else from that night, neither seeing nor hearing anything more until the next morning when the nurses rustling around her room woke her. Through parched lips, she asked them about her visitor the previous night.

"Why, my dear," the older of the two nurses told her, "there was no one here. No visitors are allowed after hours."

But the memory of her father's visit was powerfully vivid. The man had looked like Edwin Hall and had sounded like him. He had even smelled like the elder Hall, a mixture of pipe smoke and bay rum. Virginia would swear the rest of her life that he had been with her that night.

For the moment she let the subject drop. But from that point on, Virginia's recovery would proceed at an amazing velocity. Her father had asked her to fight and that was exactly what she intended to do. Marshaling the same kind of resolute spirit he and her grandfather had been known for, she became determined to survive and to live as normal a life as anyone else. After all, President Roosevelt had overcome his handicap; there was no reason why she couldn't do the same. And her dream of a Foreign Service career would merely be delayed.

AS THE DAYS PASSED and Virginia's strength grew, she had time to reflect on her life thus far. Her fascination with the world had begun at an early age. She made her first trip to Europe in 1909 at the age of three. It was a time when it was not unusual for wealthy families, like the Halls, to take an extended holiday to see the world's sights. They traveled by ship in elegant staterooms, ate fine foods, and celebrated the good life at sea. Once in Europe, the same privileged lifestyle prevailed. And although she was very young, Virginia soaked up the exotic cultures like a tiny sponge.

The family made another trip to Europe while Virginia was on vacation from her studies at Baltimore's Roland Park Country School. This trip gave her the opportunity to practice the foreign languages she excelled in. And the seed of an idea for her future began to germinate.

"The only way for a woman to get ahead in the world," Virginia told her high school chums at graduation in 1924, "is to get an education." They loved her and knew her well enough to describe her perfectly in the senior yearbook.

> The "Donna Juanita" of the class now approaches. Though professing to hold Man in contempt, Dindy is yet his closest counterpart—in costume. She is, by her own confession, cantankerous and capricious, but in spite of it all we would not do without her; for she is our class president, the editor-in-chief of this book, and one of the mainstays of the basketball and hockey teams. She has been acclaimed the most original of our class, and she lives up to her reputation at all times. The one thing to expect from Dindy is the unexpected.

So while her friends were planning marriages and families, Virginia was planning for college and a career. She went first to Radcliff and then Barnard College, but the classes held no spark for her. What was lacking, she decided, was the romance and intensity of an education in Europe.

Edwin Hall and his wife, Barbara, were very modern thinkers. Sending their young, single, unchaperoned daughter to Europe to pursue her studies was not at all exceptional to their way of thinking, even if, in 1926, it was to others. So later that year, Virginia arrived in France and enrolled at the Sorbonne and the École des Services Politiques in Paris. A year later, she was accepted at the Konsular Akademie in Vienna, where she graduated in 1929. And while the idea of becoming involved in Foreign Service had been a small glimmer back in high school, Virginia was now equipped with skills she hoped the State Department would find useful.

She first applied for a consular position in October of 1929 at the age of twenty-three, while a graduate student at American University in Washington, DC. She listed herself as being in perfect physical condition and fluent in French and German, with a fair knowledge of Italian. The ensuing months merged into years as the wheels of government churned slowly. Every aspect of Virginia's life was carefully researched. She provided reference letters from attorneys and bankers, business associates of her father's. Even the Halls' neighbors were interviewed, giving Mrs. Hall cause to wonder if the job her daughter was applying for was more dangerous than she had previously thought.

Finally, on July 27, 1931, Virginia began her first job with the State Department at the American Embassy in Warsaw, Poland. Her job as clerk earned her an annual salary of $2,000. Ambassador John Willye thought highly of her, reporting that she had a "prepossessing personality," and was "adaptable, alert and interested in her work." Never having had any previous work experience and no formal training in typing or stenography, her performance of clerical duties was a little lacking. Nonetheless, Ambassador Willye felt she had "no lack of service spirit" and her "co-operation with others on staff [was] excellent."

Virginia immersed herself in life in Warsaw, embracing its food, sights, and customs. Furthermore, the city was not just the city of her first job. It was also the city in which she fell in love. His name was Emil Stanisz. He was a junior officer in the Polish army, the son of a decorated Great War veteran who had died on the battlefield. Emil and his four younger siblings lived with their mother in an apartment not far from the Vistula River, which ran through the center of Warsaw. One of Emil's assignments included escorting Polish officials to the American Embassy and it was there that he and Virginia met.

Virginia found herself looking for tasks that would allow her to hover near the embassy's entrance on days when Polish officials were expected. Emil spoke very little English, and Virginia was not yet adept at Polish, but they discovered they were both fluent in German. What began as a friendship flowered. Their dates included strolls through Old Town Warsaw, on cobbled streets amid Gothic and Baroque buildings. They drank *kawa*, strong Polish coffee, at sidewalk cafés and had long discussions about world affairs.

Virginia would never have guessed it was possible to feel so many emotions simultaneously: the warmth and comfort of a companion, and the heady thrill that washed over her each time she saw Emil. It had to be love.

But, after a glorious Christmas season during which they were inseparable, Virginia could see strain on Emil's face. As 1933 dawned, he became more reserved with her. Finally, one snowy Sunday afternoon in January, he came to her flat wearing an extremely grave look.

Emil explained that ever since his father had died, his mother relied heavily on him; he was the eldest of her children and the family's major wage earner. His mother's health was poor, he told Virginia—a fact compounded by her fears that if Emil fell in love, married, and left his mother, no one would care for her in her old age.

Virginia understood completely. She had worried about her own widowed mother. But, she pointed out to Emil, between the two of them, and all his brothers and sisters, his mother would be very well cared for.

Emil shook his head. Each time he talked of Virginia or their future, his mother would suddenly become faint and be bedridden for days. She wouldn't see anyone, even a doctor. And she told Emile just the mention of "the American" made her heart race unnaturally. He feared that one day her heart would just stop beating.

Virginia suddenly realized that it was not the mother's heart that was in question, but rather Emil's. His mother was simply not pleased at the prospect of her son marrying an American.

They discussed it a few more times, but the conclusion remained the same. Emil said he'd be unable to continue seeing Virginia until his mother's health improved. The truth was so obvious: the elder woman's health would never improve as long as "the American" was in the picture.

This was a first for Virginia. In every aspect of her life, whatever she had wanted, she had achieved through hard work and determination. But in this matter, resolve would prove useless. Disappointment, helplessness, and a broken heart brought Virginia to what she thought would be the lowest point in her life.

Remaining in Warsaw simply became too painful. So Virginia sent a request to the State Department asking for a transfer in posts. As it happened, the consulate in Smyrna was in need of a clerk. Virginia's final thoughts as her train pulled out of the Warsaw station in April 1933 were of how life-altering her break with Emil had been. Of course she had no way of knowing that by the end of that year, her life would be drastically altered yet again.

BY MID-JANUARY 1934, Dr. Shepard felt Virginia was well enough to be transferred to the American Hospital in Istanbul. And she was pronounced fit for travel back to the United States in late February. As Virginia left Turkey, it wasn't only the anticipation of returning home that filled her thoughts. Although she was looking forward to seeing her family and home after living abroad nearly three years, her thoughts were consumed with the day she could resume her duties with the State Department.

Virginia's destination was the family's Box Horn Farm, which sat on 110 of the most lush acres in Maryland. The tranquil, rolling hills encompassed woods and orchards, a small stream-fed pond, and miles of riding trails. The barn was home to chickens, cows, goats, and horses, and the farmyard had been jail and infirmary to myriad wild animals, captured or saved, depending on one's point of view.

It was a magical place to grow up. Virginia and her brother learned to hunt, catch and clean their own fish, and milk cows. Virginia thought nothing of de-scenting a skunk or collecting snakes. In fact, her reptile companions accompanied her to school numerous times. On one occasion, Virginia arrived with what her teacher thought was a pretty new bracelet. On further investigation, she realized the "bracelet" was moving, and to her horror, realized that it was a snake.

The Hall family maintained a residence in Baltimore for the purposes of Edwin's business. But whenever they could, they traveled the twenty miles to Box Horn. The stately three-story house had a mansard roof and five bedrooms. There was running water but no central heating. The Halls relied on fireplaces and woodstoves for comfort in the cold months. Attached to the large kitchen were a laundry, storage room, and a small dairy, where milk from the farm's cows was processed for their consumption. The living room and library were filled with books to satisfy the Halls' keen appetite for reading, and the dining room cabinets displayed an impressive collection of silver and fine china.

Box Horn Farm's grounds included a sun-dappled tennis court, a small kitchen garden for the family's use, lush acres planted in soy beans, and a house for the tenant farmer who acted as caretaker.

From the moment Virginia arrived at Box Horn, she was eager to begin making preparations for an artificial leg. The idea of adapting to a prosthesis was not the least bit daunting to her. She figured it probably had the same kind of learning curve as a foreign language or any other skill she had mastered; it would simply require practice for perfection.

But before she could be fit with an artificial leg, it was necessary for the swelling in her stump to abate. To speed that process, her leg had been wrapped and massaged while she was in Turkey. In addition, the skin at the end of the stump also had to develop beyond just a postoperative scar. Because it would be in constant contact with the prosthetic leg, tender, new skin would not be able to tolerate the constant friction.

The artificial leg itself began as a block of wood slightly thicker than her own leg had been. A hole was bored into one end of the block and tapered exactly to fit and support the remainder of her left leg. A knee joint wasn't needed, as Virginia's own knee had been spared from amputation. Once a perfect fit was made at the contact point, the interior was varnished for smoothness. Then the rest of the block was hollowed out. When wearing the prosthesis, Virginia would don a "stump sock," a woolen sock that would pad her skin, reduce the friction of movement against the wood, and absorb perspiration.

Next, work began on the exterior. In preparation for a prosthesis, Dr. Shepard had taken careful measurements of Virginia's amputated leg and foot at the time of her surgery. These he sent to her doctors in Baltimore, who in turn made them available to the prosthetist.

A wooden foot was attached to the leg on an axis, giving it play. It had a rubber sole that would smooth out her gait as she walked. Once the leg had been sufficiently shaped and sanded by hand, horsehide was stretched on it and the seven-pound limb was sealed and painted. A leather corset was attached to the top of the prosthesis, which laced up Virginia's thigh. Elastic straps fastened to either side of the corset and extended up to her waist where they attached to a belt. The leg took two weeks to construct at a cost of $125.

Learning to manipulate the leg was a bit more challenging than Virginia had expected. She had to learn to stabilize her knee with her weight and to move the leg with her hip. That part was not a problem. What was most difficult was learning where her new "foot" was in relationship to space. Because she had no feeling, she did not have a sense of where the foot was at any given time.

A physiotherapist helped Virginia with strengthening her body and balancing on her new leg. She began by "walking" with crutches, then graduated to a cane, and finally managed steps on her own with a swinging gait. By early fall of 1934, she wrote a letter to the secretary of state's executive assistant, Hugh Cumming, requesting to be reinstated to her former position at an embassy or consulate.

"Any post in Spain, preferably Malaga or Seville, would be my choice," her letter read. "I want the opportunity of learning Spanish and am interested in the economic future of Spain."

The civil unrest in Spain at the time was not a concern to Virginia. As a matter of fact, she viewed it as an incredibly interesting time to be posted there. Her letter continued, "Second choice of post, Estonia; third choice, Peru."

Cumming responded soon afterward that they would be pleased to have Virginia back at work. She could be transferred to Venice, which, he said, should meet her "requirements from the standpoint of climate, etc. Unfortunately," Cumming continued, "there is at the moment no vacancy in Spain, Estonia or Peru, but I am having a note made of [your] preference for a post in one of those countries."

Virginia left Box Horn Farm soon after, bound for Venice, where she would begin work at the American Consulate on December 10. With no doubts in her mind, she was enthusiastic about picking up the career that had been so dramatically interrupted. But she could not have guessed what challenges lay ahead for the continent of Europe. Nor could she know that the ghastly accident she had just recovered from would lead her to a job far afield from her Foreign Service goal but with much greater rewards.

3

A VANISHED DREAM

VIRGINIA HALL FIRST HAD VISITED Venice, one of Europe's oldest and most elegant cities, with her family as a young child. Later, college history professors had painted vivid portraits of palaces, canals, and cathedrals. Now at the age of twenty-nine, she eagerly anticipated her assignment at the American Consulate that would allow her to work so closely to the heart and soul of Venice.

The consulate was impressive. Rich tapestries, opulent furniture, and draperies adorned the light and airy chambers. It had recently been renovated and redecorated under the auspices of the then American consul general, Terry Stewart. The decor reflected traditional Italian flavor, tempered with an American flair.

The new environment was very different from Virginia's previous post. In Smyrna, the offices had been woefully understaffed, while the Venice office had an ample number of employees, including a vice consul to lighten the workload of Consul General Stewart. The atmosphere was relaxed and very social. Virginia's work was similar to her duties in Smyrna. She preformed traditional clerking tasks, typing English correspondence, and handling the filing, postage, and notarials. She earned such a degree of Consul General Stewart's confidence with her attention to detail and overall effectiveness that during Vice Consul Charles Terry's occasional absences, Consul General Stewart assigned Virginia the various duties reserved for Foreign Service officers, including citizenship and passport work. The taste of life as a Foreign Service officer made Virginia even more determined to become a member of that private club.

ALTHOUGH WORKING ON BEHALF of the American government, Virginia and the other consulate employees were isolated from the thoughts and opinions of their compatriots. Immersed in a cocoon of foreign culture, they were unaware of the ideas, lifestyle, and trends being propagated on the opposite side of the Atlantic.

Barbara Hall sought to keep her daughter current on American developments via weekly letters. Knowing Virginia's tastes and interests intimately, Mrs. Hall filled each letter with intriguing stories and anecdotes.

In a letter sent in July 1935, Mrs. Hall covered the American sports scene. Virginia had been a tomboy as a child, holding her own playing the roughest games her older brother and his cronies conjured up. She never feared a physical challenge and never complained when she was the most bruised at the end.

"Babe Didrikson made her first appearance as a professional golfer a few weeks ago in Chicago at the Western Open Championship," Mrs. Hall wrote. "She's just twenty-two and can already out-drive any other woman golfer. She only needs to shore up her short game to be a real contender."

The letter continued. "One of the enclosed clippings will be of special interest to you, Dindy, given your current post." It was a *Time Magazine* story about a new Detroit prizefighter by the name of Joe Louis who had recently defeated the Italian heavyweight champ, Primo Carnera. Even though Carnera outweighed him by sixty pounds, the American had dropped the Italian in the sixth round.

Mrs. Hall's letter included entertainment news as well. Virginia had been interested in drama throughout her years in high school, too. She had been in the cast of every play produced at Roland Park Country Day School, and with no boys available, she often took on male roles. She even played a rogue pirate in one production, complete with a great deal of swashbuckling and swinging on ropes across the stage. Slipping into a new identity was great fun, even if it was only for a few hours.

"According to the *New York Post* last week," Mrs. Hall wrote, "Shirley Temple, Will Rogers and Clark Gable are the country's top three box office draws. Gable's new picture, *Mutiny on the Bounty*, has just arrived in Baltimore and I'm looking forward to seeing it."

Other letters Virginia received from home were of a far more serious nature. Mrs. Hall had heard a radio program discussing the mass exodus of Europeans, most bound for the United States.

"Some are Socialists and others simply feel they've offended the Nazis and might possibly be prosecuted for it in the not too distant future," Mrs. Hall wrote. "They don't feel safe remaining on the continent. What a grave injustice it is to force someone from their homes merely because of their beliefs. And despite news items like this, many Americans still view Hitler as a man with a comical mustache who really doesn't hold a position of political power."

Virginia found the last line from another enclosed *Time* magazine article very ominous. It was a quote from Italy's current Fascist leader, Benito Mussolini: "It was not Germany which lost the last war," Il Duce told the reporter, "it was Europe. The United States gained, Japan gained, Russia gained, but Europe lost its recuperative power, the vital force."

Like many of the Europeans around her, Virginia was growing more disturbed by the gathering political gloom that surrounded much of Europe in 1935. Missives and representatives bounced between Britain, France, Italy, and Germany, all with the intention of soothing ruffled bureaucratic feathers. And while the dictators of Italy and Germany strutted across the world stage like grand peacocks, vowing that their expansionist ideas were for the sole purpose of creating a better world, their actions were interpreted differently.

Such was the case with Italy's designs on the North African country and League of Nations member Ethiopia. Italy insisted that her interest in Ethiopia be viewed solely as a mission to abolish slavery and replace oppression. In reality, it was the perfect conquest. As Mussolini's dictatorship had smashed the middle class, degraded the working class, and all but bankrupted Italy's big business, Ethiopia would provide a place to send the unemployed and avail himself of the country's vastly undeveloped resources. By the spring of 1936, Ethiopia had become a part of the Italian Empire.

Once the invasion was complete, life at the American consulate in Venice became tenser. And Virginia had made no secret of her feelings about Europe's Fascist leaders. Now at the age of thirty, she had spent one-third of her life in Europe studying and working. She felt as much a part of the European continent as she did her own homeland. She knew the languages, customs, and geography of each of the countries she'd lived in. And she'd taken the time to get to know those whose lives crossed hers. It disturbed her that America wasn't taking a greater role in mediating the rising European conflicts.

A result of her outspokenness on the subject may have been the negative report she received on the consular review conducted during the summer of 1936. Mr. Huddle, the government reviewer, submitted this final inspection report with regard to Virginia:

> Virginia Hall is a clerk of . . . unbounded ambition, a lack of appreciation of her own limitations, and a most praiseworthy determination. She also lacks common sense and good judgement. She overcomes the physical disability . . . and this interferes in no way with her performance of duty . . . . She keeps up her spirits admirably. She is *not* good material for a career service because she lacks judgement, background, good sense and discriminatory powers. She also talks too much. She is a satisfactory enough clerk, and when I was at Venice, was working to Mr. Stewart's satisfaction.

Virginia was angry and humiliated. While most women of her time were content to allow the men around them to discuss politics and world affairs, she had learned at home to read and question everything. Mr. Huddle may have preferred women to be seen and not heard, but that was not in Virginia's personality. However, a personality such as hers came with consequences. This was evidently one of them. Virginia had fallen victim to a man and a bureaucracy who had no time for deviation from the norm.

Consul General Stewart's annual report somewhat took the sting off the consulate review. He reported that Virginia Hall's work was "marked by intelligence and understanding. . . . She has the capacity to develop into a good subordinate officer. She has a pleasing personality, shows proper discernment in her dealings with visitors and has no eccentricities."

Now the question was which of these two reports would have a greater influence on her future as a Foreign Service officer.

PRESIDENT GROVER CLEVELAND issued an executive order in 1895 regarding entrance to the Foreign Service. Potential candidates were required to pass two examinations, one written and the other oral, to measure an applicant's knowledge and understanding on a range of subjects deemed necessary for the position.

The written examination included essay questions about international law, arithmetic, modern history, resources and commerce of the United States, political and commercial geography, political economy, and American history and institutions. The oral examination was given in two parts. The first required that the candidate demonstrate a proficiency in a chosen foreign language and was scored in an objective manner. The second portion gave the State Department the opportunity to judge the applicant's ability to think on her feet. These answers by their very nature were highly subjective. Not many women applied for Foreign Service, and it was rumored that their scoring was often set to a much higher standard than that of their male counterparts.

Virginia had begun the process in December of 1929 when she first applied to take the Foreign Service examination. She presented herself at a Civil Service Commission examination room in Washington, DC, for the two-day written exam, and returned six weeks later for the oral portions.

Despite a warning in her acceptance letter stating that "it is essential that candidates be thoroughly prepared in all the subjects before taking the Foreign Service examination," Virginia felt her well-rounded education would sustain her. She was wrong. She failed to achieve the necessary average to be accepted. Some of her written scores were disastrous, including a 60 percent on the section entitled "Modern History (since 1850) of Europe, Latin America and the Far East." And while she rated a perfect score on the language portion of the oral exam, she only achieved a 70 percent on the second oral section.

Undeterred, she applied to take the examinations again on July 14 and 15, 1930. Her written scores improved immensely, but her oral scores were identical to those of the previous test. And again her combined scores were not up to the standards set for entrance to the Foreign Service.

By this time Virginia was in Warsaw. She took the written portion of the exam a third time in September 1932, but the questions for the oral portion of the test never arrived. Preoccupied with her relationship with Emil, Virginia did not pursue the matter.

Virginia was ready to complete the oral exam in Venice in 1937. Once again the questions didn't arrive. What came instead spelled the demise of Virginia's Foreign Service dreams.

In a letter to Consul General Stewart, Assistant Secretary of State Sumner Welles brought to light a stipulation for a Foreign Service career Virginia was unaware of:

> The regulation governing physical examinations to the Foreign Services prescribe that amputation of any portion of a limb, except fingers or toes . . . "is a cause for rejection, and it would not be possible for Miss Hall to qualify for entry into the Service under these regulations."

The duty of passing this information on to Virginia fell to Consul Stewart. He gave her the letter to read and tried to take on the job of supportive uncle. He told her he had admired her determination in applying for the Foreign Service and regretted this unfortunate conclusion to her quest.

Virginia felt as though all of the air had suddenly been sucked from the entire room. Her mind spun across the past dozen years. There had been losses. But the loss of Emil, her father, even her leg had been tolerable because of what was possible, because of the anticipation her goal offered. It was the one thing she believed could never be taken from her. It was the one thing she was certain would some day be a reality. Now that dream had vanished like a stone sinking to the bottom of a deep, dark well.

Consul Stewart gave Virginia the rest of the afternoon off. Once in her flat, she vented her disappointment, crying, sputtering, and yelling into pillows. Her leg had nothing to do with the decision, and she knew it. Of some fifteen hundred career Foreign Service officers, only six were women. Obviously she and others of her gender were not wanted or welcome, particularly if they refused to be wall flowers and preferred to hold and express their own opinions. Virginia's intellectual self told her that perhaps it was because of the economic hardships suffered by most American households. The Depression had made jobs scarce. Giving a woman a position meant that a male breadwinner with a family to support would not be hired. But her emotional self told her that the position had been put out of her reach because she was part of a gender often viewed as incapable of handling diplomacy and decision making.

Virginia didn't go quietly. Over the next twelve months, appeals were made on her behalf by Hall family contacts, including several to President

Roosevelt himself. Finally in the fall of 1938 Virginia wrote to then Assistant Secretary of State G. Howland Shaw. Her letter was a model of civility, belying her true feelings:

> When I applied for and received a position as clerk in the Foreign Service, nearly seven years ago, it was with the express intention of taking the examinations again, hoping that I might, in the meantime, convince the Foreign Service Personnel Board of my ability to handle the work and my sincerity in wishing to carry on with it as a career. Naturally when the Department in reply to my request . . . for designation to take the oral examination stated that I was not eligible on account of physical disability, I was bitterly disappointed.

In June 1938, Virginia transferred to the consulate in Tallin, Estonia, hoping that a change of venue might restimulate her interest in her work. But with no prospect for moving any farther up the State Department ladder, the pleasure she had once derived from consular work faded. She submitted her resignation in May 1939. Her exit paperwork gave her the option of all former State Department employees. She could "proceed to the United States at any time within one year after the effective date of resignation."

But for the first time in her life, Virginia's future was anything but certain. And at this point in time, her future career choice wasn't even on the government's drawing board.

4

THE BLITZKRIEG

VIRGINIA WENT TO PARIS after leaving Estonia. Although she had had the rare opportunity of seeing a great deal of the world in her thirty-three years, this city seemed the perfect choice. It was a location she dearly loved that held myriad fond memories from childhood journeys with her family and her college days. It was a place to clear her head and refocus after the unexpected and heartbreaking conclusion of her State Department career.

The tail end of spring 1939 greeted Virginia on her arrival in Paris. As May slid into June, and the Parisian summer began, solace washed over her. The quintessential French conventions, *bouquinistes* selling books and postcards at stands along the Seine, throaty French tunes pouring out of cabaret doors, and sidewalk cafés occupied from morning till night were so familiar. Paris always made Virginia think of the quote: "Every man has two countries, his own and France." She spent her days wandering the city and doing some freelance journalism for American newspapers, all the while contemplating her future.

And while she may have been focusing on the next chapter in her own life, Virginia was not oblivious to the rapidly changing political and social climate around her. Six months earlier, in November of 1938, while she was trying to reignite her enthusiasm for consular work in Estonia, shocking events had been unfolding in Germany. Adolph Hitler had been steadily enacting laws curtailing Jewish businesses and the Jewish lifestyle. The assassination of a German Embassy official in Paris by a Jewish youth on November 7 gave the Nazis a perfect excuse to further browbeat the Jews. The event became known as Kristallnacht.

The "Night of Broken Glass" was a two-day orgy of terror during which raging mobs in Germany, Austria, and the Sudetenland freely attacked Jews in the street, in their homes, and at their places of work and worship. Ninety-six Jews were killed and hundreds more injured. More than a thousand synagogues were burned. About seventy-five hundred Jewish businesses were destroyed. Cemeteries and schools were vandalized. Thirty thousand Jews were arrested and sent to concentration camps.

Following Kristallnacht, panicked German, Austrian, and Czech Jews flooded France, which had already been overwhelmed with refugees two years earlier as a result of the Spanish Civil War. Some of Virginia's new Parisian acquaintances expressed their feelings regarding the Germans: they simply and unapologetically did not like them. While the French field marshals had been exceedingly rough with their German POWs during World War I, the Kaiser was downright inhumane to the French prisoners. And thus far, Nazi behavior was following an equally odious course. The fact that German-speaking refugees were now clogging the streets of beautiful Paris pushed French tolerance to the limits.

Added to all of this was the decade's worldwide economic depression. It had caused the French to become as poor and hungry as their American counterparts. Quotas limiting jobs for foreigners had gone into effect, which caused enormous unemployment among the refugees, followed by hunger. Sharing an already limited amount of resources with the immigrants, the majority of whom were Jewish, resulted in rabid anti-Semitic feelings among many French citizens.

All of these elements collided in the summer of 1939. With increasing regularity, Virginia saw vulgar sentiments painted on buildings that housed Jewish-owned businesses. It disgusted her that the newspaper stories were becoming more sympathetic to the gangs that attacked Jews in broad daylight than to the victims themselves. And the stories she overheard from newly arrived refugees were unbelievable. In broken French, they related horrific tales of Nazi persecution against Jews and others. And every one of them, regardless of nationality or religion, was relieved to have escaped to the security of France, a security physically represented by the Maginot Line.

NAMED FOR THE FRENCH MINISTER of war, André Maginot, who had directed its construction since its inception in 1929, the Maginot Line had become known as the "Great Wall of France." It was built to protect France from Germany, her longtime enemy. The line was a fortification along the eastern frontier, extending from the Swiss border up to the Ardennes Forest on the Belgian border. The line stopped there because French military strategists believed that the impenetrable Ardennes forest would keep any invaders at bay.

Constructed mainly of concrete, the Maginot was not a particularly attractive edifice. When the ladies of Parisian society learned of its lack of appeal, they were concerned for the morale of the young men posted there and so devised a plan. They took up collections to purchase and plant rosebushes along the mighty wall.

Aside from its aesthetic shortcomings, the Maginot Line was a vast, state-of-the-art system of underground components. Dynamic and ultramodern, its interconnecting tunnels stretched for miles, housing thousands of men who trained, watched, and waited for war. Its fortifications could accomplish many goals, including the absolute imperative—protecting France's northern industrial regions from invasion.

French confidence was also bolstered by the terms of peace struck in 1919 following World War I that were designed to prevent Germany from ever being able to fight again. Her military was dismembered, she was forced to pay reparations to injured nations, and her former empire was reallocated. The map of Europe was completely redrawn.

But while the treaties signed at the close of the war overcame discrepancies on the map, national hatreds were not overcome. Germans, both by birth and by citizenship, lived in all of the newly defined areas, none too pleased at now finding themselves citizens of other nations. Upon his rise to political power in 1933, Adolph Hitler sought to change that and restore Germany to her former glory as a superstate.

Hitler rearmed his country by conscription in 1935, and in 1936 reoccupied the Rhineland, a portion of Germany adjacent to Belgium and France that was demilitarized by the Treaty of Versailles. In 1938, Germany annexed Austria, an apparent stepping-stone, to test the world waters on its road to expansion. When he met no opposition, Hitler hungrily snapped up the frontier area of Czechoslovakia known as the "Sudetenland" a year later. Acquired as a result of the Munich Agreement, "The Sudetens are the last territorial demand I shall make in Europe," Hitler vowed. Located in the heart of Europe, the area was one of the richest territories on the continent because of its natural resources and great industries, both much needed by the Nazis.

Despite the fact that these steps were in direct contrast to the earlier treaties, France and Great Britain calmly tolerated Hitler's moves. But in March of 1939, he seized more of Czechoslovakia: Bohemia, Moravia, and Slovakia. Many French and British policy makers abruptly woke up to the fact that Hitler appeared to be marching toward European, if not world, conquest.

When Hitler's plundering gaze fell upon Poland, France and Great Britain publicly guaranteed to help the country defend itself against any action considered a threat to her independence. As the summer of 1939 slipped by, French newspapers were replete with stories of words and actions protesting Germany's audacity. One edition of the Paris news organ *L'Oeuvre*, Virginia's favorite with her morning café au lait and croissant, quoted an unnamed French governmental source: "If Poland fights, Britain and France will fight, too." What a tragedy that war appeared once again to be on Europe's doorstep.

AT 5:20 AM ON FRIDAY, September 1, 1939, Adolph Hitler started World War II. The first German bombs were dropped on Puck, Poland, a fishing village and air base on the Baltic Sea. By 8:30 AM, thirty cities were in flames. Homes, hospitals, and churches were bombed along with military objectives. Shrines, museums, and libraries were flagrantly destroyed. Women, children, and the elderly were slaughtered as they fled from their falling cities.

Virginia heard the news that war had officially begun on the radio in her flat that morning. She was stunned; Hitler had really done it. Her first thoughts were of Emil. What part would he play as Poland was being ravaged by vicious invaders? And beautiful Warsaw—what would happen to that magnificent city? She thought of their long walks along the river and the hours they had spent discussing the world and their futures. Sitting at her tiny table, with the window open and a late summer breeze floating in, tears stung her eyes. The destruction of Poland and the death of thousands of its soldiers would be a tragedy. And the thought of Emil in the midst of it was overwhelming.

By evening, Paris newspapers had labeled the day "Gray Friday," as had other papers around the world. And they gave extensive accounts of French and British governmental missives insisting that Hitler "withdraw entirely from Polish soil or consider himself at war with them." Virginia and five friends had dinner that night at the Café Cluny on the Left Bank. One of the women, Claire de La Tour, lived in the flat below Virginia and the two had become good friends. It was Claire who had introduced Virginia to the others, all young, progressive thinkers. This gathering had become a weekly tradition for them.

Claire told the group that her brother, Jean-Paul, who was stationed near Metz on the Maginot Line, had written her, insisting that Hitler's days were numbered. The French army, Jean-Paul had said, was waiting for the Führer to take one step too far. The result would be war. It was Claire's opinion that the invasion of Poland might be the last straw.

Claire's prediction proved accurate. France officially declared war against Germany at 5:00 PM the next day, September 3. Great Britain had done so six hours earlier. The newspapers dubbed this day "Black Sunday."

At dawn on Monday, heavy guns up and down the 250-mile-long Maginot Line began talking. By nightfall, France had launched two high-powered attacks into Germany. French newspaper stories extolled the power of the French military, proudly stating that for an invasion of Germany, the country was in a much better position than it had been in 1914. The Alsace-Lorraine area along the border was now in French hands, unlike the last war, and the region's high escarpments that jutted east toward the enemy would make for excellent cover. These reports did a great deal to bolster French confidence.

The following Friday at their weekly dinner, Virginia and her friends discussed Great Britain's new leaflet campaign. The week before, British planes had dropped millions of circulars over Germany containing messages to the German people. Statements such as "This war is unnecessary," "You are on the edge of bankruptcy. We have unlimited reserves of men and provisions," and "The Reich is not threatened from any side," were printed in German in the hope that the people themselves would rise up against the war.

But Virginia didn't believe the campaign would be successful. She told her friends that, based on what she had heard when she was still working at the consulate in Estonia, Hitler had made many improvements in what had been a sorry state of affairs in Germany. He had put the country back to work, although most of the jobs, she conceded, were probably related to war production. He reorganized the educational system and forced the young people to join his youth groups. On the surface, it all sounded wonderful. Why wouldn't the German populace be thrilled with the progress?

But a recent letter she had received from her mother told of the Nazis' atrocious treatment of Jews in Germany and elsewhere. The reports came from those who had hurriedly immigrated to the United States. Nazis were rounding up whole families and forcing them to move to camps.

Claire volunteered a story she had heard from her rabbi, who had a cousin living in Munich. The last letter the rabbi had received from the cousin described how the family had lost their apartment and was moved to an all-Jewish area, where they shared a smaller flat with two other families. The cousin had been a successful dentist, but was now only allowed to treat Jews. Since most of them were out of work, there was very little money changing hands and everyone was living near poverty. Sadly, that letter from Munich had arrived three months ago. The rabbi hadn't heard anything from his cousin since.

HITLER'S CAMPAIGN AGAINST POLAND lasted twenty-seven days; Warsaw surrendered on September 27, 1939. During that time Germany deployed one and a half million men and tested a newly devised tactic known as "blitzkrieg" (lightning war). Blitzkrieg consisted of fast-moving armored thrusts, penetrating deep behind enemy lines, supported by air strikes. The concept had been an even greater success than was expected.

On September 17, Russia also entered a war with the Poles. Fully aware of Germany's probable intentions to invade Russian territory at some point, the Russians began what they called "armed interventions" from the east to protect their frontiers. Within two days they had crossed half the country, repositioned themselves on what had been their border before the First World War, and sent the message to Berlin that Nazi aggression into the Baltic and the Ukraine must stop immediately.

The day of Poland's surrender, while Germany seized 72,500 square miles, Russia took 78,000 square miles. That same day, Hitler announced to his generals that his next plan was to attack the west. He demanded a strategy from them that would allow him to accomplish his goal before winter.

French and British generals were conferring as well. They felt confident that Hitler would soon make a move westward since he had created his own defensive bastion facing the Maginot Line called the Westwall. Soldiers of both armies were reported bathing in the Rhine River in plain sight of one another. The Germans had even posted signs announcing to their French counterparts, "We have orders not to fire on you until you fire on us."

However, aside from minor skirmishes, neither side did much fighting. This bizarre nonaction was dubbed *"la drôle de guerre,"* the phony war, or more accurately, the funny war. Hitler's goal of attacking the west before winter, however, was not met and as 1940 dawned, the worst winter of the century settled in. Temperatures fell dangerously low and mountains of snow covered the continent. Hitler's plans for a massive attack were postponed again and again. On the French side of the border, the army used the time for training exercises and lectures. Across the channel, the British did the same.

Virginia and Claire decided that it was out of the question for them to sit idly by while preparations for war were going on all around them. They enlisted in the Services Sanitaires de l'Armée, a Red Cross–type organization. Volunteers were gladly accepted, regardless of nationality or the number of legs they possessed. They received basic medical training, such as how to bandage wounds and how to apply a tourniquet. Additionally they were given a brief course on how to defend themselves should the need arise. Kicking, scratching, and stomping on insteps were all acceptable in time of war they were told. None of that, of course, would have stopped a bullet, but then no one expected a protracted war at that point either.

When they had completed the four-week training course, Virginia and Claire were given the rank of private, second class, and assigned the duty of ambulance drivers. Virginia didn't tell her mother about her decision to volunteer. When the real fighting broke out, the French victory would be quick and decisive and when it was all over, she would simply write a letter home telling her mother about the minor part she had played in the French victory over the Nazis.

Throughout the winter and the drôle de guerre, Virginia and Claire lived in a barracks outside Paris. Their monotonous days consisted of rolling bandages and sharing their sketchy first-aid knowledge with citizen groups that were anxious to be prepared. But as winter melted into spring, French-German skirmishes accelerated. Virginia and Claire assumed their duties as drivers in March and were assigned to cover an area outside the city of Metz, about twenty miles from the Maginot Line. They lived in a little cottage near town that had been donated to the war effort by its owner. The accommodations were rustic but adequate and food was available from nearby farms. The two worked the day shift, and tried to meet back at the cottage each evening for supper.

Since her accident, Virginia did nearly everything she had done previously. But admittedly, the ambulance work was physically difficult. The vehicle was a pared-down Deux Chevaux. Already spartan, it was made even more so with nothing in the interior but a hard bench seat in the front and room for two stretchers in the back. And of course it was a straight shift, which meant Virginia had to use her artificial leg and foot for the clutch pedal.

Every night, when she returned to the cottage, she massaged her stump and took care to dry out her stump sock to prevent blisters the next day. Virginia had told Claire about the accident long before the war began. Although Virginia wasn't ever comfortable talking about or displaying her amputation, Claire didn't make a fuss over it. And for that, Virginia was grateful.

The ambulance job was emotionally draining as well. At each stop, Virginia helped the attending medics load the blood-caked men, some crying out in agonizing pain. Then she sped off, with the patients bouncing in the back, across the rough terrain to field hospitals. And when the need arose, she took the patients from the field into Metz, where more complicated procedures could be performed at the hospital.

Even at this stage, war was ugly. It wasn't the blood and gore that bothered Virginia. It was the faces of the young men, grimacing in pain. It was the knowing look of the medic when he recognized that his patient would not survive. And it was the knowledge that through this misery and death, the future of an entire generation of French was being changed forever.

Still, it was very gratifying work. And with every day that passed, memories of Foreign Service exams and being told that her disability was limiting became more distant. They hardly mattered now. She was needed; and she was secure behind the insurmountable defense of the Maginot Line.

The issue of security changed on May 10, 1940. The Low Countries—Holland, Belgium, and Luxembourg—had hoped that Hitler might ignore them out of respect for their neutrality. It was not to be. At about 3:00 AM the Nazi blitzkrieg swept in. The Germans announced they were advancing to protect the Low Countries from an invasion by Great Britain and France, and gave the latter two countries notice that any resistance would be crushed. These announcements, however, came well after the attack had begun.

By May 14, Holland, which hadn't fought in a war since 1830, had surrendered. Belgium, having been attacked the same day as Holland, made no forward progress against the German onslaught and began to fall back only a day into the fighting. France and Great Britain responded to Belgium's cry for help by sending powerful forces, led by General Charles de Gaulle, to hold off the Germans at one end of the border. Like all of the French, de Gaulle believed that the Ardennes Forest and the Meuse River would protect the other end.

Such positioning was precisely what the Germans had counted on. The Nazi army had spent months training in order to be able to cross the raging Meuse, one of Europe's most difficult rivers, and to penetrate the previously deemed impregnable Ardennes. By tackling them both, the Germans effortlessly avoided the Maginot Line and took the Allied army by complete surprise. The massive armies of Nazi tanks swept across the river and through the forest. In the midst of the fighting, on May 28, Belgium's King Leopold III surrendered his army. This left the Allies fatally outnumbered.

Likewise, the fighting had also increased in the east where Virginia and Claire were working. Now their jobs were overwhelming. They drove for hours at a time, the notion of "shifts" having completely disappeared. They worked until they dropped from exhaustion only to begin again after a quick nap.

Their comfortable little cottage became a distant memory. They slept wherever they could in infantry camps, without the benefit of cots, sheets, or pillows. A blanket was considered a luxury. They lived out of small, canvas duffel bags that contained life's bare essentials: a toothbrush, a comb, slivers of soap. Personal hygiene was a near impossibility. There was no time or place to bathe, so splashing in a pail of river water had to do. They only had a few extra items of clothing, and laundry was out of the question.

Food was simple and scarce, but there was little time or energy to eat it anyway. They lived primarily on bread and potatoes, with an occasional piece of sausage. They were tired, dirty, and sickened by the carnage they were witnessing.

Virginia's amputated stump had merely been stiff when her work hours were fewer. But now, the continuous use of the clutch made her whole left thigh ache. The skin was often rubbed raw where it met the artificial limb. To make matters worse, the summer heat and humidity were now as intense as the winter's cold had been. Virginia had only two stump socks. If she wore them both at once, the extra cushioning greatly alleviated her discomfort, but her increased perspiration soaked the socks. Wet wool between her leg and the wooden prosthesis was almost worse than no wool at all.

When she allowed herself the time to sleep, Virginia would drift off, thinking she had seen the worst injuries possible. But when she awoke and began working again, she came across even more gruesomely wounded men. By 9:00 AM on May 30, Virginia had already made the trip between the front and a newly established field hospital three times.

She returned to her pickup point for her fourth run and, as was her custom, immediately climbed out of the ambulance to assist the waiting medics and patients. While many of the men were writhing in pain, one lay motionless on his litter.

Virginia walked over and knelt down beside him. His entire head was bandaged, the blood beginning to seep through the gauze. As Virginia approached, the medic who had been attending him scurried off, she presumed in search of more bandages. As she studied the patient, who was unconscious, she realized there was something odd about his bandaged face. There were no contours where his eyes and nose should be. Rather, the bandage was almost level, so much so that she looked down at the rest of his body to see if he was perhaps lying face down. The toes of his muddied boots were pointing skyward. He was definitely lying face up.

The medic returned with more bandages and reached for the man's wrist to feel for a pulse. He sat still for a moment and then looked at Virginia and shook his head.

"He's gone, poor guy. Took one in the face. It blew the whole front of his head off. I can't believe he made it this far; he got hit over an hour ago."

Virginia stood and looked at the dead soldier's face, understanding now why it appeared as flat as a tabletop. The medic reached for the soldier's dog tags and read the name out loud as he printed it on a card pinned to the man's shirt.

"Jean-Paul de La Tour."

Virginia spun around to where the medic was crouched. "What's his name?"

"Jean-Paul de La Tour. Why, you know him?"

"Does he have identification papers or anything with him?"

"Fellas usually keep that kind of thing in their helmets. But he didn't have a helmet when I found him," the medic answered. "Sometimes guys keep things in their boots." He picked up the man's left leg, pulled off the boot, and felt inside. He found a small packet of folded paper and opened it up, sorting through the contents.

"Here's a photo. Anybody look familiar?"

Virginia took the picture from the medic's outstretched hand. Laughing gaily at the camera was a handsome young man in uniform. Standing next to him, laughing just as gaily, blonde hair ruffled by a breeze, was Claire.

5

VIVE LA FRANCE

ANGUISH IS A CLOUD that settles on each person differently. For some it becomes so dense that even breathing is a struggle. For others, it's a fine mist, easily cut through and left behind. Virginia knew how she had handled her anguish. It was easiest for her to just jump back into life. But she was not at all certain how Claire would handle the pain she would surely feel at the news of her brother's death.

Virginia simply hadn't considered French stoicism. Claire was understandably shocked at first and wept. But in less than an hour, she dried her tears, squared her shoulders, and was ready to throw herself back into her war work. The army told her it would make every effort possible to return Jean-Paul's body home. Claire chose not to accompany it.

She told Virginia there was nothing she could do for Jean-Paul at home, preferring instead to continue working. She felt certain that would be what her brother would have wanted. Their belief, she told Virginia, was that only a body died. The spirit lived on in the hearts of those left behind. She felt that her brother's spirit would be with her, working beside her. Furthermore, Claire declared that for her, the war was no longer just a fight for France, but a fight for religious freedom.

France had once been a model of religious tolerance, repealing anti-Semitic laws in 1790, shortly after the Revolution and well before any other Western country. In the ensuing 150 years, the French had been true to their priceless heritage, *liberté, égalité, fraternité*. Liberty, equality, and fraternity were what the country offered the oppressed of other, less tolerant, European

39

nations. But unemployment, poverty, and dismal living conditions gave rise to resentment against the three million immigrants living on French soil at the time. Throughout the late 1930s, Nazi-inspired prejudices grew in neighboring countries, and the immigrants' numbers in France, many of them Jewish, increased as thousands fled to escape Nazi cruelty.

Resentment and rumors soon became news stories in French papers. "Only Jews want conflict in Europe," they reported. "German Jews clutter up French streets, telling us to fight on their behalf." Soon all Jews, even those whose families had been French for generations, as Claire's had been, were regarded suspiciously.

But very few newspapers reached the bloody battlefields in early June 1940. Their only reality was transporting the never-ending number of wounded soldiers from the fields of slaughter to makeshift hospitals. At one point, the gory scenes reminded Virginia of the poem she had memorized in grade school about the bloody Civil War battle at Shiloh:

Dark forms were strewn thickly all over the field,
Whose hearts were now still and whose cold lips were sealed;
And streams crept slowly through torn, trampled grass
That they tinged such a horrible red, alas!

Every French roadway and forest trail Virginia turned her ambulance down was now choked with refugees fleeing the German juggernaut. The masses of humanity had left behind most of their possessions, their burning homes and farms, and their friends and relatives who had fallen victim to the carnage. It was heartbreaking to watch the traumatized throngs making use of every vehicle they could commandeer to carry themselves and their belongings to safety. Bikes, wagons with or without horses, dogcarts, and wheelbarrows were pressed into service. Those who had no vehicle stumbled forward on foot.

Virginia watched men and women carrying terror-stricken children, and the elderly taking turns supporting one another. Like Virginia, they were tired, hungry, and war weary. And like her, they were sickened by the bodies that littered the road after each pass of the German warplanes. The bombers' goal was to destroy the roads to prevent the French military from making use of them. They appeared to have little concern for any civilian casualties—that was the price of war.

German military strategists had expected to find as worthy an adversary in the French as they had seen in the previous war. But Hitler was convinced of the opposite. He believed that the French had become lazy and were incapable of mounting the same kind of offensive they had exhibited in 1917 and 1918. Sadly, the Führer's prophecy proved the more accurate.

By late May 1940, many of the French army divisions had been lost in Belgium and the nation's air force was practically wiped out. The Germans arrived with powerful tanks, while the French had only machine guns. The British reinforcements were not arriving fast enough. Although the Allies attempted to hold their ground, the German drive continued. Their objective was obvious—Paris. Their battle plan was simple: keep pushing the Allies southward, like a giant broom sweeping breadcrumbs toward the door.

Virginia heard rumors in the field about German troops approaching Paris from the Belgian border. They were seventy miles away, then sixty-three, then fifty-seven. Meanwhile the lines her ambulance serviced became just as fluid, falling back five miles, then fifteen, then twenty. Six hundred thousand German soldiers, followed by thirty-five hundred of their best tanks, were storming toward the capital from the east. In their wake they left husbands, fathers, and sons dead or dying. There was little time to bury the dead. And the fuel shortage hindered the number of wounded she and Claire could move.

All ambulance drivers were responsible for finding fuel for their own vehicles. Occasionally Virginia and Claire stumbled upon a small surplus an army unit might have saved. But for the most part, they were forced to plead their case to farmers and villagers who had remained in their homes, keeping their last drops of gasoline in the event they needed to make a quick escape. When lack of fuel precluded driving, the two women willingly rolled up their sleeves and helped the doctors and medics treat the wounded in the field. They saw limbs amputated with little anesthesia and bellies ripped open by shrapnel, internal organs spilling out like glistening sausages.

The furious pace and constant cloud of dust and smoke caused the days and nights to run together for Virginia. She and Claire had established a small stable, the remains of a burned-out farm, as their meeting place every twenty-four hours. It was an attempt to assure one another of their safety, as they were now directly in the line of fire.

On June 10, the French government left Paris for Tours, 140 miles southwest of the capital. Winston Churchill, who had become the British prime minister on May 10, the same day that Hitler began his attack on Belgium and Holland, met French Premier Paul Reynaud in Tours on the eleventh. Churchill was perhaps the greatest friend France had among the Britons. He urged Reynaud to continue to resist the Germans, and he took General de Gaulle, now the French undersecretary for war, back to London. There, de Gaulle was to act as Churchill's ally against the peace party in his cabinet.

On June 13, the American ambassador to France notified the Germans on behalf of the French that Paris had been declared an open city. No resistance would be put forth against German invasion, and therefore no force would be needed on their part. Although the declaration preserved the city's priceless art and architecture for the Germans, the citizenry itself had all but disappeared. The few who remained on June 14 were subjected to a degrading display of Nazi triumph. Dusty tanks clanked savagely down the Champs-Élysée, followed by goose-stepping infantry and blaring German bands.

On the same day, as the thrust of never-ending German military might surged southward, the French government left Tours for Bordeaux, two hundred miles farther south. Throughout the eastern and central regions of the country, the French were in retreat, pursued relentlessly by the Germans. Half of Premier Reynaud's cabinet favored a surrender, while the other half urged him to fight on. Rather than deal with the dilemma, Reynaud resigned. Eighty-three-year-old Philippe Pétain, former World War I hero, assumed his position. Just hours after France's new government was formed on June 19, Pétain formally petitioned the Germans for an armistice.

Pétain's wishes were delivered in a radio broadcast to France's forty-three million inhabitants, as the rest of the world listened in:

> People of France: As requested by the President of the Republic, I shall henceforth be the leader of the French government. Being convinced of the affection of our admirable army, whose heroism stands as testimony to our long military position as they fight an enemy which outnumbers them, convinced that our army's resistance has fulfilled our duty towards our allies, convinced of the support pledged by the former soldiers I've led, convinced of the French people's faith in me, I give France the gift of myself to ease its troubles.
>
> In these difficult times, I think of the poor refugees, who, in the depths of despair, trudge across our roads. I extend my

compassion and concern for them. My heart is heavy as I tell you today that the fight must end.

Last night I spoke with our adversary and asked if they were prepared to help me, between soldiers, after the fight, with honor intact, to find a way in which to end the hostilities.

The country and the world stood still at that moment. With France now a part of the new German empire, a mere twenty-one miles of water separated Great Britain from a fanatic Nazi dictator bent on world domination.

Later that day, Virginia was attempting to take a short nap on a bed of moldy straw in a farmyard that had been turned into a makeshift field hospital. She sensed an increase in activity around her and forced herself to get up. She assumed that the enemy was on a fast approach.

She stopped a distraught medic to inquire about the commotion in camp. "Reynaud's resigned and Pétain's taken over as premier. He's asked the Krauts to let us surrender. *Mon Dieu!* The hundreds of men I've watched die—and all for what?"

Virginia was incredulous. What had happened to liberté, égalité, fraternité? How could feisty France, the first nation to extend aid to the American Revolution and the nation who had been victorious over the Germans in the war a little over two decades before, now be willing to send up a white flag?

Virginia looked around her at the wounded men. They lay on straw beds, with little in the way of blankets. The bandages covering their wounds were rags, often having been made from the clothing of another soldier who had died. Their splints were tree limbs and little beyond water and bread was available to sustain them. There were no drugs to ease their pain or stave off their infections. The medic had been right: these men had made enormous sacrifices for their country. And now they were being asked by that same country to live under a tyrannical dictatorship, driven by a madman whose goal appeared to be global domination.

This was not the French spirit Virginia loved. The French she knew were outspoken, proud, and resolute against the dilution of their culture by any outside force.

AT 3:30 PM ON JUNE 22, in railway car number 2419D, in the city of Compiègne, north of Paris, the supreme commander of the French army, General Charles Huntzinger, signed the armistice with Germany. The railway car was significant. It was where, in 1918, at the eleventh hour on the eleventh day of the eleventh month, the French had demanded that the Germans appear as supplicants. There, the armistice ending the Great War had been signed, the armistice that had fractured the German empire and had gnawed at Hitler's gut for nearly twenty-three years.

The morning after the signing, General Charles de Gaulle spoke solemnly from a BBC studio in London:

> *La France a perdu la bataille; elle n'a pas perdu la guerre* [France has lost the battle; she has not lost the war]. For the honor of the country, I demand that all free Frenchmen continue to fight wherever they are and by whatever means they can. . . . I invite all Frenchmen of the land armies, the naval forces, the air forces, the engineers and the specialists and the workmen of the armament industry who may be in British territory or who can come there, to join me for this purpose. . . . I invite the leaders, the soldiers, the sailors and the airmen . . . to get in touch with me. . . . *Vive la France!* Long live France, free in honor and in independence!

Virginia listened to General de Gaulle's speech on a radio in the café of a village near the stable where she and Claire had spent the night. The two had come to the village in search of food for the wounded, and were bundling up what they had begged from the residents when the general's address began.

De Gaulle's words removed only some of the sting of Pétain's armistice. Virginia learned the terms of that armistice over the next several days. Germany would occupy approximately three-fifths of the country, including a wide strip along the whole of the Atlantic coast. The *zone libre*, the unoccupied area, began south of the Loire River and ran to the Mediterranean, minus the Alpine frontier and the aforementioned Atlantic coast. Furthermore, all military, naval, and air forces, except police forces, would be demobilized. The Germans were granted the rights to all arms and implements of war in the occupied area.

Pétain's government was given the choice of setting up its capital in Paris, well within the occupied zone and the center of the German military administration, or anywhere it chose in the zone libre. Pétain selected Vichy, a small town east of Lyon, known for its curative mineral springs.

Ultimately, the new *État français* became known as Vichy France and from there, Pétain declared de Gaulle and all who followed him as traitors.

SO THAT'S THAT, VIRGINIA THOUGHT. La belle France, like a former lady of leisure who suddenly finds herself penniless and in rags, had fallen to her knees before the conquerors. About two hundred thousand Frenchmen had died in an effort to keep the country free. She was certain that she, herself, must have aided at least a thousand, many of whom did not survive. She had witnessed the death of her friend's only sibling. The magnitude of it all left a tightness in her chest, along with a feeling of personal failure that she could have done more.

As with the other French army units, hers was disbanded once the armistice became official. Not sure what her next move should be, Virginia decided to join Claire, who was headed south to her family home in Cahors, a small town north of Toulouse. The city lay within the borders of Vichy France.

The rucksacks the two women had dragged around with them the previous months were just about void of anything of value. Still, they gratefully stowed away the small chunks of sausage and bread that the unit's quartermaster had given them and began their journey in the back of an open-air troop transport truck. When it ran out of gas, they found a bicycle and took turns riding one another on the handlebars. Although having only one strong leg to power the bike, Virginia insisted that she take her turn peddling, with Claire riding. Their progress was slow but steady.

At nightfall, they came upon a farmer and his hay wagon. Unlike others they had passed that were being pulled by humans, this farmer was still using his horse, and the animal looked fairly sturdy. Virginia negotiated a deal with him. He would take them to Cahors (he was going in that direction anyway) and they would give him the bicycle upon their arrival. They spent a surprisingly comfortable night on beds of hay, sharing the wagon with the farmer's wife, toddler, and dog. At sunrise, Virginia, Claire, and the farmer's family pooled their food for a meager breakfast and then continued down the road.

The two women, still in shock over the capitulation, tried to guess what the future would hold for France. Virginia insisted that Britain's determination to repel the Germans, along with President Roosevelt's strong feelings about supporting America's longtime ally, would make the Nazi hold on

Europe brief. But Claire wasn't appeased. Americans, she told Virginia, were often unrealistically optimistic. She was ashamed of the collapse of France.

The women arrived in Cahors a day later, dirty, tired, and hungry. Claire's father owned the Boucherie de La Tour, a butcher shop that had been opened by his grandfather seventy years earlier. The family lived in an apartment above the shop. Claire's mother burst into tears the moment her daughter walked into the kitchen.

For the first time Virginia realized what a sight they must have been. Their hair had not been combed in three days and bits of hay from the wagon stuck out between the strands. They still wore their uniforms, which were soiled with dried blood and dust. Virginia's had a tear in one elbow and the right shoulder of Claire's had ripped out at the back. They wore grimy anklets and shoes, which were caked with mud. Their legs were dirty, bruised, and scratched from the dry hay they had been sitting in for two days.

Like her daughter, Mme de La Tour reigned in her emotions as quickly as they had gotten away from her. She insisted that the women take baths immediately, a luxury they hadn't experienced in ages. And a short while later they sat down to what looked like a feast.

The meat and hearty gravy melted in Virginia's mouth. She couldn't quite place the flavor, but figured it had been so long since she had eaten a decent meal, she just wasn't accustomed to good food. She asked Mme de La Tour what kind of beef it was. Claire's mother chuckled and told her apologetically they hadn't had beef in quite a while. They were eating rabbit—an animal that had not only become France's new plat du jour, but a lucrative enterprise as well. M. de La Tour had followed the government's urging and begun raising them several months earlier. He had sold quite a few of them to the army, she told Virginia proudly. They grew quickly and needed very little space. And after all, they reproduce like rabbits, she said with a laugh.

As good as the meal was, Virginia had to fight to stay awake to finish it. She would be sleeping in the room that had belonged to Jean-Paul. It was peacefully quiet in the cozy bed; there were no guns booming from far-off turrets, no sharp cracks from sentries' rifles, no cries of pain from nearby wounded. Virginia was clean, well fed, and comfortable for the first time in months. The horrible war she'd been in the midst of just a short week earlier was a nightmare from a different time. But it was a nightmare she would soon revisit.

6

THE DARK YEARS BEGIN

WHAT VIRGINIA AWOKE TO the next morning, and what she would see in the days and months to come, was a nearly unrecognizable France. Newspapers reported that the German military had taken over Paris, using the former French governmental buildings as their own and taking up residence in the grand apartments and hotels. Except for German army cars, everyone else in Paris traveled on foot, by bicycle, or braved the suffocatingly overcrowded Métro. Nazi flags fluttered in the summer breeze across the city, including those at the new Gestapo headquarters on the Rue des Saussaies. Furthermore, Paris's Le Bourget airport was now the new home of the Luftwaffe wing in France.

Virginia felt anger and sadness at the same time as she read about France's new status as a conquered nation. The happy times she had spent in Paris as a child, a student, and an adult flooded to mind. How could that have melted away so easily?

In Vichy, there were also reports of commandeered hotels. Pétain and his new French government occupied the popular resort the Hôtel du Parc to work hard at re-creating a nation. Pétain had empowered his vice premier, Pierre Laval, to draw up a "new kind of constitution," giving France an "ultramodern version of democracy." The old motto of *liberté, égalité, fraternité*, born during the French Revolution, was junked and replaced with a new version, commensurate with the near-Fascist values the new government stressed: *travaille, famille, patrie*—work, family, fatherland. In other words, the job of the French was, as it was for the rest of the Nazi empire, to produce goods and future soldiers for the Reich.

Over the next few days, Virginia witnessed Gallic emotions running the gamut. Some French people swallowed Pétain's story. He was, after all, a hero of World War I. If he told Vichy France, via his radio addresses, that the Germans had grand plans that would make the country strong and powerful again, there was no reason not to believe him. Perhaps the Germans really were dedicated to improving French lifestyle.

Other citizens reasoned that Pétain's advanced age was an advantage and a great deterrent from waging future wars. Still others were fearful of their new government and its German influence. In any event, it was obvious to Virginia that the French were traumatized, dazed, and anesthetized from their recent defeat. A fog of passive isolationism seemed to have settled over the country, a country suddenly closed off from the rest of the world.

Stories abounded of Germans living the high life in France's large cities. But they weren't alone. Some French police officers had taken possession of prime apartments in the occupied zone as well. They weren't required to use the newly issued ration cards and didn't have to stand in food lines. They ate at the expensive restaurants alongside the Germans, restaurants where there were never any food shortages.

If they were nothing else, the Germans were organized. They divided the country into twelve regions, each with its own prison camps. A total of eighty of them opened, their purpose supposedly to house the thousands of prisoners hauled off to Germany during the fighting who were now being returned to France. But it wasn't just prisoners who were filling the camps. Suddenly, Jews from Alsace were being sent to the camps in the Pyrénées. This news was disconcerting and the topic of conversations at the de La Tour residence centered around the Germans' treatment of France's Jewish population.

First, there was the "surrender on demand" clause in the armistice that dictated that the Vichy government must assist the Nazis in tracking down "undesirable" people and deporting them to other "more suitable" areas of the country. Next came the "Laws of Exception and Exclusion," which revoked rights Jewish citizens had enjoyed for generations.

Virginia knew that French Jews had never been completely integrated into society. She'd read more than one newspaper editorial with an anti-Semitic slant. And she knew that the friendship she and Claire shared, one between a Gentile and a Jew, was rare. Most Jewish families were close only to other Jews and had very few Gentiles they could turn to in time of need. This was definitely becoming a time of need.

Virginia encouraged her friends to consider relocating, but the de La Tours were not interested. Jews had been discriminated against for centuries, M. de La Tour told Virginia. It was not new and certainly nothing to uproot the family over. Furthermore, the Nazis couldn't possibly round up all the Jews in the country.

But the Germans accelerated their anti-Jewish movement. The Law of July 17 forbade anyone not born of French fathers from becoming a civil servant. This affected the great number of Jews who had come from other countries in the previous decades, as well as those fleeing Nazi Germany. Regardless of who had become a French citizen, bloodlines were considered before citizenship.

A short time later, Pétain repealed the Marchandeau Law, which outlawed racial libel. Vichy journalists, heavily influenced by the Nazis, were now able to express their venomous judgment regarding the Jews.

"Every French citizen should be aware," one writer penned, "that since the Jews were in such high number in the previous government, and as such were directly responsible for this country's supplies, it is their poor planning that has caused the gross shortages we face today. And can we be completely certain that they, in the greed for which they are so well known, did not stockpile food and clothing for themselves in order to create such an atmosphere of want?"

Another wrote: "Why should we, the citizens of France, be responsible for the dirty Jews of other countries? They flocked here like noisy geese and now we must give them food and shelter, already in such short demand. We are taking bread out of our children's mouths to feed theirs."

These words disgusted Virginia, and they terrified the de La Tours. Hatred against Jews was growing, even in Cahors. Claire persuaded her parents to move to a farm in the country owned by her father's cousin. Meanwhile, Virginia had learned via the grapevine that the war-wounded were still being transported toward Paris and that experienced drivers were in great demand. The Services Sanitaires was now under the auspices of the German government and Nazis now provided fuel for ambulances. Virginia applied and was rehired as an ambulance driver.

Virginia and the de La Tours left Cahors the same day, headed in opposite directions. The de La Tours went southeast toward Carcassone while Virginia took a northern route. She hitched a series of rides in the medical transports up to a base in Valençay, a town 134 miles south of Paris. Although she no longer had to pick up wounded from the battlefield, and the constant din from the bombing was absent, the job was familiar: help load the wounded at the field hospitals into her ambulance and transport them to permanent health care facilities.

Shortly after arrival, Virginia heard disturbing rumors. More and more Frenchmen were being drafted to work in German factories, replacing former workers now wearing Nazi uniforms. Virginia realized that as soon as the men she was transporting were able, they would be packed off to turn out more Nazi war materials, which would in turn cause more men to be wounded in other countries. The seemingly never-ending cycle was maddening to Virginia, but it also served as the impetus of a plan. There had to be groups organizing somewhere to eradicate the Nazi stranglehold on Europe and she was determined to find them.

By the time her ambulance work was completed at the end of August, Virginia had decided that Great Britain would be the best place to launch some kind of work against the Nazi regime. As the United States was not involved in the European conflict, Americans were still free to leave France. Virginia's exit strategy was to take a train from Paris to the border town of Irún, Spain, and then take a ship to London. Spain was neutral and not engaged in any military action against the Nazis. Virginia had heard, however, that it had become quite a destination for the throngs fleeing France.

Prior to boarding her train, Virginia queued up to present her papers to the German guards at the station. The emblem on her American passport was visible to all who stood nearby, and of particular interest to a man who later sat down next to her in the second-class compartment. The compartment's other occupants were a young mother and her four children.

Minutes after the train pulled out of the station, the man congenially started up a conversation with Virginia in English, wanting to know if she was heading back home. His forwardness startled her. Her former friendly nature had given rise to caution with strangers in light of the sudden political changes in France. She studied this pleasant-looking man warily and told him simply that she was going to London. The man was undaunted by her chilly reception. He introduced himself as George Bellows and told Virginia he lived in Spain and had been in France checking on some friends. Having seen that they were doing as well as could be expected under the circumstances, he was now returning to Spain. He chatted amiably about the beauty of the French countryside and how difficult life had become for most of the people.

Virginia decided Bellows was British, at least his accent was British. She relaxed gradually. He appeared to really love France and its citizens. His descriptions of happier times spent with friends sounded familiar to Virginia. His sympathies seemed genuine. They shared the same feelings that all the Nazis stood for was fundamentally wrong and that the Nazis' actions were nothing short of sadistic.

Bellows went on to tell her a story that had unfolded at a Renault automobile factory near Paris that was now being used to manufacture Nazi war materials. The workers had complained to their new bosses that their working conditions were simply insupportable. The Germans suggested that perhaps they would like to form a delegation to discuss the problem further. When the delegation presented itself, the Germans lined them up against a factory wall and shot them all. It was a horrific mental image.

The longer they talked the more candid both of them became about their feelings for the Nazis and the war they were waging against Europe. By the time the four-hundred-mile train trip was coming to an end, Virginia was encouraged: surely there would be other Brits who felt the same way Bellows did.

Bellows took out paper and pen and told her he had some great chums in London she should look up. He wrote down their names and numbers, and then suggested it would be a good idea for her to drop by the American Embassy when she got to London, just to let them know she was there.

The train came to a noisy halt at Hendaye on the French side of the border with Spain. Porters, moving through the aisle, told passengers to collect their belongings and prepare to cross the border on foot.

After she had descended, it occurred to Virginia that Bellows's British citizenship might be a problem for him. She turned to speak to him only to find they had become separated in the throngs crowding the platform. She moved along with them and when it was her turn, handed her passport to the Nazi guard standing smartly in front of her. He thumbed through it, looking carefully at each page. He studied the picture and then looked hard at her face. Without a word, he shoved the passport back at her, which Virginia took as the sign he was satisfied she was legitimate.

Virginia's first impression of the Irún train station was that it was noisy, dirty, and the perfect place to remind those who passed through that there was a new world order. Hanging on the walls were enormous canvas portraits of Franco, Hitler, and Mussolini.

Suddenly Bellows reappeared beside her as if he'd been there all along. He suggested she stay at the Hotel del Norte and invited her to join him for dinner with some friends. Virginia accepted both the recommendation and the invitation. Later that evening, she found the three men and three women, two Brits and the rest Spanish, as engaging as Bellows had been. It was almost midnight by the time they parted.

Virginia left Spain at 11:30 the next morning. When she arrived in London two days later, it was with a mixture of emotions. It had been years since she had spent any time in an English-speaking country. Hearing the language being used all around her was odd. And it seemed as though everyone was in a great hurry.

She took a day to settle into a room at Mrs. Tipton's Boarding House in Westminster and then presented herself at the American Embassy at 1 Grosvenor Square as Bellows had recommended. But she never expected the near celebrity status she received. Once word spread through the embassy that she had spent so much time in France and been close to the fighting, she was whisked into a conference room where a group of diplomats streamed in bombarding her with questions. "What is the situation in occupied France?" "What is the reaction of the French to their occupiers?" "What did you observe during the course of your journey out of France?" They reminded her of pigeons flapping at tossed bread crumbs. Had the occasion not been so serious, their frenzy might almost have been comical.

Virginia told them that all of France, occupied or not, was facing an enormous food shortage, as most of it was being diverted to the German army. It was worse in unoccupied France, she explained, and catastrophic in the eastern regions like Alsace.

There was a strict curfew in Paris, she continued. Everyone found on the streets after 7:00 PM was arrested, and provided nothing could be found to hold these people further, they were released the following morning at 7:00 AM. Only a single industry continued to thrive: prostitution. Virginia paused here with the briefest of smiles, causing several in her audience to blush. She explained that the prostitutes now had a whole new clientele in the Germans.

Asked how the French felt about the Germans, she responded that her observation was that the Germans were attempting to ingratiate themselves with French society, thus far with only marginal success. Her opinion was that a good many of the French were ready to revolt, particularly those in what was called the "*nono*"—the unoccupied zone.

Virginia's debriefing lasted about an hour, after which she was offered a position in the office of the embassy's military attaché. While another embassy job wasn't exactly what Virginia had planned on, being an underclerk meant a paycheck of $1,260 a year; more than enough for a single woman living in London in September 1940. And being close to governmental affairs might give her a better chance at finding the anti-Nazi work she was really interested in.

THE BRITISH HAD BEEN PREPARING for war since 1937 when the Royal Air Force buildup began. In 1939, a nationwide blackout was imposed and plans were made for the evacuation of cities presumed to be primary targets. Once France fell, thousands of British citizens were evacuated, primarily children. Thinking they were embarking on a grand holiday, the children saw their train trip to the southwest of England and Wales as a lark. They were sorely disappointed when they learned that schools awaited them at their destinations in an effort to give them as normal an existence as possible.

At the same time, all men between the ages of eighteen and fifty received notification of their liability for military service. Certain occupations were exempt, as their skills were needed in factories to keep up the furious pace of the industry of war. Material resources were mobilized as effectively as was labor. Consumption of every kind was cut and massive rationing was put into place, with gasoline leading the way in September 1939. Food rationing began in January 1940. Bacon, ham, sugar, and butter became available only with a coupon book.

By the time Virginia arrived in London in late August of 1940, other foods had been added to the ration list. Spam canned meat became a meal staple and powdered eggs replaced the genuine article. Mrs. Tipton served them periodically to her boarders and when Virginia first tasted them, she was shocked by their runny consistency. The gentleman boarder across the dining room table was watching her face and chuckled softly.

Mrs. Tipton's war efforts went further than runny artificial eggs. She, like most of her neighbors, had turned her flower bed into a vegetable garden, raising as much of her own produce as possible so that the farmers' crops could be reserved for the troops. The British government's "Dig for Victory" program made every Londoner a patriot.

Britain had not sued for peace after France fell in June as Hitler had expected, so the Führer launched Operation SEELÖWE, or SEALION, whose goal was to overpower the Royal Air Force (RAF) to prepare for the invasion of Britain. SEALION had begun in July 1940 with the Luftwaffe attacking British airfields and radar stations. But rather than achieving Hitler's goal, the attacks allowed the world to see that the Luftwaffe was poorly prepared for the conflict. And although the sheer weight of their bombardment was sometimes overwhelming, the British prevailed.

Hitler next approved a heavy bombing offensive "for disruptive attacks on the population and air defences of major British cities, including London, by day and night." At 4:00 PM on Saturday, September 7, just two weeks after Virginia had arrived in the capital city, 348 German bombers along with 617 fighters began blasting London and continued until 6:00 PM. Two hours later, using the fires set by the first assault as guides, a second group began another attack. The first targets were the docks and the East End, but soon the entire city fell within the Luftwaffe's crosshairs. The blitzkrieg of London had begun. And the city's 8.5 million people would experience a hell they had never seen before.

Virginia and her six fellow boarders, along with Mrs. Tipton, had just settled in to enjoy their Saturday tea when the first air raid siren shrieked. Two of the women jumped up and shrieked along with it. A discussion ensued on whether or not the siren was a warning or the real thing. The debate halted abruptly when a second siren sounded with a simultaneous thunder that Virginia felt throughout her body.

"It's the real thing!" one of the men shouted, and the eight of them hightailed it to the door leading to the basement. Just weeks earlier, following the advice of government radio announcements and flyers, Mrs. Tipton had outfitted a well-reinforced corner of her basement with mats, blankets, water, and tins of food. They hadn't even made it to the corner when the next bomb hit.

The timid woman who lived in the room next to Virginia's began praying immediately. A couple of the men paced like caged lions and the other boarders just sat staring into space, seemingly pondering their fate and that of friends and family living elsewhere in the city. Mrs. Tipton was particularly distraught over the fact that her cat, Raleigh, had been out in the garden when the bombardment began. Virginia sat next to her, and tried to be reassuring.

In truth, soothing Mrs. Tipton was a welcome personal diversion. Throughout her months on the French front, although she was near the fighting and certainly saw her share of its destruction, Virginia never felt as though she, personally, was a target. Here in London, the situation was vastly different. The Nazi bombs would not spare her simply because she held an American passport.

After several hours, and as suddenly as it had begun, the deafening roar was replaced by a deafening silence. The men looked at each other and silently agreed to chance a look upstairs. Virginia rose as well, and Mrs. Tipton pleaded for her to check on Raleigh.

The house was untouched, although some of the windows in the parlor and dining room had been shattered from the bombs' concussion. They ventured out the front door to the street. The sight was indescribably horrific. But it was the smell that Virginia most noticed. The air was thick with an acrid smoke caused by the explosives. Gritty dust from powdered brickwork and masonry made breathing a chore. A dark haze swirled around them as fires burned hot at several houses up and down the street. And the smell of sewer gas from broken pipelines leached up from the gutters, combining with the other foul odors. Before the scene had fully sunk in, Virginia and the men felt, rather than heard, another round of bombardment moving in their direction. They raced back into the house and down the basement stairs.

This drill repeated itself multiple times over the course of the night. Each time the bombing subsided, a group from the basement would timidly climb the stairs to check on the status of the house and the cat. After the third foray, it occurred to Virginia how ludicrous it all was. It made little difference whether the house had been hit or not—there was nowhere else for them to go and at least they had shelter and water and food.

Finally, at four-thirty the next morning, the quiet extended beyond its previous five or ten minutes and the group in Mrs. Tipton's basement agreed that the bombing had subsided for the night. They were further put at ease when the all-clear siren sounded shortly after the last of them had climbed the basement stairs. Wandering around the still-standing house, they all marveled at how little damage it had suffered. Save for the broken windows and one shattered teacup in the parlor, nothing had been disturbed. And much to Mrs. Tipton's delight, Raleigh made an appearance from under the divan he had used as his evening's bomb shelter.

The blitz continued for fifty-seven consecutive nights. The German goal was to kill and destroy as much as possible. Hitler figured that the carnage and the constant terror of the prospect of more bombing would bring the populace to its collective knees. The Luftwaffe dropped about three hundred tons of high explosive bombs on Mrs. Tipton's borough of Westminster alone. Even the British government expected the worst. In addition to hospitals preparing to accept the wounded, they also expected patients who would be driven mad by the air raids.

But quite the contrary occurred: the bombs tended to heal psychological maladies. Many people who were neurotic about the prospect of war were cured by its reality. They had too much to do to have time to be frightened. And they enjoyed finding themselves braver than they ever knew they could be.

As defense against the death raining from the sky, more shelters were needed in the city. Some buildings weren't fortunate to have sturdy basements like Mrs. Tipton's. Those that did have basements weren't sufficient to house all of the population. And although the Nazi raids seemed to occur only at night, it wasn't out of the question that an attack might also come during the day. It was vital, therefore, for citizens going about their daily business, to know precisely where the closest shelter was no matter where they were in the city. The official shelters were insufficient, but the vast network of Underground stations supplied just what was needed. While the trains continued to run through most of the city, seventy-nine stations were adapted and could accommodate up to 177,000 people each. The British government boarded up the tracks and equipped the stations with running water. An entire city burgeoned beneath London's surface.

The Underground shelters did, however, take some getting used to. The stench of so many humans and so little fresh air was overwhelming at times. Initially, fights broke out as people vied for space to camp out on for the night. But soon routine set in and families would roll up their blankets and pillows and make the pilgrimage, often before dark each night. Some brought food and had dinner, others brought diversions to share: a har-monica or guitar to serenade the crowds, or books to read aloud.

The only bright side to the all-out attacks on London, and later, other British cities, was that it gave RAF Fighter Command a much-needed break to rebuild outlying damaged airfields, train new pilots, and repair air-craft. As Winston Churchill said, "It was therefore with a sense of relief that Fighter Command felt the German attack turn on to London."

Oddly, in the face of this new round of death and destruction, the ritu-als of everyday life continued for Virginia as they did for those around her. The milkman picked his steps carefully across the newly ruined street in front of Virginia's boarding house to make his rounds each morning. The postman routinely collected mail from a letter box mysteriously left intact in the middle of the wasteland that had once been a café on the corner. And Virginia went to work each morning at the embassy as if the rubble in the streets were nothing out of the ordinary.

The newspaper reports from Paris were just as surreal. The German sol-diers, hated by generations of French, were behaving like perfect gentlemen. The picture of culture, the Nazis were frequenting bookstores and cafés. An air of normalcy reigned by day, while fear was supreme in the dark of night. A knock on the door could mean one or all of the inhabitants would be carted off for questioning by the authorities. Overt actions of resistance al-ways brought immediate death.

And there was much to resist. The Reich had installed a ministry in Paris to control all press, radio, and film. Only word of mouth brought any news about Vichy government failures or the war waging with Britain. Food shortages among the French increased, while the Germans consumed whatever they pleased. With the complicity of Vichy, manufacturing was redirected to the German war effort and rural areas became the target of acquisition. A dismal winter had descended over France.

VIRGINIA HAD MADE CONTACT with most of the people whose names George Bellows had given her. They, as well as several other clerks at the embassy, had become great chums and she saw them frequently at parties and gatherings, such as the one held at the home of Vera Atkins on January 14, 1941. Another of Bellows's friends, Larry Pulver, had suggested Virginia accompany him to Vera's soirée.

The home, not far from Virginia's boarding house, was a tall, narrow Victorian, painted a pale blue with yellow awnings, as yet untouched by Hitler's bombs. The owner was as distinctive as her house. Virginia judged Vera to be close to her own age. While Virginia was tall and lanky, Vera was petite. Pulver had told Virginia that Vera worked for the War Office in some capacity. Virginia watched as the hostess buzzed from guest to guest like a hummingbird, anxious to make certain all were having a good time and well supplied with grilled Spam appetizers and bad wine. It was a particularly special night as both the water and the electricity were working in Vera's home. Since the bombing, most homes experienced outages of some sort nearly every day.

As the evening continued, one of the guests shared his experiences as an ambulance driver during the height of the blitz. He worked in the East End, around the docks. The people there were truly something, he said, warm, affectionate, rather reckless, and incredibly brave. He once came across a young boy who was crying and when he asked what the matter was, the child said, "They burned up me mum today."

The man assumed the boy was speaking about injuries his mother had suffered so he asked if the child's mother had been badly burned. The boy looked at him through tears and said, "Oh, yes sir. They don't muck about in crematoriums."

The guest's story was followed by head shaking and chuckles and then another man who had been on the fire brigade spoke up. They were hauling people out of a burning building that had collapsed, he explained, bringing them out on anything they could find, even corrugated metal. One man he had helped bring out had lost an entire side of his body: half of his face, his arm, and his leg. He looked up at the volunteer and asked for "a cigarette, mate." The volunteer lit one for him and put it between his lips. He took a couple of drags and said, "Will you tell me landlady I shall not be home to tea?" Then he closed his eyes and died.

This story brought an awkward silence to the group, quickly broken by the gravelly voice of their hostess asking Virginia to tell them what she thought of the Nazis when she met them. While Virginia might have been cautious about her feelings months earlier on the train with Bellows, she had long given up the need to be circumspect. She told them after what she had seen in France and lived through in London, she'd like nothing better than to go back and take on "the filthy Jerries."

While anyone at the party, including Vera, might have been a Nazi sympathizer, or even a spy, Virginia continued with customary outspokenness. She had heard that the Quakers were being allowed into France on goodwill missions. She figured she could get back into the country via Barcelona or Lisbon on a fictitious benevolent undertaking. It would be fairly simple as she was a citizen of a noncombatant country. Vera didn't comment, but Virginia's words did not go unnoticed. The hostess merely smiled sweetly and offered her another appetizer.

7

THE MAKING OF A SPY

THE MORNING AFTER HER COCKTAIL PARTY, Vera Atkins typed a
memo and filed it in her folder marked, "Prospects."

> Miss VH who works at the American embassy talked in my
> house last night of wanting to go to France via Barcelona or Lis-
> bon. She talked of joining the Quaker organisation as an excuse.
> I am getting fuller details and will put her through the cards at
> the same time continuing approaches.

Two days later a message arrived at the embassy for Virginia. It requested her to join Vera for lunch the following day and included a phone
number to which she could RSVP. When Virginia called, a woman answered the phone saying, "Inter-Services Research Bureau." When asked,
she told Virginia that Vera wasn't in, but she was happy to take the message
that Virginia would be at the appointed place at noon.

As Virginia strode up to the restaurant the next day, Vera was arriving at
the same time. She was smartly dressed, but like so many other women, including Virginia, Vera had taken to wearing stockings with ladders in them,
the British name for a run. Silk had to be preserved for parachutes, and
women were doing their part for the war effort.

Once they'd settled at a table and began to consult menus, Vera told Virginia that she would take care of lunch with her ration coupons. She had
found a couple of extras, she said, and encouraged Virginia to order whatever

she liked. Such an extravagance was quite a treat and Virginia nodded a thank-you to Vera.

Once their soup had been served, Vera leaned in closer to Virginia to speak in a softer voice. There were many positions in the British government she felt that Virginia would be uniquely qualified for, she said. Virginia waited as the waiter came and went and then asked what she meant.

Vera summarized what she perceived as Virginia's assets: she was self-confident, had said she spoke French fluently, and knew the country. She looked strong and healthy. No one, Vera said, would ever guess Virginia was missing a leg. Virginia was shocked at this bombshell, but Vera squinted slyly through a haze of cigarette smoke and simply said she had a great many connections who knew a lot of things about a lot of people.

Their lunch conversation then took a different course. Vera said she was interested in Virginia's work with the French ambulance service. How had she found the position? For whom specifically did she work? What was her training? Sympathetic clucks and nods were woven in among her questions, and her comments about the ugliness of war were peppered with expletives. More questions followed, about Virginia's acquaintances in France. Without ever being aware, Virginia had given Vera her résumé, and it contained exactly the kind of information the latter was seeking.

As they were parting, Vera told Virginia that if she was interested in further discussions about aiding the war effort, she should meet her at the Northumberland Hotel at two o'clock the next day. With a curt nod that assumed Virginia's consent, Vera turned and walked away.

CLANDESTINE OPERATIONS ARE AS OLD as warfare itself, the Trojan Horse being probably one of the most famous examples of an early paramilitary undertaking.

The British government had been considering such operations when it developed Section D in 1938 under the authority of the Foreign Office. The organization's purpose was as nebulous as its name. Its employees were "to investigate every possibility of attacking potential enemies by means other than the operations of military forces."

Section D was to consider sabotage targets within Germany and to look into employing those who might be persuaded to undertake these actions, such as the Jews or the Communists. Meanwhile in France, everyone in the government refused to consider the possibility of the country's collapse. But someone in Section D had the forethought to leave ten small caches of sabotage stores in northern France, each with two Frenchmen in charge of them. They were scattered over 150 miles between Rouen and Chalons-sur-Marne.

When the fall of France became apparent to the British government in June of 1940, and Nazi Germany's ruthless dealings with their captured nations were publicized, Winston Churchill became highly enthused over creating an organization to specialize in irregular warfare. It wasn't until later that he was informed of the existence of Section D. On July 16, 1940, Churchill invited then Minister of Economic Warfare Hugh Dalton to take charge of subversion, and the Special Operations Executive—the SOE—was born.

SOE's purpose was, in the words of its founding charter, "to co-ordinate all action, by way of subversion and sabotage, against the enemy overseas." Simply put, Hitler had presented the world with a very unorthodox war. It was necessary to create an unorthodox organization to fight such an enemy. Once SOE had been officially created, Churchill gave Dalton a simple directive: "And now set Europe ablaze."

The very existence of this body was one of the most closely guarded secrets. Yet a team of administrators had to be formed, people with vision and connections. Recruiters had to be found who could identify individuals with the right combination of skills and personality traits. The new organization couldn't advertise for laborers and secretaries in the want ads. Trainers and instructors would be needed who could impart the knowledge necessary for agents to carry out their missions, jobs which would certainly be different from their current occupations. The scope of the task was immense. As one veteran said later, "Examining such an enormous task, one felt as if one had been told to move the Pyramids with a pin."

Sections were organized within the SOE to handle different areas of work and different parts of the world. Since the newly fallen France was geographically the closest Nazi territory to Britain, it appeared logical that operations should begin there as quickly as possible. Thus F Section came into being at the same time that SOE was formed. Leslie Humphreys was the original head of the section. The leadership then passed to H. R. Marriott in December of 1940, and finally to Maurice Buckmaster, who retained the position until the end of the war. Into their capable hands fell the task of recruiting French-speaking individuals who could infiltrate the country behind enemy lines.

The RF section was formed in the spring of 1941 when de Gaulle insisted on having a section that would be manned only with French and would answer directly to him. F Section was prohibited from recruiting any Frenchmen or Frenchwomen, although to do so seemed the most logical step. The DF section handled escapees from France, primarily through Spain. The EU/P section acted as liaison between the Polish government in exile in London and SOE and dealt with the large number of Poles living outside of Poland, half a million of them in central France. The section dubbed AMF was based in Algiers and worked in the southern areas of France. In addition there were country sections for the Middle East, the Balkins, and Scandinavia.

This profusion of sections and personalities quite naturally caused occasional friction and confusion, made all the more difficult by the number of Resistance organizations sprouting up throughout France. In one instance, F Section agents arrived at an appointed parachute drop location, only to find RF agents already in possession of the goods sent from London. On another occasion, an SOE group was surveying a potential German shipping target at the Bordeaux docks only to watch it blown up by Royal Marine canoeists who used mines that had been supplied to them by none other than the SOE.

In order to run a successful clandestine operation, an army of support people was needed. Their work was done at "stations," each designated by a Roman numeral. The stations were located throughout Great Britain in office buildings, manors, schools, and halls. And their work covered a broad spectrum.

Besides training for the newly recruited agents, new weapons and implements were needed that could be mass-produced, dropped by parachute, or deployed underwater. To that end, a creative research and development team came up with such devices as booby traps, miniature motorbikes, and tiny submarines. Cryptologists devised codes and communications experts developed a staff to receive incoming agents' messages. Eventually even forgers were hired to begin work on counterfeit French francs that could be taken back into France to purchase whatever was necessary to carry on missions. In addition to the need for intelligence analysis, counterintelligence was also needed, and staff was recruited for both of those areas as well.

SOE personnel came from all walks of life and worked slavishly, sometimes around the clock. This included, of course, Vera Atkins. She was an intelligence officer and deputy to the F Section chief. Their operations began at offices at 64 Baker Street under the cover name of Inter-Services Research Bureau. The location was a tongue-in-cheek nod to Britain's most famous detective, Sherlock Holmes, whose offices were also located on Baker Street. In fact the SOE was occasionally called, as was Holmes' fictional group of spies before them, "the Baker Street Irregulars." A great deal of effort went into keeping the locations of all SOE work secret, even among the various sections. New recruits were never taken to Baker Street. Rather, SOE officers met them in other locations.

THE NORTHUMBERLAND HOTEL was a dingy building near Charing Cross, in the heart of London. A pub anchored the first floor, while a sitting room and restaurant were located on the second, and two floors of hotel rooms sat above that. It would have been a completely unknown location to Virginia except for the fact that she had been an avid Sherlock Holmes fan in her youth. The Northumberland figured prominently in Sir Arthur Conan Doyle's classic *Hound of the Baskervilles*.

Virginia asked for Vera Atkins at the hotel desk inside the pub. The man behind the counter gave her the once-over, then escorted her to the lift. The two of them rode silently up to the third floor, where he led her down the hall to a closed door. He rapped on the wood paneling and waited for a response from within. Upon Vera's raspy acknowledgment, the door was opened.

Virginia took in the room. Despite the fact that the windows were boarded up from outside, the shades were partially drawn in further preparation for the evening's imposed blackout. Cigarette smoke hung in the room like London's famous fog and ashtrays overflowed with the remnants of Vera's virulent habit. There was no bed as would be expected in a hotel room; in its place was a desk and a round table cluttered with used plates and teacups. The room was devoid of any accoutrements or color.

Vera sat in a chair on one side of the desk with a file folder lying open in front of her. She smiled pleasantly and motioned toward the chair opposite her, asking Virginia to sit down. She began promptly by telling Virginia that she was not really with the War Office, but with another organization looking for people who might consider going to France.

Before Virginia had a chance to respond, the room door opened and a very tall, handsome man near Virginia's age strode in. He nodded at Vera who said in French, "*Je voudrais vous présenter Mlle Virginia Hall.*" Upon hearing herself introduced, Virginia held out her hand. The man took it and smiled warmly, responding, "*Bonjour, Mlle Hall. Le capitaine Jacques de Guélis.*"

Vera explained to Virginia that de Guélis was a newcomer to the organization. He had been in France as a liaison officer with the British Expeditionary Force and was captured the previous year. He had been able to escape and found their organization when he returned to Britain.

De Guélis said that he was interested in hearing Virginia's story. How had she, an American, come to be in England during a war? What were her experiences in France? Where had she gone to school and what languages did she speak? The questions continued for thirty minutes, and Virginia responded calmly to each one in flawless French.

When she finished, he told her she had a perfect command of the French language, despite a decidedly American accent. In a soft, confidential voice, he explained that the organization he and Vera were a part of was planning on sneaking British agents into France. Their purpose would be to gather information about the Nazis' positions and begin to organize whatever kind of resistance among the French they might find. De Guélis said Vera had told him about Virginia's desire to return to France, but he was confused as to why she would take up a fight that wasn't even hers.

Virginia bristled at this, explaining that she had spent most of her adult life in Europe. She loved the countries she'd lived in and the people she'd met. In no uncertain terms, she told him, a fight against the Nazis was as much hers as it was theirs. Or his.

Her outspokenness startled de Guélis and he studied her. Virginia never blinked or wavered, looking directly back into his eyes. A long silence ensued, after which he told her that taking action against the Nazis would require not only desire, but an organized effort with help from both inside and outside the country. And that was where their interest in Virginia lay.

He and Vera believed, he said, that women agents would be able to move more freely and would be less suspect than male agents. Virginia had been highly spoken of. She had the wit, courage, and attention to detail that they believed would be the hallmarks of a good agent. And it was obvious, he said, that she didn't step down from a challenge.

Her familiarity with the country and the language was an enormous asset. Plus, as an American, and therefore a noncombatant, she would have complete freedom to move about. Finally the question Virginia had anticipated came. Would she be willing to go back to France working undercover for the British government?

Virginia was elated. For ten years she had struggled to get a job in the Foreign Service of her own country. The response had essentially been that women weren't right for the job, that *she* wasn't right for the job, and that amputees weren't up to the challenge. Now, suddenly, a foreign government saw something in her that her own government had not. She was indeed mentally and physically capable—in some ways more so than those who currently held even loftier governmental positions—and she cared very deeply about Europe's position in the world community and its very survival. In short, the British government saw her as a valuable asset.

Virginia needed no time to think over her answer.

GREAT BRITAIN'S PLAN TO INFILTRATE France with special agents was crucial, in terms of both helping to free France, as well as to defend the British homeland. There were many Brits, and as in the case of Virginia, non-Brits, willing to volunteer at the very mention of it. But in order for such a plan to work successfully, the agents had to be trained to absolute perfection. Their lives and those of their colleagues would depend upon it. The training was demanding. Recruits had to learn demolition, field craft (clandestine survival), Morse code, weapons training, map reading, canoeing, parachuting, bomber receptions, security, and the general organization of an underground circuit.

The SOE was very selective and many of the volunteers washed out for various reasons: the training was more rigorous than they could physically handle, they were unable to guard secret information, their personality was not suited to espionage. Those who didn't make it went from the training facilities to "the Cooler," a lonely manor in northern Scotland where they remained a number of weeks until the information they had learned was no longer current and any slips they might make couldn't harm the program.

Virginia had been identified as having the qualities the SOE was seeking. Their agents would need to be leaders, but also have a team spirit. They needed organizational skills and to be efficient and industrious, but also had to know when to delegate. They needed versatility and resourcefulness as well as common sense, and they needed to be able to mix in well but to be discreet and not draw attention to themselves. Most of all, they needed to understand that there would be no applause for a job well done. Recognition would mean exposure, making it impossible for them to take on future missions and endangering other agents in the field.

While Vera Atkins, Jacques de Guélis, and others believed that Virginia possessed the much sought-after qualities, she still had to be trained and tested. Virginia understood that the training alone would be a full-time job, making it impossible for her to carry on with her job at the embassy. She officially resigned her position on Wednesday, February 26, 1941, listing her reason as seeking other employment.

Working for a foreign government's intelligence division would most certainly be frowned upon by her own government, however, Virginia dealt with the conflict in her own way. She always preferred asking forgiveness for something she'd already done, rather than ask permission—and face the risk of being turned down—before she took action.

Not qualifying for a mission in France wasn't something Virginia could envision. But at this early stage, her exact insertion date behind enemy lines couldn't be predicted. So she held on to her room at Mrs. Tipton's, telling her landlady that she was taking a position with the First Aid Nursing Yeomanry, the FANYs. Her FANY training would take her away from London for a time, she explained, but she would continue to pay for her room from her savings to have a home to come back to once the training was complete.

The following Monday, Virginia was on a train heading south to the town of Guilford. The twenty-five-mile trip took just an hour and when she arrived at the station she met a young woman in a FANY uniform who walked up to her and called her by name. I'd better do something about my appearance, Virginia thought, if I'm that easy to spot. After arriving at Wanborough Manor, the estate that was to be her home in the weeks to come, she mentioned the incident to one of the hosts that first night at dinner. He told her it wasn't that her *looks* were anything out of the ordinary, but probably that her *look* was. One must never look as though he he were searching for someone or something, unless of course, one wanted others to think precisely that. By the end of training, he assured her she would know just how to differentiate between the two.

Training at Wanborough began immediately and was continuous. Virginia tore into it with a kind of dynamism she hadn't felt since high school, the kind she employed when learning a new sport or the lines to a play. Every waking hour, the recruits were instructed, right down to simple table manners that would give them away as being British. They learned how to hold their eating utensils in the French way, with fork in left hand and knife in right, just as they're set at the table. They had to be taught not to pour their milk into their teacups first, but after the tea or coffee had been poured. Smoking was prohibited for women in France during the war, so female recruits who smoked had to do so surreptitiously. Any one of these simple missteps could be deadly under a watchful German eye.

Immediately upon their arrival at Wanborough recruits received code names that they would use for communications with other SOE members and headquarters. Virginia's was Germaine. They were instructed to use these names exclusively from then on. Only French was to be spoken at meals and after that first morning, Virginia was amazed at the command of the language her recruit colleagues had. It was comforting as well—survival in the field would rest not only with her own expertise, but also with that of those around her.

Their course work began that first day with Morse code. All the recruits were slow and sloppy, and Virginia was not alone in her frustration. Just when she thought she'd burst, the whole group was trooped outside into the winter sunshine, where they began lessons on demolition. Two hours later, they were all back in the large dining hall, lunching on an excellent sausage cassoulet with crème brûlée for dessert. Then it was on to a canoe class followed by an introduction to the weapons they would be issued.

"This is a Browning repeater," Leslie, their weapons instructor told them. "It's the lightest gun available and is clip-fed. This is the gun you'll use in the field, and by the end of three weeks, you'll be very comfortable with it."

Virginia knew from the start that the weaponry class would be her favorite. It brought back fond memories of the hunting and target practice she'd done with her father and brother at Box Hill.

"Never kill a German," Leslie told them a few days later. "Put him in the hospital for six months instead. He's more bother to his commander alive than dead. A wounded soldier has to be looked after. A dead soldier is buried and forgotten." The class stood silently considering this comment. "You're truthfully better off not being caught with anything that could be used against you in a fight. Furthermore, it's not easy explaining away a weapon—those Nazis are highly suspicious of anyone who has one."

The only other female, a recruit code-named Delphine, leaned over to Virginia and told her she thought the weapons business was ghastly. She said she had never considered until just then that she might have to actually use a weapon against another human. It was rather a sobering thought.

Virginia nodded and they moved on to their next lesson: knife fighting. "A knife should be used daintily," Leslie told them. "To defend yourself, you don't stab. Rather, you cut." The recruits were given wooden knives the exact shape and weight of the real thing. The knives were tipped with red lipstick and the recruits used them first on hanging dummies and later on one another. The telltale lipstick smears identified how accurate the cutting would have been had they been attacking another person.

Virginia became very adept using a knife against a dummy. The day they graduated to working on one another, the drill was to sneak up behind one of the other recruits and slit the throat. Virginia accomplished the task with no problem. But when the man turned and Virginia saw the lipstick smear on his throat, reality sunk in, just as it had for Delphine several days earlier.

If the agents were caught without a gun or knife, they were taught how to defend themselves nonetheless. They were to forget any fistfights they'd ever seen in the movies, nor did they need to use their knuckles to fight. Knuckles, the instructor said, were comparatively fragile. Rather, he instructed them to use the heel of their open hand. Landing on a man's jaw will break it neat as you please.

If they happened to be caught holding an umbrella or walking stick, they could use those as well. But they shouldn't slash with them like a sword. Instead, they should thrust. He demonstrated on a hanging dummy. And the golden rule in hand-to-hand combat, the instructor said, was to get close. The nearer they were, the harder it would be for their opponent to get out of their way.

Virginia participated in all of the courses her colleagues did. Her disability was never an issue, although some of the physical training, like running up and down Hog's Back Hill, was made difficult by her wooden leg. Had her instructors allowed her to pass on those exercises, and they did not, Virginia would not have agreed to it anyway. After all, the Germans were certainly not going to make any exceptions for her.

The course work continued seven days a week, although the schedules varied and recruits worked at their own pace. The SOE discovered that pushing someone too hard to learn something he feared did not accelerate the process. In fact, it often had the opposite effect. Furthermore, instructors were constantly evaluating the recruits on their physical and mental stamina and their overall attitudes. The instructors met on a weekly basis to assess the recruits. And as they saw a personality emerging, they paired that person with a particular job in France.

With each passing day, the recruits' skills improved. Their shots became truer, the lipstick smears deadlier, and the hikes and runs livelier. Even the Morse buzzer tapped more accurately.

The recruits lived two to a room at Wanborough. Virginia's roommate, Delphine, said she joined because her husband was in North Africa and she was home by herself. Her brother had been an RAF pilot and was killed a few months ago. That, she said, pretty much pushed her over the edge. Her goal was to be a radio operator.

Radio operators were the only agents who routinely carried around physical evidence of their job. It was the most dangerous of all positions, but Delphine said she wasn't worried. She was getting the hang of Morse code and was almost up to receiving the required twelve words a minute. Then came the question Virginia had now explained multiple times. What was she, a Yank, doing in British intelligence?

Virginia smiled and gave Delphine the same answer she'd given de Guélis and others who had asked. Virginia's determination and loyalty amazed Delphine. She told Virginia she thought she was very brave and hoped she didn't wash out, as she was just the kind of person Britain and the rest of Europe really needed. Flattery made Virginia uncomfortable, so she changed the subject and suggested they quiz one another on stripping down their guns and then rebuilding them.

The two worked for several hours before lights-out was called. But night did not mean that training stopped. One of the most important elements for the agents in the field was their cover story—who they were, what they were doing, where they had come from. They couldn't walk a single step in enemy territory without a series of lies that could flow out of their mouths as naturally as if they were the truth. And the lies had to be ready, regardless of time of day or circumstances.

Instructors routinely stormed into recruits' rooms banging pans and flashing on the lights. Recruits had been told repeatedly they couldn't jump up and scream, "Bloody hell!" The correct response was "*Nom de Dieu!*" And once they'd taken the Lord's name in vain, they had to be able to answer questions.

There were other true-to-life lessons as well, including "dead drops." The recruits dropped into nearby towns to leave and pick up messages from one another without being detected. The messages were left in mailboxes, under newspapers on café tables, and among produce at the fruit stand. But again, speed and stealth were of paramount importance.

Training involved every facet of the recruits' lives. They were taught that agents should never travel together in the same compartment on a train, and that meetings between them and other agents had to be kept to an absolute minimum. Since they couldn't write anything down behind enemy lines, they were given extensive memory tests to sharpen their recall. They had to burn any received messages if they could do so without arousing suspicion, or tear them into small pieces and scatter them over a large area. These seemingly insignificant acts, they were told, could very well be the difference between life and death for themselves and others.

At the end of the three weeks at Wanborough, Virginia felt as though she'd been in training for months. Just after dinner one night, while she and Delphine were washing out a few things in the bowl, a two-man team of instructors knocked on their door. The men told them that they had both passed the preliminary phase of their training and that they would leave first thing in the morning for the second phase.

They left at 6:00 AM, heading north into Scotland. Virginia and Delphine joined two other women who had also passed the preliminary courses. That's a pretty stiff attrition rate, Virginia thought. Twelve women had arrived at Wanborough three weeks earlier and now there were only four of them left who arrived at their destination, Arisaig, near Inverness.

This phase of training was to last four weeks. "Group A," as it was called, consisted of a variety of country houses, scattered throughout the wild and beautiful Scottish countryside. The activities were much stiffer, dealing with in-depth paramilitary training: more knife work, pistol and submachine-gun training on British and enemy weapons, map reading, and advanced raiding tactics. Some days they worked through the night, executing railway demolitions with plastic explosives and a great deal of cross-country hiking.

As the second phase of training drew to a close, Virginia, who had always been confident in all that she did, felt certain that she could take down an enemy, male or female, by surprise. She had no doubt that she could ward off an attacker with a variety of judo moves. Only she and Delphine remained of the four who had come to Scotland together.

Delphine was headed next to Ringway Airfield, near Manchester in central England, for parachute training. But Virginia broke from the normal regimen. She wouldn't have to drop into France, nor would she have been able to with her wooden leg. She would be entering legally as an American citizen. So she was off to the Group B schools near Beaulieu, an estate very near the English Channel. She and Delphine wished one another Godspeed and went their separate ways.

I wonder if I'll ever see her again, Virginia thought as she boarded the train. They'd been warned in the first phase of their training that friendships and romances among agents were dangerous on several levels and therefore strongly discouraged. But living in such close quarters and enduring the demanding training had created a need in all of them for companionship on some level, even if only to complain about their aches and pains.

Recruits attending the Group B schools lived and worked in the eleven buildings on the Beaulieu estate. The soon-to-be-agents were allowed to abandon the commando mentality they had acquired in Scotland and adopt one of a clandestine existence. They were required to do extraordinary things, all the while looking as though they were carrying on an ordinary life. As one of Virginia's instructors put it, "Remember, 'He that has a secret to hide should not only hide it, but hide that he has to hide it.'"

It was at this point that each of the recruits' cover stories were developed based on their skills and their situation. Virginia's story was that she was a French-speaking American newspaper reporter, Brigitte LeContre, sent to write articles to keep the Americans apprised of the situation in Vichy France. It was a feasible story and it wasn't too much of a stretch. Virginia had done some freelance writing off and on mingled in with her State Department clerking. But she needed to land an actual job with an American paper without divulging the work she would really be doing—helping downed pilots and escaped prisoners out of enemy territory as well as keeping close tabs on the comings and goings of the Germans in her area. For this, Virginia called on an old family friend in the editorial department at the *New York Post*. Her cable to him was responded to almost immediately in the affirmative. Certainly she could have a position, the response read. However, was she certain she would be comfortable in such a dangerous part of the world? His words made her laugh out loud.

She'd been dodging bombs for two years and was about to become involved in espionage, and this dear man wondered if a little reporting in France was too dangerous. She sent one more cable assuring her new employer that she would be careful, and she had the job.

As the days passed, Virginia decided that her training at Beaulieu was the most rigorous of all. It was no longer about physical agility, but mental agility, which culminated in a rough mock interrogation. The recruits had had a single message burned into their heads on the subject of arrest and interrogation. "If you are arrested, particularly by the Gestapo," they were told, "do not assume that all is lost. The Gestapo's reputation has been built upon ruthlessness and terrorism, not intelligence. They will always pretend to know more than they do and may even make a good guess. But remember that it is a guess; otherwise they would not be interrogating you."

In the middle of the night during her third week at Beaulieu, two German soldiers rudely awakened Virginia from a sound sleep and dragged her from her bed to a basement interrogation room.

"What is your name?" a disembodied voice asked from the darkness. Virginia was standing in her nightgown under a bare lightbulb. She had been allowed to fasten her wooden leg, but was not given any other concessions. The room was cold, damp, and dark.

"My name is Brigitte LeContre."

"And what is your business in France?"

"I am a reporter for the *New York Post*. I write stories about Vichy France."

"Are you trying to help those who would resist against the Germans?"

"No, not at all."

"But you were seen with someone we suspect of doing so. How can you explain that?" The voice had become progressively louder and was now shouting. The two soldiers appeared from out of the darkness and forced what looked like electrical wires into each of Virginia's hands.

"I don't know who you're talking about. I simply write stories; I told you."

"And what kind of stories do you tell?"

"True ones."

At that somewhat smug answer, an immense shock traveled the length of her body. She couldn't believe they were actually electrocuting her, and a split second later she realized they weren't. It was the shock from a bucket of ice-cold water that had been thrown at her.

The voice continued, ever more threatening. "What kind of stories do you tell? Are you trying to convince the Americans to enter the war?"

"I'm only a reporter, a civilian," Virginia gasped. "Our citizens are interested in what's happening overseas, including here in France."

"Do you work for the American government?"

"No, I'm a reporter."

Another shock wave from another bucket of cold water.

"Stop lying!"

"I'm telling you the truth!" she panted. "I have no reason to lie to you. You have my papers. You can see they're all in order."

Silence followed. Virginia was frozen to the bone, but stood firm. A bucket of cold water was mild compared to the techniques the Germans might use.

Suddenly more light filled the room. She saw the source of the voice: a mild-looking, bespectacled man seated at a table. Several of her instructors surrounded him.

"Very well done, Germaine," one of the instructors said. "You're free to go now." Someone handed her a blanket, which she wrapped around her shoulders and then made her way out of the basement and up to her room. She later learned via the Beaulieu grapevine that professional interrogators, policemen, and ex-policemen, had volunteered to come in for these exercises. They were good, Virginia thought. Damn good.

VIRGINIA WAS ONCE AGAIN sitting opposite Vera Atkins in the dingy Northumberland Hotel room. She had returned to London earlier in the day from Beaulieu and found a message waiting for her at Mrs. Tipton's to come to the hotel at her earliest convenience.

Vera was pleased to see the reports and that her intuition about Virginia was right. The American was clearly everything she and Jacques thought she was. A rap on the door was followed by it opening, and Jacques de Guélis strode in.

De Guélis shook Virginia's hand congratulating her on her success in SOE training. Virginia smiled inwardly. Much of what she'd done in training wasn't too different from what she and her brother did during childhood summers at Box Hill. Hunting, camping, hiking . . . all of it had come flooding back. Not that her training hadn't been difficult at times, but it was certainly nothing more than she expected the real thing would be.

Vera exhaled a veil of cigarette smoke and told Virginia it was time to make her official by signing a few documents. Next to her signature, Virginia added the date, April 1, 1941. She filled in her mother's name and address on another document that designated where her pay should be sent.

That bit of business done, Vera told her she would begin the most difficult part of the job: waiting. Her cover was in place, but they had to wait for the diplomatic wheels to turn. She had Virginia sign the visa application for passage into unoccupied France and gave her the cover letter to the American Embassy to read over. It requested them to expedite matters by cabling the application to the American Embassy in Vichy.

The waiting was not something Virginia was looking forward to and she asked Vera what she should do in the meantime. Enjoy London in the springtime, came the answer. But be sure to be back inside by blackout, Vera cautioned. They certainly didn't want to lose her now.

8

INTO THE WOLVES' LAIR

"HITLER BEGINS WAR ON RUSSIA, with Armies on March from Arctic to the Black Sea," the June 22, 1941, *New York Times* headline screamed. The lead article began:

> As dawn broke over Europe today, the legions of National Socialist Germany began their long-rumored invasion of Communist Soviet Russia. . . . Adolph Hitler, in a proclamation to the German people . . . termed the military action begun this morning the largest in the history of the world. It was necessary, he added, because in spite of his unceasing efforts to preserve peace in this area, it had definitely been proved that Russia was in a coalition with England to ruin Germany by prolonging the war.

Sitting in Mrs. Tipton's parlor and listening to the BBC reports on Hitler's advance into Russia, Virginia was exasperated. She was trained and ready. Hitler was increasing his stranglehold on the world. And yet, there she sat waiting as the appropriate paperwork for her return to France inched its way through governmental offices.

Much to Virginia's surprise, the invasion of Russia delivered two unexpected benefits. One to the morale of the British: they were no longer alone in the battle against Nazi Germany. The second benefit was to the SOE, which Virginia learned about from Vera. The Communists in France had remained neutral since the country's fall a year earlier. It was assumed in

Britain that they would have no interest in resistance or collaboration. But this changed drastically with the new Nazi assault. According to agents already in the field, the Communists, who named themselves Francs-tireurs et partisans (FTP) were now eagerly seeking Resistance groups as allies. A clandestine existence was familiar to them, which would make them naturals as underground participants. Although relationships between them and other French political parties were strained by years of mutual unfamiliarity, the additional manpower would indeed be a comfort to both sides. After all, their goal was the same: to obliterate the Nazi regime.

BY THE END OF JULY, Virginia thought she'd go mad from the waiting. Since her cover was a journalist, it seemed only logical that she should hone up on her writing skills, which occupied some of her time. In addition she worked with the SOE code specialists on how to get her information out of France and back to them. She would write letters that, to the casual observer, were simply chatty missives discussing the weather and her sightseeing trips. They would be sent to London via other agents. Once there, SOE cryptologists would pull certain letters out of certain words to produce the vital information.

She kept fit with walks through the London bombing rubble and made several trips out to the Beaulieu manor where she could use their target facilities and update her identification skills. The SOE drilled their agents on recognition of German military insignias and Nazi and Gestapo personalities of note. Since new information arrived almost daily, Virginia needed to be on top of things when she finally got her traveling papers. And she kept abreast of SOE issues that were pertinent to her through meetings with Vera at the Northumberland.

At one such meeting, Vera told her that SOE had organized the infiltration of a number of agents into France; the first going in by parachute on May 5. The work done thus far had been good, very good, she said. And, there was an ingenious new method of communication. Those first agents realized they needed to limit the amount of time they were actually transmitting and receiving messages. German wireless interception service jammed the radios, and hunted them with their direction-finding vans. Agents were concerned about sending or receiving for longer than a minute. The solution lay with the BBC.

Despite the Nazis' best efforts at blocking the signal, agents could almost always raise the BBC's powerful overseas service. SOE's first agent in France suggested using it for communication. At the end of each evening's broadcast, the *messages personnels* would be announced. This would be followed by a plethora of phrases like, *Roméo embrasse Juliette, La chienne de Barbara aura trios chiots, Marcel n'aime pas le mouton.* Some sounded like family notices and some were just gibberish, but they were actually code phrases. Agents in the field listened carefully each night, already having been told which coded message would pertain to them. They could receive news of new arrivals, the safe return to England of others, and even supply drops.

To Virginia, it was one more example of one of the SOE's greatest strengths: creating solutions to problems, quickly and efficiently. However one problem that still plagued the agency dealt with new recruits.

It wasn't that there weren't enough of them. Plenty of men and women were happy to sign up when given the opportunity. But many washed out when they became security risks. They were careless, leaving delicate items, like codebooks, out in the open. Worse still, some talked too much. In one incident, a recruit told a barman at a pub near the manor that he was involved in secret government work that would win the war. The barman happened to be on the SOE payroll and reported the event immediately. The recruit's excuse was that he wasn't thinking, which was exactly the problem. Thinking was the number one job when working undercover. Talking too much in France would be fatal.

FINALLY, ONE MORNING IN EARLY AUGUST, the call Virginia had not-so-patiently awaited finally arrived. Virginia was to meet Vera at noon at the Northumberland. When she arrived at the now familiar hotel room that served as Vera's office, a pleasant looking, middle-aged gentleman was there as well.

Vera introduced him to Virginia as Selwyn Jepson, one of F Section's right-hand men. The three of them sat around Vera's desk with cups of tea and Jepson explained that it wasn't just paperwork that had caused the delay in Virginia's being sent to France. Jacques de Guélis had gone in a few weeks earlier, and, among other jobs, had set up contacts for Virginia and paved the way for her cover story. All was now in place and the time had come for her to take center stage.

She would go first to Vichy, Jepson told her. As soon as she arrived, she was to go to the American Embassy to officially register, and then do the same at the Vichy government headquarters. De Guélis had suggested she stay at the Hôtel Thermalia on rue Jardet. Jepson told her to always ask for streetside rooms in hotels. It would enable her to observe who was coming and going, plus allow her to alert other agents that she was in by leaving something in plain view on the windowsill.

Her SOE assignment was not unlike what the newspaper was hoping to receive from her: reports on the general situation in France. The mentality, among both the French and the Nazis, what there were great stores of and what was lacking, was vital information to the British military.

A week or so after Virginia's arrival in Vichy, Jepson told her she was to move on to Lyon, two hundred kilometers to the north. De Guélis recommended the Grand Nouvel Hôtel in Lyon. There, she would serve as a human depot. All incoming agents would be instructed to contact her when they first arrived in the area. Virginia would inform them of conditions at the time and give them whatever assistance they required. London would make sure that she always had an ample supply of francs to fund their needs, and would send her off with a wad of cash as well. Although the money was printed in England, it all went through an extensive "dirtying" process to make it look as though it were well circulated. SOE expert forgers even went so far as to pin stacks of it together through the watermark with large hat pins, just as the French banks did.

In addition to finding hotels for her, de Guélis had also identified two Resistance sympathizers in Lyon who were prepared to assist her. From those two, she was to build a network. Jepson gave her a paper with their names and addresses, told her to memorize them, and then burn the paper. The contacts had been told to expect one Brigitte LeContre to contact them sometime in September. To confirm her identity when she met them, she was to say, "*Je viens avec des nouvelles de Marie.*" They would respond by saying, "*Voulez-vous dire Marie Renard?*"

It was a lot of information to take in all at once. Acting the part of another person would come easily for Virginia. After all, she'd been the star of many high school productions. But this wasn't playacting. Would she be able to remember how to protect herself in an emergency? Could she maintain her cover under intense questioning or torture? Could she live a lie for months on end? Worrying about it at this point would do her no good, now or then.

She asked Jepson how she was to contact London with her reports. The lengthy ones he told her to send out with agents who would be moving through Vichy and Lyon. As she was the hub of the SOE wheel in that part of France, practically everyone would be in contact with her at one time or another. Shorter messages could be relayed via radio transmission. There would be a wireless operator in the area at her disposal.

And the most important thing, Jepson reminded her, was not to forget she had a carte blanche entry into the country because of her American citizenship. It was invaluable to the SOE and their work and they were willing to go to great lengths to protect it. Her job, he said, was not to fight the Germans, but to organize a Resistance network that would fight the Germans by any means possible.

Virginia wondered what she should do if she needed approval for anything, but Jepson waved her aside. They had faith in her keen sense of leadership and knew she possessed the resourcefulness to handle whatever came her way. She was her own boss, he said, she was to make the decisions. And she wasn't to worry about doing things by the book. There was no book.

Virginia was filled with a fusion of emotions. There was a small amount of apprehension, of course, coupled with excitement, anticipation, and even a little pride at the fact that the work she would be doing could have an outcome on France's future.

Vera slid a small box across the table to her, explaining that it was a token of their appreciation. Virginia opened the box and revealed a gold powder compact, inscribed with *Bonne Chance* (good luck). Jepson echoed the inscription and told her England was grateful for her service in its noble cause. And, he added, if she had to, she could always pawn the compact if she needed extra cash.

There were just a few more details Vera needed to complete Virginia's paperwork. Correspondence with her mother was no problem. To the outside world, Virginia was a stringer on assignment with the paper. But if she was detained for any length of time, Vera asked, how did she want them to contact Mrs. Hall? And even more important, did she have a will?

In the confident way her colleagues at SOE had come to expect from her, Virginia told Vera to contact Mrs. Hall only in the case of her death. And since she wasn't planning on that happening, there wasn't really any need for a will. Her pay was already going to her mother and she didn't own property anyway. Vera smiled and handed her the tickets for her ship to

Lisbon, Portugal, and the train from there to Vichy. She would leave first thing in the morning.

BRIGITTE LECONTRE, CODE-NAMED Germaine, arrived in Vichy, France, on Saturday, August 23, 1941. She was the first woman field agent the SOE had sent into France. Inside her dress, she wore two money belts, one over each hip, both heavily laden with her stash of counterfeit French currency. The money belts on top of the waistband connected to her wooden leg made her feel as though she'd suddenly taken on an additional ten pounds—a very precious ten pounds. The one million francs she carried would be used to build her Resistance unit, bribe those so inclined, and fund her own living expenses. Being caught with so much cash would mean a lot of answers to some very tough questions.

This was Virginia's first visit to Vichy, a lovely town in the heart of France, sitting on the banks of the Allier River, three hours south of Paris and four hours north of the Spanish border. Virginia had read up on the town while she was still in London. Its curative sulphurous springs attracted thousands of aging and ailing visitors, or *curistes*, every year. Before the war, they had come to drink the water, wallow in it, inhale its steam, and be sprayed with it.

But a curtain of tension hung heavily in the former spa town now. It had been a ten-minute walk along the rue de Paris from the train station to the town's center. Despite the bright summer sunlight, most passersby Virginia saw looked preoccupied and anxious. They spoke to their companions in hushed voices and none of them were smiling. Virginia's first stop was the office of Ambassador William Leahy at the American Embassy.

The embassy was created almost immediately after the government had formed in Vichy. This act recognizing Vichy as a neutral, sovereign entity by the United States government mollified the majority of Americans who wanted to remain out of the war, continue to provide aid to Great Britain, and refrain from appeasing Hitler. But in addition to these political reasons, there was also the underlying feeling in America that France had been defeated because of her internal weaknesses. By recognizing Vichy—and allowing Gaston Henry-Haye to take up residence in Washington as Vichy ambassador—America sent a message of reproach to France.

Ambassador Leahy was not available when Virginia arrived at the embassy, but his clerk took all of her information and gave her directions to her next destination: the Vichy *gendarmerie*. Her first impression of the Vichy police was better than she expected it to be. She felt completely confident with her new identity and answered all of their polite questions as if it were information she'd been giving her entire life. They, in turn, were very solicitous to her, and appreciative of her adherence to their laws regarding the registration of all newly arrived foreigners. But neither their manners nor their smiles diminished her contempt for their collaboration with the Nazis.

WHEN PÉTAIN AGREED TO AN ARMISTICE with Germany in 1940, it was with the understanding that some type of cooperation with the former enemy would be necessary for his *État français* to succeed. Pétain and his vice premier, Pierre Laval, believed that collaboration with Germany would ensure France a better place in Europe, the new German Europe, once Britain fell and the war ended. They hoped that it would bring a rapid return of the 1.6 million French prisoners of war taken to Germany, who were now really being held as hostages; that it would decrease the indemnity France was required to pay for the German army's upkeep—four hundred million francs per day, the equivalent of nine million dollars. And finally they hoped that it would ensure the sovereignty of the occupied and unoccupied zones.

But the French people weren't sure what to think. A sarcastic new slogan circulated in hushed voices across France, *Donne-moi ta montre, je te dirai l'heure"* (Give me your watch, I'll tell you the time.) It was a tongue-in-cheek criticism that the Nazis were taking everything, and giving very little in return.

Holding all this over the Vichy government's head, Nazi Germany was easily able to force Pétain and Laval's hands. The two men, of course, were quick to conceal this appearance of a puppet show, and were able in many cases to guess in advance what the Germans' next demands would be. They then instituted new laws, making changes look as though they were their idea. Unfortunately, a great many of these new laws were at the expense of France's Jewish population. The Statute des Juifs, which had passed on October 3, 1940, pronounced Jews to be second-class citizens and limited all of their rights. It was a classic reaction.

The Vichy government told its citizenry that France was recovering and that they had done themselves a great disservice by trying to defeat Germany in the first place. The German presence in France was to be welcomed with open arms, because such collaboration would ensure that the Reich would take care of them in the future. For some, the promise of position and wealth after so many years of economic depression was too great a temptation. Renouncing a Jew or a Resistance member was such a small service to exchange for so much. And thus collaboration arrived in the homes of the common man and woman.

VIRGINIA'S HOTEL ON RUE JARDET was small but cozy and her room faced the street exactly as de Guélis had suggested. From her third-floor window, she was able to see quite a distance up and down the street and beyond. Her investigation of Vichy in those first few days revealed that the subject at the forefront of everyone's mind was food, or more accurately, the lack thereof. The majority of France's meat and produce, not to mention the wine and champagne, was going to the Nazis. Even tobacco was rationed: women were still unable to smoke and men were limited to two packs a day.

"Back in May there was plenty of butter on the Swiss border, much more than people could use or buy with their ration cards. But exportation was forbidden," a man in a café confided in her. "Women were to be given an extra ration of sugar in June to preserve strawberries, but it didn't arrive until July, long after the berries were gone. The wine growers needed chemicals to fight bugs in the vineyards, but the chemicals were so delayed that by the time they arrived, the bugs had spread and the grapes were ruined. Transportation and distribution has been as troublesome as the food shortages. If we continue down this road, what shortages are in store for us next year?"

Virginia also got a quick lesson in black market economics from her hotel's owner. "I hear that many food dealers hold back quantities so they can sell them on the black market for greater profits. Black market commerce is dangerous, though. The police are stopping everyone who carries a package or basket and making them show proof of purchase. If they don't have it or their package has more than their allotment . . . Poof! Off to jail! So the black market profiteers have gotten clever—they're using school children, hollowing out their books and moving their contraband that way." To make matters worse, black market prices were eight to ten times higher than they would have been in street markets, if the same foods were available.

It seemed obvious to Virginia that her first *Post* article, which appeared in the Thursday, September 4 issue, should address these matters of privation.

I received my ration card for the month of September today. As I understand it, I'm allowed 10 ounces of bread per day. Beyond that, my allotments for the month are as follows: 2 ounces of cheese, 25 ounces of fats, 20 ounces of sugar, 10 ounces of meat, and 6 ounces of coffee. And by coffee, they mean 2 ounces of real coffee and 4 ounces of some kind of substitute material. . . . No rice, noodles or chocolate are available during the month of September as these are reserved for the colder months. . . . France would be paradise for a vegetarian if there was milk, cheese and butter, but I haven't seen any butter and there is no milk.

Shortly after she sent her article off to New York, Jacques de Guélis contacted Virginia and asked her to join him at a Vichy café. He told her he was returning to *chez nous* soon. Agents never mentioned the word England, but simply referred to it in French as "our place." Virginia handed de Guélis a sealed envelope, which, once decoded in London, would reveal her observations about the Vichy government, the police activity, and the overall climate regarding resistance.

They discussed in guarded language what they both agreed was great potential for the Resistance, as well as what appeared to be a new French attitude toward the British. Those who embraced the British were saying, "If only the English win," while those who still weren't fans were saying, "If only the *goddamned* English would win."

Next they talked about Blacktown, SOE's codename for Lyon. Virginia told him she was headed that way on Saturday and assured him she had memorized the names and addresses of his friends there. De Guélis wished her luck and left. He would begin his trip back to England and hoped to be home by the time Virginia arrived in Lyon.

LYON WAS THE LARGEST CITY in the unoccupied zone and was an important rail and industrial center. It was built around the meeting place of two large French rivers, the Rhône and the Saône. The city's center was a narrow strip of land that lay between the two rivers and on it were the main square, Place Bellecour, and many of the major hotels, including the Grand Nouvel, which Virginia would call home.

The trip from Vichy had taken just over two hours and she arrived midmorning. She took the tram from the railway station, the Gare de Perrache, to the hotel at 11 rue Grolée. She registered as Brigitte LeContre for a room facing the street and lugged her valise up to the third floor. She freshened up and left the hotel to contact the man Jacques had felt would be her best ally in Lyon, gynecologist Dr. Jean Rousset.

Rousset's home and office was at 7 place Antonin Poncer. She gave the man who answered the door her pass phrase, "*Je viens avec des nouvelles de Marie.*" He looked at her closely and asked, "*Voulez-vous dire Marie Renard?*" He smiled then and told her how glad he was to finally meet her. He was a middle-aged man of slight build with round, horned-rimmed glasses and a pleasant face. He had been very busy since de Guélis had left, he said, and had made the acquaintance of several individuals who were eagerly waiting to help the cause.

Virginia became instinctively cautious. Falling into a trap so early in the game would not only be potentially hazardous, it would be embarrassing. She asked Rousset about their trustworthiness. His answer was reassuring. He had known these people since they were all *petits*, he said. It would not be difficult for him to determine if they were lying. And these friends, in turn, had recommended others, although Rousset deferred to Virginia to make the final determination about them.

Virginia wondered what skills this man thought she possessed that would allow her to see into the souls of others. She was a good judge of character, but in this arena it was vital that she judge carefully. Nonetheless, she was anxious to meet them. Rousset suggested they all meet at the Café de la République on rue de la République that evening for dinner around 7:30. The group would consist of his longtime friend Robert, who lived near the restaurant, and M. and Mme Joulian, who lived a few streets over.

Virginia told him she knew the restaurant and that the time and place would work for her and then asked him if he would be willing to make his office available as a letter box. Having somewhere that they could leave written messages for one another was one of the first things they would need.

Her timid approach at asking about his willingness of involvement amused Rousset, and he asked her if she thought that resistance was something only recently invented in England. Many Frenchmen, he told her, had thought of nothing else for months. They were devoted to freeing their country of invaders and collaborators and they wanted liberation at all costs. He was, he said, grateful that she was willing to risk danger in the same cause and he put himself and his office at her disposal.

Virginia was delighted to find such a gem of a man. De Guélis must have recognized all of the same characteristics. After she left Rousset's, she took the rest of the afternoon to explore Lyon. It was about four times the size of Vichy, and dominated by two hills. Atop one sat a beautiful basilica. The other hill was home to many of the city's famous silk shops. But despite the picturesque setting, the city's inhabitants closely resembled those of Vichy. Everyone she passed appeared to be guarded, looking straight ahead with a somber fixation. Children peeked out from behind their parents, seemingly sensing that all was not right with their world.

Virginia found the Café de la République with no problem that evening and arrived just as Rousset did. He led her to a table where a tall man had waved them over. Already seated with him was a middle-aged couple. The three smiled at her and shook her hand when Rousset introduced her. It was a *jour sans alcool*, a day when no alcohol was allowed, yet one more of the inconvenient rationings plaguing the country. Sweet aperitifs were allowed, however: *grenache*, *banyuls*, or *muscat*. They each ordered their favorite and began to size one another up.

Robert Le Provost was the tall, lanky chap who had waved. He appeared to be in his midthirties. His face had a sad appearance, even when he smiled. He told Virginia that he had worked for the French Service des Renseignments (Information Bureau) for fifteen years. He finished his monologue by telling her that his father had owned a small fishing company in Marseille and that he therefore had quite a few friends in the south of France. Virginia wasn't sure whether Le Provost was trying to assure her that he was congenial despite his cheerless countenance, or that she might find his friends interesting.

The middle-aged couple, M. and Mme Joulian, were the exact opposite of Le Provost. They were short, round, and jolly. They owned a small factory that produced pots and pans, they told Virginia. They had never had any children and so both worked long hours in the factory.

For her part, Virginia explained that she was in France as a stringer for the *New York Post*. No one flinched at that statement and Virginia wondered if Rousset had told them what her real purpose was in France. When the waiter appeared with large menus, they all began reading. Lyon was famous for its cuisine, but Virginia expected little. Amazingly, everything on the menu was marked as available. She asked her companions why.

Rousset explained that they were in a black market restaurant and that the owner, also their waiter, was an old friend, and a Resistance sympathizer.

They could order anything they wanted, regardless of what food coupons they had available. If, however, someone came in without a connection, they'd get a pretty meager meal.

When the owner returned for their orders, Rousset introduced him to Virginia and told him Mlle LeContre was a very good friend and needed to be taken care of. The man smiled broadly and said cryptically that friends were important in times like these.

As soon as the ordering was completed, Le Provost told Virginia quietly that one of "her" pilots was living at his house. She gathered he assumed from her accent that she was British. The pilot had been shot down, was uninjured, and was anxious to return home. He asked her if she could help, saying he had connections in Marseille to get him out, but needed money in order to pay for the transportation.

Virginia was taken aback. The conversation had turned serious so quickly. Le Provost had evidently developed an immediate confidence in her and was willing to take Rousset's word for it that she was the genuine article. She asked him if the pilot had false identification papers and ration cards. He didn't, but Le Provost had a friend who worked in the Food Office and could get ration cards. Another friend printed identification documents all day long for the Vichy government and would be happy to oblige them with what they needed. All it took was the right number of francs.

It was incredible. The underpinnings of a strong Resistance circuit were being presented to Virginia on a platter along with the excellent French cuisine. Greased with the cash she had brought from England, the wheels of resistance could begin to turn immediately.

Virginia told Le Provost they could get to work on the project right away. The pilot would have valuable information that would no doubt help them down the road. Everything learned from that moment forward would build the foundation for the future.

The five of them next discussed how the Joulians' factory would come into play. M. Joulian enthusiastically told Virginia they would be able to keep her up to date on the availability of strategic materials, things that would not seem uncommon for them to inquire about. From there, they could guess how much the Germans were getting and what was running in short supply. Mme Joulian interrupted him to say that their home would be open to anyone who needed it.

Virginia cautioned them about communication. She explained the value of using Rousset's office as a letter box. And she told them they would need to use code words occasionally. Anyone passing through their homes would be referred to as "brothers." And they were being sent to *chez nous*. By the time her first dinner in Lyon came to an end, Virginia felt as though she had forged a wonderful group of allies.

The next morning, Virginia contacted the other name de Guélis had recommended, Mme Germaine Guérin, whose address was not far from the hotel. Jacques had been accurate in identifying Rousset as a sound aide in their work. Virginia hoped that his second suggestion panned out as well.

A maid answered the door, and Virginia gave her name. The maid left for a moment, then returned to ask Virginia to follow her. The apartment was beautifully appointed with rugs and artwork. The furniture was lavish and the draperies were yards of fine silk. Mme Guérin was seated in a drawing room sipping a café au lait.

Virginia gave her the pass phrase as soon as she entered the room. Mme Guérin responded and once the maid left told Virginia how glad she was that she had finally arrived. The woman was fiftyish, with blue-black hair swept up in a twist. She wore a morning coat as sumptuous as her surroundings and already had on an ample coat of rouge and lipstick.

Virginia thanked her for the welcome and accepted the café she offered. It was *real* coffee with *real* milk. And it was wonderful after several weeks of consuming the brown liquid that had replaced the authentic brew. The *café national*, as it was called, was one quarter coffee to three quarters ground acorns.

Mme Guérin told Virginia that the only thing she knew about her was what she had been told by the gentleman who'd stopped by some weeks earlier. He said that Virginia was an American journalist in France to collect money to help General de Gaulle. She was a Gaullist to the end and was happy to help however she could. Virginia thanked her and told her there may also be a need for used clothing and extra food in the future. Would she be willing to donate those as well?

Mme Guérin agreed immediately, telling Virginia that one of her hobbies was finding things for those in need through her black market contacts. In addition, through her business of providing comfort to others, she said her employees were occasionally made privy to information. She would be happy to pass that along as well if Virginia thought it might be of help.

Virginia was confused about where the information would come from, and Mme Guérin explained that her clients, many of them Vichy officials, sought out girls of the right beauty and class. And those were the only kind she employed.

A light went on for Virginia. Mme Guérin was the proprietress of a brothel. But her vocation was of no concern. Virginia felt confident that the woman was sincere and accepted her offer graciously. Furthermore, she was willing to work with Virginia without knowing any additional details about her than she already did. That would work to her favor if she were ever questioned about Virginia. She wouldn't be able to give any more information than she herself had been given.

VIRGINIA'S SECOND ARTICLE for the *Post* appeared a few weeks later in October 1941. It was titled "Odd Bits," its humorous tone quite a contrast to the seriousness of Virginia's real mission in Lyon.

The war has caused most of the people in France to change their ways and customs in greater or lesser degree. Everybody eats less than before, of course; most people wear less. The most honest have their little peccadillos now-a-days about getting a piece of cheese without tickets, or a pair of socks on the black market. Whether morals will snap back once the situation returns to normal or not is the question. For the present, practically everyone is cherishing and condoning dishonesty in some degree. . . .

Everyone mops these days so that not a drop of good sauce escapes. . . . The more uncouth take a large chunk of bread in their fingers and go to it with vim . . . sopping and rubbing until the plate is clean. I foresee that the ordinary glaze (on the plate) is not going to be able to withstand such onslaughts. . . . Once the glaze is gone it would not take long to mop a hole clean through to the other side. So I foresee new life in the ceramic industry, the end of cheap pottery and china.

Then there's the question of fishing. . . . It has changed from a sport to a means to an end. The end being dinner—God willing. . . . I was fascinated by a cheery gent with a cherry nose, a very bright eye and a lively tongue who spread at his feet on the platform by the side of the [tram] car some black moist earth on newspapers. "Worms, worms," he cried. "Nice, fine, dainty worms, come and get 'em." And they did! . . . One old chap got in the car, sat down ahead of me, looked out the window at the worm man for a bit, then couldn't bear it any longer and out he went. He came back with a most stained little bundle of black earth and red "dainty" worms. Another fisherman across the aisle engaged him in conversation. "Fine but solid—that's the secret of fishing. They're fine ones too, and hard to get now." (Do even worms disappear with the occupation?)

Virginia's November 24 article was of an entirely different nature, painting a clear picture of the ever-tightening noose the Nazis and the collaborators were throwing around the necks of all French Jews. It was titled "Vichy Bars Stock to Jews: Further Economic Bans Expected."

A law forbidding acquisition of stock by Jews without special permission has just been passed. . . . Jews are not permitted to be bankers, stockbrokers, publicity agents, merchants, real estate agents or owners, owners of gambling concessions, nor are they allowed to earn a living by working in the theatre, movies or for the press. . . . The Lyon regional office of the General Jewish Commissariat announced on Friday the placing of 36 Jewish enterprises under temporary administration. This means that "Aryans" have been appointed to direct the firms until sale or other liquidation. . . . Among the firms dealt with are banks, movie companies, textile, gas and iron companies and one newspaper.

9

RESISTANCE IS BORN

AS DR. ROUSSET HAD POINTED OUT to Virginia in their first meeting, the seeds of resistance were alive in some French people from the very moment Pétain's government capitulated. They preferred death to accepting German domination. In fact, according to SOE estimates, only one French citizen in one hundred was ready to resist in 1940. Those who felt the fire were united in their belief that Nazi ideology was depraved, but they operated informally and in small groups with no long-term strategy.

The groups began with modest gestures of resistance. They furtively affixed posters to city buildings calling for others to resist. They redirected freight cars loaded with supplies for Germany. They sabotaged German equipment and vehicles.

Passive resistance existed, too. In an attempt to delay production of goods needed by the German army, workers carried out their tasks as slowly as possible and employers observed the last letter of the complicated bureaucratic regulations.

The groups' membership had no age or gender biases. From young women, their faces hidden by umbrellas, to aged men feigning blindness, the few did what they could to hamper the invaders and encourage others to join them. Retribution by the Nazis against those who were captured was swift and sure: execution, with a recognizable red and black public notice containing a photograph of the dead.

One of the earliest organized groups in Paris grew from a group of scientists and lawyers. They called themselves the Musée de l'Homme

(Museum of Mankind). These brave men published an anti-Nazi newspaper, helped downed RAF pilots, and were even able to make contact with the SOE in London. But mere months after development, their ranks were infiltrated by a Vichy agent. The entire group was arrested and most were executed by firing squad. As he was about to die, one of the resisters screamed at his Vichy executioners, "Imbeciles, it's for you, too, that I die!"

In the zone libre, organized resistance took root in Lyon. The city had always had a political bent, and a handful of individuals took it upon themselves to counteract the propaganda being spread by the Vichy-controlled radio and newspapers. In 1940, Henri Frenay, a former French army officer, organized the Libération Nationale in Lyon and oversaw the publication of two papers, *Les Petites Ailes* (Little Wings) and *Vérité* (Truth) in early 1941.

At the same time, Émmanuel d'Astier formed a group of left-wing saboteurs in Lyon that became known as the Libération-sud (Liberation South). The publication of the group's paper, *Libération*, debuted in July 1941. A third Resistance newspaper appeared in Lyon as well, titled *Franc-Tireur* (Sniper), which was published by Jewish lawyer Jean-Pierre Lévy.

The publishers all had to beg, borrow, or steal ink, paper, and presses to create their newspapers. Once they were printed, they were sealed in plain envelopes and hand-delivered to sympathetic individuals, especially those who would be in contact with the public, such as doctors and priests. And, of course, being caught in possession of one of these periodicals was considered an absolute crime. The guilty were hustled off to jail, where they were first beaten in an effort to gain information about other Resistance members, then sent to a prison camp.

Lyon's underground newspapers gradually drew their readers into a single group with common goals: reclamation of their country and their dignity. They had great faith in their ideals, and for many, dying seemed but a small price to pay. The groups were divided into cells, or circuits, for greater security. If Vichy or the Nazis infiltrated one circuit, the entire operation would not have to shut down. They met where and when they could, making use of the hidden passageways in Lyon, the *traboules*, as a means of escape when pursued by Vichy authorities. The *traboules* connected the buildings of old Lyon and had been created by the city's early inhabitants as shortcuts to the river for water. In the dark days of the early 1940s, they became blessed sanctuaries for Resistance members.

With Virginia's arrival in Lyon signaling the promise of Allied help for their cause, those who were willing to risk all came gladly out of the shadows. And, as a cavalcade of agents arrived from Baker Street, bringing with them cash, radio transmitters, and training, the French Resistance became a self-assured force to be reckoned with.

One day, a month and a half after Virginia's arrival in Lyon, Le Provost showed her a notice that had run in that day's Vichy newspaper. The notice, from General von Stulpnagel, the military governor in Paris, had been published in the capital's newspaper the day before.

> Notice: any male person directly or indirectly helping the crew of enemy aircraft landed by parachute or having effected a forced landing, or assisting in their evasion, or hiding or helping them in any way whatever, will be shot immediately.
>
> Women guilty of the same offence will be deported to concentration camps in Germany.
>
> Any persons seizing crew members having effected a forced landing or descended by parachute, or who, by their attitude, contribute to their capture, will receive a reward of up to 10,000 Francs. In some special cases the reward will be even higher.

Le Provost had heard via the Resistance grapevine that the Vichy government had already announced it would follow a similar path with regard to downed airmen. The *gendarmes* and the collaborators would be eager to turn in whomever they could to get their hands on the money and the prestige, Le Provost told Virginia. His guess was that many of Vichy's pseudo officials were men who had been picked on when they were *petit*. Now they had been given positions of power and could potentially receive big favors from the Nazis if they turned over a member of the Resistance or a Jew. And there was double the reward for someone who was both. The man after whom all the other Vichy officials had patterned themselves, Le Provost said, was Secretary General René Bousquet.

Bousquet supervised the Vichy gendarmerie. In 1930, he had become a national celebrity at the age of twenty when he helped in rescue efforts during a flood near Toulouse in southern France. The next year he went to work in a government office and remained there after the armistice between Pétain and the Germans.

Bousquet became a fanatical administrator who was quick to embrace the German victory and who appreciated the Germans' commitment to order and anti-Communism. He hunted Resistance members with gusto. He ordered those captured turned over to the Gestapo, which tortured them using horrific means. Their toenails were torn out one by one. They were burned with hot pokers. They were electrocuted with wires attached to the breasts of the captive women and the genitals of the men. Other preferred means included filing down prisoners' teeth, slitting the soles of prisoners' feet and forcing them to walk on salt, and of course food, drink, and sleep depravation.

Bousquet's plan with regard to the Jews in France was simple: rid the country of them by any means. He made certain that anti-Semitic propaganda ran on the radio, in the newspapers, and on the newsreels. And he supported the great campaign to distinguish the Jews from the French. "Ninety percent of old French stock are pure-bred whites," the campaign's brochures maintained. "The Jews are the result of thousands of years of inbreeding between the Mongols, blacks and whites." Because of this racial mix, the campaign contended, Jews have unique faces, bodies, attitudes, and gestures. The public was told to study these characteristics to learn to recognize them.

Gradually, the positive Jewish presence was removed from the public eye. Jewish actors' and directors' names were erased from the credits of French films. Most pre-Nazi films were melted down, the remains made into nail polish and shoe polish. Replacing them in the cinemas were overt, anti-Jewish propaganda films, some made solely by the Nazis and others a collaboration of the Germans and Vichy. Such was the case of the documentary *The Jewish Peril*. "The Jew is like a rat," the film proclaimed. "He is sly and cruel. He feels the irresistible need to destroy. The Jews' power lies in their superior numbers and, like proliferating rats, they are a danger to human health."

Anti-Semitism, it appeared, was one of the ominous common bonds between the German conquerors and the spineless Vichy government. It was accompanied by anti-Communism and good old-fashioned self-interest.

BY LATE NOVEMBER 1941, Virginia was performing a juggling act as she continued to establish Resistance contacts, help downed British pilots, and welcome newly arrived SOE agents from England. But unlike keeping mere circus balls in the air, there were deadly consequences should any one of these drop.

Dr. Rousset's office was being used regularly as a letter box where agents and Resistance members could drop off and pick up communiqués to one another. Mme Guérin's promise of money, food, and clothing had proven to be better than Virginia expected. The woman still had not asked her about the destination of the donations, although she had made numerous comments regarding the Resistance to which Virginia would simply smile. And the information that her "girls" gleaned from their clients kept them all aware of Vichy surveillance of particular areas and persons. With the help of Le Provost's friends in the printing offices, Virginia was not only able to supply papers to those in need in France, she was also able to send out current samples of ration books and *cartes d'identité* (identity cards) with agents returning to England. The appearance of these documents changed regularly and it was crucial that incoming agents have exact forgeries.

A friend of Mme Guérin's, Paul Genet, joined Virginia's group shortly after the madam. He was well connected within the Vichy gendarmerie and feigned support of Pétain's government. In reality, he was repulsed by it and was only too willing to pass on the names of officials whom he believed could be bribed into any number of things provided the price was right.

Virginia suggested to Genet that she would like to interview some of the Vichy officials for the *Post*. She was interested in hearing their stories in order to better understand what made them tick. Her premise amused Genet. He understood only too well that what she was really after was what they knew and whether they might be willing to sell their information. He set up the meeting as a lunch two days later, choosing a pro-Vichy restaurant. Despite the fact that the French population at large was going hungry, Vichy officials ate very well in certain establishments in exchange for protection from persecution.

One of the individuals at the luncheon was the director of the press in Lyon. It was his responsibility to make sure that only the "correct" news, that is, news with a German slant, was printed. The second man was a major in the gendarmerie, and had been a police officer before the war as well. The third was associated with the mayor's office, although Virginia never completely understood what his job was.

The director of the press asked Virginia right away how she liked the city. Virginia answered that she thought the city was beautiful, but felt badly that she had come at such an unpleasant time. She hoped by offering an opening for criticism of the current regime, the men's answers would give her a good idea where they stood.

The director waved aside her comment, saying it was the perfect time to be in Lyon. It was because of people like her that the world would soon see all of the wonderful changes occurring in France. He expounded on this comment, while the other two men sat in silence. When he excused himself to use the *toilettes*, the representative from the mayor's office leaned forward to tell Virginia that there were some who would like other facts to be told in America. The food shortage, for example, was troublesome and was having a great effect on the people, mentally and physically.

Virginia thought this was a very brave statement to make in front of the major, who said nothing. In fact he didn't speak much during the entire luncheon. When they shook hands and parted ways, Virginia concluded that the newspaperman was too pro-Vichy to be of any help. The silence of the major bothered her as it could be read either way. But the representative from the mayor's office had possibilities and she filed his name away in her mind for future contact.

As she rounded a corner on the way back to her hotel, Virginia came across a shocking commotion. Three gendarmes were viciously beating and kicking an elderly man on the sidewalk. Each time he tried to rise, they kicked him down again. Blood from his nose and mouth stained the snow. When he stopped resisting them, the gendarmes dragged him out to the street and threw him into the back of their police van. Shopkeepers had come to their doors to watch, and other passersby had paused briefly, but none of them had tried to intervene. When the van left, they all resumed their activities.

The brutality of the scene sickened Virginia. Her father, had he been alive, would have been approximately the same age as the man the gendarmes had just hauled off. What had his crime been? Surely it couldn't have been so grave as to require three officers to publicly beat him to bloody unconsciousness.

The Vichy authorities were equally merciless whenever they captured downed RAF airmen wandering the zone libre. The lucky ones came in contact with Resistance circuits and a steady stream of them kept Virginia's group busy. The best way for them to get back to England was through Spain, but they needed connections. Virginia's Resistance organization, code-named HECKLER, had become well known among the other groups as a circuit with many ties. Lyon, they were told before leaving England, was the place to go if they ran into trouble.

If they were wounded, Dr. Rousset, whose code name was Pepin and whom Virginia called Pep, tended to them. He was willing to undertake just about anything Virginia asked of him. He worked tirelessly and Virginia knew he would die before divulging any secrets about their organization. She wanted to feel the kind of emotion for him that would be normal for one friend to feel for another. But she didn't dare. The cardinal rule in espionage, they had repeated during her training, was never to get involved in any way with anyone else.

Virginia's life was a bizarre jumble of paradoxes. She was constantly surrounded by people with whom she could never become close. They thought she was someone she wasn't. None of them could ever know the exact nature of her mission, nor the missions of one another. Whether or not Virginia trusted them was not the issue. The fact was that affection, or love, or whatever one chose to call it, could cloud decision making. And that was not a chance she was willing to take. For a gregarious American who loved people, this self-imposed detachment from others was one of the toughest parts of her mission.

Equally challenging was assuring the downed pilots that she really did know what she was doing. Dropping into a hostile country, barely speaking the language, and running for one's life were all very unnerving. Being turned over to a woman and told to trust in her to assist with their escape was more than some of them could stomach. But they had no choice. Until the right opportunity for passage to Spain arose, they were virtually under Virginia's command and housed with Lyon Resistance members or at Mme Guérin's brothel. Those whose French was not passable had their throats bandaged by Dr. Rousset. And the good doctor provided them with a card that explained they had suffered a war injury that affected their ability to speak.

Escape routes out of France were limited. The Germans controlled the north and the west, the Italians the east. Warships patrolled the Mediterranean and most of the ports were blockaded. Sometimes, however, Le Provost's contacts in Marseille would be able to receive them. In that case, the pilots were shipped out in a truck belonging to fleet owner Eugène Labourier. Once in Marseille, they would board a local watercraft, usually some kind of fishing vessel, which would take them to a Spanish Mediterranean port. The most preferred method of exfiltration, however, was a trip in one of Labourier's trucks to Perpignon, a French city on the Spanish border, where the pilots connected with a guide who led them across the Pyrénées.

Virginia worked primarily behind the scenes and she rarely met face-to-face with the escaping pilots. But one cold day in early December, it was left to her to give a pilot his final instructions before he began the journey to the Spanish border. Although there was no more heat in the cafés than in any other building, warmth from human bodies helped make up for the lack of it coming from the furnace, so eateries became preferred meeting places. Plus, cafés and restaurants gave the HECKLER members a reason for congregating; sipping a beverage of choice, limited as the choices were, remained a national pastime.

The Brit spoke French very well, with a much better accent than Virginia's. He could very easily have passed for a Frenchman. But he had been in the country only a week, spending most of his time in hiding. His lack of familiarity with the new French laws became apparent when he ordered a beer. The waiter looked at him in surprise and pointed to the sign hanging over the bar. It pictured a beached whale expiring on the sand. Below it were printed the words *Jour sans alcool.*

Virginia ordered two grenaches, as if she hadn't even heard the pilot's order. When the waiter left, she quietly explained the law to the pilot. But his faux pas did not go unnoticed, and a few minutes later two men in suits walked up to their table and demanded to see their papers.

Virginia and the Brit produced their identification documents and sat quietly as the officials studied them. Virginia felt her pulse pounding in her head. Her papers were authentic, but the pilot's were forgeries, hastily produced for him to use in his border crossing. The agonizing seconds ticked off. Finally, one of the officials bent very close to the pilot and asked why he had ordered a beer on a *jour sans alcool.*

The pilot opened his mouth, but no words came out. He turned his wild eyes to Virginia. She looked directly at the officials and lied with complete sangfroid, telling them that the man suffered from a mental condition. He had no idea what day it was or what changes had occurred in France over the past couple of years. Her lie was picking up steam.

She was interviewing him, she said, for an article she was writing for the *New York Post.* Once the interview was completed, she would return him to the care of his doctor. She waved her hand airily in the direction of the official still holding the papers saying her nationality and profession were explained quite clearly, if the men would care to read them more closely.

They studied Virginia's credentials again and looked back at her, seemingly memorizing her face, before moving away. When their grenaches arrived, Virginia and the Brit drank them in relative silence, and as quickly as they dared without seeming obvious. When they left the café, they took a circuitous route to Pep's office on the off chance that they were being followed, but it appeared as though they were alone. Virginia told Pep about their encounter, while the poor airman, visibly shaken, tried in vain to light a cigarette.

But the whole incident gave Virginia an idea. She suggested to Pep that they establish an asylum as a cover for all of the other "mentally unstable" who might pass through his doors. After all, the collapse of France had been traumatic and there must be myriad French soldiers who were affected. An asylum would be the perfect excuse to give to Pep's housekeeper and neighbors to explain the number of strange men suddenly visiting the clinic. And it would give them the opportunity to keep these men close until they could escape through Spain.

As he had with all of Virginia's requests, Pep agreed without hesitation. But ideas such as these were always accompanied with setup costs, paid for with large amounts of mostly counterfeit francs brought to Virginia by arriving SOE agents. Some of these agents came ashore in watercraft, but many of them arrived by parachute.

Parachute drops had become quite commonplace for SOE and the Resistance. The plane of choice in 1941 was the Westland Lysander, a small, single-engine monoplane that could cruise up to 165 miles per hour. If it was stripped of all arms and armor and equipped with an extra fuel tank, it had a range of 450 miles, more than enough to travel across the channel and back again. Besides the pilot, it could seat two passengers comfortably, three or four if absolutely necessary.

Flights to France occurred during the fuller phases of the moon, its light being the only one pilots had available. They navigated using landmarks like rivers, as well as dead reckoning. Initially, agents were dropped in blind, with no one to meet them. But once the Resistance and agent population grew, reception committees were commonplace. The circuit leader chose a landing strip and its coordinates were determined by placing a clear plastic device on a map of the area. The device had numbered grids on it, and it was the chosen grid number, rather than a city name, that was transmitted to London as the drop location.

The reception committee met at the agreed-upon location, and when the plane arrived, it was signaled in code from the ground using a flashlight. Once the plane flashed a response, the rest of the committee illuminated the landing strip with their lights. Their positions on the field always took into consideration the direction and speed of the wind, the goal being that the arriving agent would arrive exactly in their midst. Depending on the situation, occasionally bonfires were used in place of flashlights. Once the incoming agents had floated to earth, their flight suits and parachutes were buried and the whole group dispersed in minutes to avoid attention from nosy neighbors, passing gendarmes, or Gestapo agents.

SOE parachuted in supplies as well. Weapons and ammunition, explosive supplies, wireless sets with repair pieces, clothing, medical supplies, K rations, and anything else that was necessary could be packed into large cylindrical containers. Rarely was the total weight over one hundred pounds. Some containers were six feet tall, with three smaller cylinders inside. Others consisted of five separate cylinders bound together. SOE's packing staff was top notch; rarely did items arrive in poor condition. One of their finest achievements was a drop of two hundred bottles of printer's ink for a Resistance newspaper. Not one bottle was cracked.

One agent to parachute in during the full moon of September 1941 was thirty-three-year-old Ben Cowburn, a Lancashire oil technician. His mission was to travel through France making a study of potential oil targets, finding out which were being used by the Germans that could become bombing objectives. When his tour finally took him to the vicinity of Lyon in December, he went to the Grand Nouvel Hôtel to look up Virginia.

The two of them went to dinner at a black market restaurant along with Pep. Cowburn told Virginia how highly thought of she was back in London. He commended her for her work, in light of her leg. Pep asked Cowburn what he was talking about. Cowburn was embarrassed at the slip, but Virginia only shrugged it off telling Pep she had had an accident a few years back and in order to save her life, she lost the leg. She simply didn't think it was important enough to mention to him. It was just one of those inconveniences one had to deal with in life. She told them she refused to let "Cuthbert" hold her back, and when they looked confused, she explained she had long ago bestowed her leg with the name.

Virginia steered the conversation back to business asking Cowburn about new piano players. Agents used the term to refer to wireless operators, calling the radios pianos. As there was no one within earshot and their waiter was keeping a discreet distance, Virginia told Cowburn of her concern at being out of touch with London. The HECKLER circuit had been cut off since an entire group of incoming agents, including a wireless operator, had been picked up a couple of months earlier.

Not coincidentally, Cowburn told her he had been asked by London to enlist her help with a group of agents whose mission had been code-named CORSICA. They had parachuted into France on October 10, the first combined drop of men and arms into the zone libre. One of them landed badly a mile or so from his comrades. He was knocked unconscious and picked up by the gendarmes the next day. In his pocket they found the address of a safe house near Châteauroux, the Villa des Bois. The Vichy police went to the villa and arrested everyone there. Among them, in fact, was a Frenchman, Gabriel, who had been recruited by de Guélis.

The gendarmes waited, and as the "Corsicans" arrived one by one, they were arrested as well. A total of a dozen men were picked up, two of whom were wireless operators. It was a huge setback to lose so many men at one time.

Since her arrival, one of the things Virginia had refused to give in to were thoughts of "what if?" What if she was putting her Resistance friends at too great a risk? What if any of them were arrested? Could they hold up under torture? And what if agents she had given information or money to were stopped? She had been incredibly careful, even protective, of all those under her watch. Cowburn's story turned those worries into a reality. She had seen what the Vichy gendarmes were capable of. What the Corsicans would probably endure as enemies of the state was unthinkable. The only way she could remain effective was to maintain a distance from her emotions.

She asked Cowburn where the men had been taken. His answer gave her chills. They were in Beleyme Prison in Périgueux, whose reputation was one of the worst in France. Hygiene and sanitation were nonexistent, little food was provided, and most of it was rotten. Disease and vermin ran rampant. SOE was buying information from a guard, who told them one of the wireless operators had already been shot, after having been tortured for several days.

Virginia was ready to help any way she and her circuit members could. Cowburn told her she might be asked to help with bribes or an escape. He said he felt badly about burdening her with one more job, as he had heard just about everyone in the zone libre came to see her for one reason or another. But Virginia made it plain to Cowburn that his request *was* her job just as all the others were.

ON DECEMBER 8, 1941, Virginia stopped in at the shop of Labourier's girlfriend, Andrée Michel. Maggy, as her friends called her, had joined the Resistance with Labourier and had become invaluable as a courier. She was the first to deliver unthinkable news to Virginia: the United States had been bombed by the Japanese.

It had happened the day before on December 7, Andrée explained. A naval base in Hawaii was the target. Most of the ships were sunk and many people were killed. President Roosevelt had just asked the American Congress to declare war against Japan, and Congress accepted.

Virginia's life had been so involved with the war in Europe that an attack against the United States by Japan was not something she had ever considered. The days that followed were filled with an even more amazing series of events. Britain also declared war against Japan on the eighth, as several of their territories had been bombed at the same time as Hawaii. Then, on Thursday, December 11, first Mussolini and then Hitler declared war against the United States. Making his announcement at the Reichstag in Berlin, Hitler said he had tried to avoid direct conflict with the United States, but under the Tripartite Agreement signed on September 27, 1940, Germany was obliged to join Italy to defend its ally Japan. He accused President Roosevelt of waging a campaign against Germany since 1937, blamed him for the outbreak of war in 1939, and said the United States had a plan to invade Germany in 1943.

President Roosevelt's response was swift and Congress voted to declare war on Germany and Italy. Virginia heard excerpts of the president's speech to the American public that night on the BBC's French broadcast:

> On the morning of December 11, the Government of Germany, pursuing its course of world conquest, declared war against the United States. . . . Delay invites great danger. Rapid and united effort by all of the peoples of the world who are determined to remain free will insure a world victory of the forces of justice and of righteousness over the forces of savagery and of barbarism.

This put Virginia in an unusual position. She was living legally in unoccupied France, but it was an entity within a country now occupied by a nation that had declared war against the United States. Diplomatic ties between Washington and Vichy France had remained intact. And Virginia's only close call with the Vichy authorities thus far had been with the Brit in the café. Still, she didn't know whether or not that incident put her name on a watch list. It was crucial now that, while she continued to lead her dual life, she pay close attention to any clues that might suggest she was an arrest target.

Virginia's December article for the *Post* appeared lighthearted, given the gravity of events around her. But reading between the lines, her message was quite serious. It was a commentary on the sorry condition of her surroundings and the verminlike regime under which they all struggled. It was titled "La Charmante."

> La Charmante has returned to France in a big way after an absence of over a century. . . . La Charmante is the soubriquet given by Napoleon's soldiers to the mange which they knew so well and so fondly. . . . Mange is a cowardly disease, veritably the soul of pusillanimity, and appears to plague man and beast alike when they are suffering from fatigue, under-nourishment with resulting bad physical condition, and are not as clean as they might be.

The mange that Virginia wrote about was an affliction caused by microscopic mites that burrow under the skin to lay eggs. The resulting rash itches horribly, particularly at night, and often causes the sufferer to scratch so radically that sores appear. Animal mange can't be passed to humans, but the condition is extremely contagious between humans. She continued:

> Hannibal, ever solicitous for the well being of his men and horses, discovered this cowardly character of mange too. . . . The cure which Hannibal used so effectively was to wash his troops in wine. . . . Such a delightful cure would, alas, be impossible in France today. . . . Its reintroduction into the country was slow, but with the progressive difficulties of food and consequent deterioration of the health of the population, with fatigue burdening people who no longer ride in trams, busses and taxis but

who walk and bike and stand in food queues for hours at a time, with the increasing scarcity of soap and the decreasing frequency with which personal or household linen can be washed, mange has found an ideal terrain in which to flourish and spread.

WHILE VIRGINIA CAME FROM a fairly privileged family, other SOE agents came from elevated social circles as well. Baron Pierre de Vomécourt was one of them, a genuine landed gentry and a handsome fast-talker who was a good shot and a fast thinker. His family had rendered great service to France, most often in the form of combat against Germanic armies. His great-grandfather had been tortured and killed by Prussian invaders in 1870, his father died early in World War I, and his elder brother, Jean, lied about his age to join the fighting in 1917 and was seriously wounded. In short, the recent German invasion was more than Pierre could stomach. Attached to a British Army regiment as Anglo-French liaison officer, he was evacuated from Dunkirk just before France fell in 1940. In London, he was recruited into a British military regiment, and then, for obvious reasons, by the SOE. He knew the country, the language, and had contacts.

Of SOE, de Vomécourt believed that "the ultimate goal was to provide the French with the means to share in the liberation of their country, but the immediate objective was to thwart the enemy's war production in France—by disrupting the transport and delivery of raw materials, sabotage at the work place, deliberate errors in the administration and planning munitions production, etc."

More than a year passed before he was sent back to France and much had changed in the country, most of which British intelligence was not yet aware. Pierre was to discover that when, as the first Free French SOE agent, he parachuted in blind on May 10, 1941, there was no reception committee to meet him. He ordered a coffee with cognac the next morning, not understanding it was a *jour sans alcool*. He managed to escape the officials called by the café owner and eventually found his way to his younger brother, Philippe's, château. Jean joined them at the château and Pierre recruited them both.

The de Vomécourts divided France into three parts to recruit anti-Nazis willing to take part in the Resistance. As Philippe's château was near Limoges, he became responsible for the part of the country that lay south of the Loire River and started the ANTOINE circuit (*réseau*). Jean lived near Pontarlier, near the Swiss border, so he began the AUTOGIRO réseau in eastern France, while Pierre headed back to Paris to start up the GARDENER réseau. Although SOE normally funded its circuits, these men used a great deal of their own money for their réseaux.

Pierre arranged for SOE's first parachute drop to be made near Philippe's château. The latter enlisted the help of his gardener's son-in-law to handle the reception and together they hid the stores. Included among them was a good deal of explosives, meant to create havoc on the railroad system. Moving it across the demarcation line into the occupied zone and his brother's waiting réseau would be difficult. Shipments of goods by train were next to impossible, even for Philippe, who was employed as a railroad inspector. And all trucks were carefully searched. But Philippe had a farmer friend who was an apiarist and was sympathetic to the Resistance. They loaded the farmer's truck with bees and beehives, hiding the explosives in one corner. No German guard wanted to thoroughly search among the bees, and the explosives arrived safely at their destination.

Although he had almost been picked up with the others in the raid against the Corsicans, Philippe had thus far remained untouched by the Nazis or their sympathizers. Having been in Paris on railroad business in January 1942, he passed through Lyon on his return to the zone libre and met with Virginia to give her a report on the situation in France's sad capital. When the Nazis first arrived, they made quite an impression on the Parisians, Philippe told her. Their dress and demeanor were nothing short of perfect. They looked fresh and well fed. One elderly World War I veteran told him that the Germans really deserved their victory and if one had to lose, it was something to be beaten by such an army.

The Parisians were pleasantly surprised. The soldiers and officers let the women exit the Métro cars first and they offered to carry heavy loads for the elderly. But it wasn't long before the Parisians realized that the Germans' propriety did not make up for the fact that they were taking the food right out of the Parisians' mouths.

Now, only the Germans rode in the first-class Métro cars, Philippe said. And if they rode in second class, no one sat on either side of them. Most people preferred to walk to their destinations, so Paris streets had become a popular place for conversations. The Germans soon figured this out, and the Gestapo sent over an army of well-dressed, French-speaking German women to infiltrate the streets and stores and eavesdrop on the conversations.

Worst of all were the food shortages, which were so dramatic that Parisians were literally starving daily. Some collapsed on the street, while others sat in doorways and stared vacantly into space. Food would arrive at the markets through the front door and was immediately taken out the back door to the awaiting Germans.

Paris, Philippe said, was two cities. Besides the city he had just described, food was plentiful in the other Paris. At the big restaurants, Maxime's, Fouquet's, Le Boeuf sur le Toit, one could have anything, as long as one was a German officer, one of his concubines, or a significant collaborator.

Not long after Philippe's visit, Pierre also arrived in Lyon to see Virginia. His GARDENER réseau had lost its radio operator to the Gestapo shortly after he arrived, and Pierre was obliged to cross the demarcation line every time he wanted to send a message. And the message he needed to send this time was of extreme urgency. Just days earlier, Pierre had been in Caen in northeastern France when, sitting in a café, he recognized another agent from his training days in the Scottish countryside. The two made eye contact and left the café separately only to join up again shortly afterward.

The agent had valuable information regarding a nearby airbase. Because of its proximity to the coast, the airbase was vital to the Nazis both in defending France from the British and in continuing the bombing runs into Britain. The agent not only knew the strength of the Luftwaffe there, but also potential sabotage targets to knock it out of commission.

Virginia was able to send the information on to London with a departing agent. But the communication with London, or more accurately, the lack thereof, was troubling. Radio operators were being picked off by the Gestapo within days of their arrival as the Nazis' direction-finding equipment continued to improve, and collaborators continued to keep watch for telltale antenna wires hanging out windows.

VIRGINIA'S LAST ARTICLE for the *Post* appeared on January 22, 1942. It was now too risky for her to continue to flash her press credentials, and she was concerned that even the venerable New York newspaper may have been infiltrated by spies. The article's title was "France's Rabbits on Strike" and the dateline read "Somewhere in France."

> Buck rabbits have gone on strike. . . . The prospective fathers
> of thousands of rabbits have apparently lost interest in their

wives and their pride in numerous progeny. They are listless and disinterested.

The rabbits' unbalanced diet is at the root of the trouble . . . his vitamin intake is insufficient and unbalanced.

Pigeons haven't gone on strike, but they are being eaten up rapidly. Bordeaux, for example, used to pride herself on its friendly pigeons, estimated at 5,000. . . . But now it is reported the latest pigeon census in Bordeaux is only 91. . . . Man, in France, doesn't disappear in quite the same way. . . . He suffers from diminishment. His girth shrinks and shrinks. From statistics compiled last summer by a well-known doctor in Lyon, the average loss of weight at the time was 12 pounds, 12 ounces per person. . . . This doctor however, insisted that not lack of food alone was the cause of the loss of weight. Two other factors play a great role: increased physical activity and mental strain coupled with moral suffering.

People who used to ride in taxis or private cars or even street cars now walk or ride bicycles, and housewives spend hours standing in line to get provisions for the kitchen, all of which is very slimming.

Then, too, many families are divided brutally, part living on one side of the demarcation line, part on the other. . . . And many sons, brothers, fathers and fiancés are still prisoners in Germany.

Naturally, people who are separated from those they love, whose relatives are still prisoners, are living under constant mental strain, which reacts upon their physical condition.

As she wrote the article, Virginia thought of her friend Claire de La Tour and the marvelous meal they had had from the family's new rabbit industry. Where were the de La Tours now? Were they safe, still living with relatives in the country? Or had they, too, fallen victim to this war that had already ruined so many lives?

10

NO REST FOR THE WEARY

THE GEHEIMESTAATSPOLIZEI was everywhere. They dressed in suits and skulked in darkened doorways or hovered in the corners of public places. Their eyes and ears were keenly attentive to any slip that a man or woman might make that would incriminate them as "enemies of the state." They were notorious for insidious prying and remorseless brutality. They were known simply as "the Gestapo."

Under the direction of chief murderer Heinrich Himmler, this secret police force had more than had twenty-five thousand agents roving Europe. Many came from the criminal underbelly of Germany and all were absolute Nazi disciples. The Gestapo operated without any restrictions by civil authority. Its members could not be tried for their police practices; whatever actions they took, no consequences would arise. This unconditional authority gave them a chillingly elitist air.

Gestapo agents were as omnipresent in unoccupied France as they were in the occupied areas of Europe. While Vichy and the collaborators were happy to root out Resistance members, they preferred to leave the really dirty work to Himmler's depraved secret police. The Gestapo became notorious for the ruthless torture they used to extract information from the unfortunate souls they arrested.

Once the United States became involved in the war, any immunity Virginia had had from the Gestapo evaporated. She risked what all Resistance members did: arrest, secret and unexplained, followed by a mock trial without defense, all of it punctuated by torture. If she survived, she would be shipped off to a prison or concentration camp, where more torture, disease, starvation, and death awaited. These constant threats hung over her head like the sword of Damocles, just as they did for everyone in France. She portrayed the ironclad lady to those around her, but the facade didn't protect her from her own thoughts late at night.

On January 12, 1942, a new agent arrived in Lyon. His name was Peter Churchill, no relation to the British prime minister, but equally gregarious. His code name was Michel. He was to deliver cash and orders to SOE agents as well as to supply and evaluate the CARTE réseau, led by Frenchman André Girard, who promised London an army of a quarter million men. Churchill landed on the French Mediterranean shore about twelve miles west of Cannes on January 9, having been brought to within eight hundred yards by a submarine. His family had vacationed in the area when he was young and he knew it intimately. He paddled a canoe to land and made his way to his first contact and then on to Lyon.

Churchill met Virginia in the lobby of her hotel one evening. He had checked into the Hôtel de France on rue de la Charité at de Guélis's suggestion and had been in Lyon all day with no current ration books. He was starving, he told her. London was expecting him to bring back samples for the forgers. All he'd been able to consume since dinner the previous night was an unlimited quantity of grenache.

Virginia took him to a restaurant run by a friend of the HECKLER circuit and the owner hugged her as if she were his long-lost daughter. Virginia explained that this was a restaurant where no food coupons were needed and Allied agents were always welcome. To prove her point, she ordered her favorite cocktail, a Cinzano gin, which prompted Churchill to order one for himself. Virginia gave him an overview of life in the zone libre, and he brought her up to speed on news from Baker Street.

His purpose in France, he explained, was multifaceted. He was carrying a great deal of cash, as Virginia had, which was to be distributed among the various circuits, including hers. He was to collect current ration books and cartes d'identité to take back for the forgers. And he was to go to Marseilles to meet with a French colonel about releasing a group of captured agents and Resistance members.

Churchill told Virginia he needed some assistance with contacts in Marseille and asked if she would accompany him. Her life in Lyon had become a revolving door of incoming agents, all with requests for aid in their missions.

Going to Marseille would be just one more task on her already long list, but she relished the work. It was exactly what she'd come to France to undertake. That and to prove to herself that she was not the outspoken, crippled woman the American State Department seemed to think she was.

Virginia and Churchill agreed to take two different trains for Marseille the next morning on the off chance that if one of them was stopped by Vichy agents or the Gestapo, at least both of them wouldn't be picked up. Virginia took the early train at 7:10. They were always crowded now, because of the lack of fuel for cars and buses. Every seat was taken, and those individuals without a place to sit stood where they could, many spilling out into the aisles. An atmosphere of gloom and despair filled the car, replicated by the dark, gray scenery that sped past them. Passengers around Virginia either buried themselves behind newspapers or stared out the windows, avoiding making eye contact with others. Their expressions were grim in anticipation of yet another difficult day.

The train arrived in Marseille a little after eleven o'clock and Virginia waited on the chilly platform for Churchill's to arrive an hour later. Once they found one another, she guided him into the station's restaurant and out the exit door. Her Marseille contact, Olivier, had told her about the exit. The Gestapo hasn't discovered it yet and it allowed agents to avoid their reception committee.

Marseille had become notorious among agents as one of the worst places in which to operate. It was an important port and had a mixed population of more than a million people, many from the low end of the social ladder. Added to that were the refugees from all over Europe who had poured into the city seeking escape from the Nazis. The Gestapo's presence was evident. Official black Citröens cruised the streets, their passengers scrutinizing passersby. If someone looked particularly suspicious, they were dragged into the car and hauled off. Many never returned. The people on the streets looked terrified, starving, and cold. There was no snow, but the bitter temperatures had invaded France's southern provinces as well.

As they walked, Churchill asked Virginia if the stories he'd heard about her leg were true. She admitted that she had a wooden leg but said she was sure the stories' drama had grown in proportion to the number of times they had been retold. His praise for her work in spite of her disability made her uncomfortable, as that kind of thing always did. To distract him, she played tour guide, pointing out the Hôtel Splendide, Marseille's Gestapo headquarters.

They met Virginia's contact, Olivier, in a café on one of the city's squares. After Churchill got directions to his destination and set off for his meeting, Olivier and Virginia went to see Le Provost's fishing contacts who provided passage to Spain for the HECKLER circuit's people. Virginia chatted with the three men amiably, as if they were old school chums. She gave each of them a bonus of one thousand francs for the outstanding work they had already done.

They had agreed to meet Churchill at another café. Once they arrived, they found a table and signaled the waiter, but before they could place their order, a dozen gendarmes stormed in, guns drawn. A cacophony filled the place: screams and shouts, chairs and tables overturning, glasses shattering on the floor. The men and women, their faces tense with fear, were ordered at gunpoint to stand against the bar and produce their papers. An eerie silence descended.

A minute later, the district police commissioner swept in and began stalking down the row of frightened café patrons, pointing at most of the men. It was what the French called a *rafle*, a raid, and the lucky selectees were being chosen for mandatory labor in Germany. Vichy had made a deal with the Nazis to send three workers in exchange for the return of every French POW. The chosen men were dragged out of the café and would be immediately trucked to the station, locked in trains, and taken away, without being given a chance to pack or bid their families good-bye.

Virginia and Olivier were near the end of the line. He was holding her arm protectively. The commissioner was now only half a dozen people away. Virginia was not about to waste her time with the self-inflated Marseille gendarmes, and was conjuring up a distraction. She glanced over at Olivier. He was making eye contact with one of the inspectors who had accompanied the commissioner.

The inspector motioned to one of the gendarmes and pointed at Virginia and Olivier. He told the gendarme to take them into the back room where he would question them as soon as he was done.

The two were hustled off unceremoniously and shoved into a little, dark room behind the bar that smelled of stale beer. Judging from the number of wooden kegs lying around, Virginia guessed it was where they kept their stock. Olivier dragged a keg over to the wall beneath a window, telling Virginia that he knew the inspector and they just been given a head start. Olivier helped her up onto the keg. She pulled herself into a sitting position on the windowsill and swung her legs out, dropping to the sidewalk below. He followed her seconds later. They ran to the corner and saw Churchill striding toward the café from the other direction.

Olivier signaled him to cross the street. He did and then crossed back to meet them at the corner. The three of them got away from the café as quickly as possible. As they charged along, Olivier gave Churchill a quick description of their close call in the *rafle*. Churchill was already distraught and explained he wasn't able to enlist the colonel's help in springing the men from prison.

When they were a good five blocks from their original meeting place, they slipped into another café. Olivier felt they were safe there. *Rafles* only occurred in a couple of cafés in a day and always in the same area. They ordered three grenaches to buy themselves some time and to calm their nerves.

Virginia told Churchill his dilemma might not be as grave as he assumed, depending on how much he was willing to spend on some bribes. He was authorized to go as high as a million, he told her, at which point Olivier nodded to Virginia. They all had unscrupulous lawyers up their sleeves, she told him. And prison guards could be bought, too.

They worked out the details and went back to the train station. As before, Virginia took the first train back to Lyon and Churchill followed on the next one. He was leaving the next morning, but promised to pass her regards to the new head of F Section, Maurice Buckmaster, who had worked for the Ford Motor Company in France in the 1930s. Buckmaster knew France well and had extensive contacts, all of whom would prove to be useful. His enthusiasm about the work SOE was doing was contagious and his leadership qualities were unparalleled.

THE CORSICANS' SITUATION was becoming grave. This was the case that Ben Cowburn had told Virginia about, and the one she had alluded to when she was with Churchill. Pierre Bloch, the Frenchman in the group who had been recruited by Jacques de Guélis, was occasionally able to see his wife, Marie. The couple lived in the nearby village of Villamblard and the guards allowed Marie to give her husband food packages. Pierre had been told by the British prisoners with him to send Marie to Lyon to find the woman they knew as Mlle LeContre.

The prison conditions, Marie told Virginia, were beyond description. They were thrown in with deserters, thieves, and murders. Pierre had described other men he'd seen, weakened by disease and starvation, who were actually being eaten by rats they were unable to repel. He'd heard stories about the German guards who, in a never-ending search for sadistic treatment methods, occasionally amused themselves by forcing the prisoners to eat their own feces. At the present time the Corsicans were maintaining their spirits, but their physical condition was deteriorating.

Her husband's face had been badly beaten, she told Virginia. The guards beat them all the time, sometimes to glean information, and sometimes just for sport. Virginia had heard stories about Beleyme Prison, sickening stories of the same kind of abuses Marie was describing. Almost any place else would be better, she told Marie. So their first order of business was to get them out of that prison and into another. Then they'd worry about planning an escape. While HECKLER had many contacts, Virginia's first instinct was to go to the embassy the United States still maintained in Vichy to ask for help through governmental channels.

She met with Ambassador William Leahy two days later and filled him in on the details. His initial response was as she expected. There was really nothing the American government could do, as the captives were Englishmen. Deciding to take a chance, Virginia divulged a deeper layer of the story. These men were vitally important in helping to fight the Nazis, she explained. They were part of an ever-growing assemblage within France's borders. Their nationality mattered little, as both the British and the United States were now fighting a common enemy and would soon need every means available. This revelation got Leahy's attention. He would see what he could do, he promised, and would contact her as soon as he had news.

AT THE SAME TIME Virginia was meeting with Ambassador Leahy, another conference was taking place, this one outside Berlin at Wannsee. An exquisite château on the shores of a lake, once a private residence, was opened and staffed for the event. At about 11:00 AM on January 20, 1942, the forum convened with fifteen men in attendance, representatives of the Nazi governmental offices involved in Jewish affairs. Only the chairmen knew of the meeting's agenda: General Reinhard Heydrich of the Schutzstaffel (an elite paramilitary unit of the Nazi military known as the SS) and his special assistant SS Lieutenant Colonel Adolph Eichmann. The topic to be discussed was *endlösung*: the final solution.

Heydrich explained he had been given "the responsibility for working out the final solution to the *judenfrage*," the Jewish question. The conference participants agreed that the Jews, by virtue of their mere numbers, represented a major problem. With the standstill in Russia and America in the war, the German military was being drained, as was the Reich's food supply. They simply could no longer store the Jews within the German sphere of influence.

Heydrich then outlined his plan: make a major and thorough sweep of the estimated six million Jews throughout Europe, depositing them in one of the five major camps at Auschwitz, Belzec, Treblinka, Sobibor, or Majdanek. His presentation ended with a revelation, delivered so callously that even some of these most hardened Nazis flinched. Once taken to the camps, the men, women, and children, would be exterminated by the most expeditious means possible. Heydrich's final solution, *vernichtung*, represented the systematic annihilation of all of the Jews in Europe.

AMBASSADOR LEAHY AND VIRGINIA worked for weeks on the petition to move the nine Corsicans from the Beleyme Prison, each using the means they were most familiar with. The ambassador contacted Vichy political acquaintances, making promises to some and calling in favors from others. Virginia used the francs printed in England to glean information from gendarmes and guards who could be bought. Marie's weekly reports to Virginia were tearful—the Corsicans were becoming alarmingly weak.

It was now mid-February and Virginia was working almost nonstop. There were agents in need of money, contacts, or a shoulder to lean on. There were RAF pilots, anxious to return to the fighting, who needed safe transport back to England. And there were other prisoners whose lives were perilously at risk in the custody of the Nazis.

The darkness of the winter days were depressing and the cold reached its icy fingers into every building and body. Virginia had not planned on such harsh weather, but had fortunately brought enough clothes so that if she wore many layers at a time, she would be able to endure. However, the soles of her shoes had become worn, one to the point of a hole and there was no leather to be found for repairs. In this, Virginia's luck was holding out better than her shoes. The sole with the hole in it was the shoe she wore on Cuthbert.

Baker Street had given Virginia the okay to move from the Grand Nouvel Hôtel to a flat on Place Ollier because of the concern that the number of visitors she had received at the hotel might appear suspicious. The flat was furnished and had two rooms, one that served as the kitchen, dining room, and parlor, and the other, separated by a curtain, which served as the bedroom. The bathroom was down the hall, shared with the floor's other residents.

Like the hotel, it had a window facing the street. Whenever she was home, Virginia put a flowerpot on the windowsill as a signal to those on the sidewalk that it was safe to visit. Given the fact that it was winter, the pot was now empty. But she had every intention of planting something in it in the spring. Flowers of any kind would brighten up the lives of those under immense tension, including hers.

IN PARIS, PIERRE DE VOMÉCOURT had continued to build his GARDENER réseau as well as help develop others. At dinner one winter night in 1942 in Paris, he met a beguiling woman named Mathilde Carré. A relationship developed between the two of them and she ultimately confided in him that she worked for a Resistance organization called Interallié. She had a radio operator at her disposal, and she would be happy to transmit messages to London for him. De Vomécourt was thrilled as he had had such difficulties staying in touch with SOE.

But as time passed, de Vomécourt discovered that Mme Carré, known as LA CHATTE, was a double agent for the Germans, as was her radio operator. She confessed that all of the messages she had sent and received were also being read by the Nazis. Her only choice, he told her, was to become a "double-double" agent and go to work for the British. He had to warn London that the radio transmissions were being monitored, and she had valuable information about the Nazis the British would be quite happy to have.

De Vomécourt told her she was to convince the Germans that she had talked him into taking her to London to help him organize a grand meeting of all of the Resistance groups thus far. The Germans fell for the idea, pleased that they would have an agent inside SOE.

On February 26, de Vomécourt and LA CHATTE left for London from the rocky shores of Brittany, to cross the channel by torpedo boat. Once there, the now double-double agent sang like a canary. She told SOE all

The Hall's 110-acre farm, Box Horn, in rural Maryland. *Photo courtesy of Lorna Catling*

Virginia and her brother John, circa 1910. *Photo courtesy of Lorna Catling*

Virginia, circa 1918. She had an interest in all wildlife from a young age. *Photo courtesy of Lorna Catling*

Virginia, her brother, John, and an unidentified friend in the barn at Box Horn, circa 1919. *Photo courtesy of Lorna Catling*

**Virginia loved the outdoors, here with an
unidentified friend, circa 1922.** *Photo courtesy of
Lorna Catling*

Hiking, circa 1922. *Photo courtesy of Lorna Catling*

She became an accomplished horsewoman, circa 1920. *Photo courtesy of Lorna Catling*

One of Virginia's
identity cards, listing
her address as the
Place Ollier in Lyon
and dated April 20,
1942. *Photo courtesy
of the International
Spy Museum*

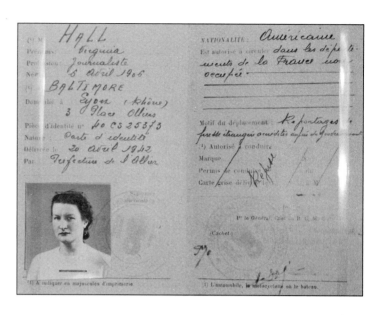

Robert Alesh, who called
himself Abbé Ackuin. He
was responsible for
betraying Virginia and
her entire circuit in Lyon.
*Photo courtesy of
National Archives*

The French tri-color flies over the Centre de l'Histoire et de la Résistance in Lyon. Formerly it was the Ecole de Santé Militaire, Klaus Barbie's headquarters and the site of his torture chambers. Today it's a museum and library. *Author photo*

ICI·EN1943 ET 1944·LA GESTAPO
NAZIE·AIDEE PAR DES TRAITRES·
A TORTURE DES MILLIERS DE
RESISTANTS ET D'OTAGES·
AVANT LEUR MORT OU LEUR
DEPORTATION+LEUR SACRIFICE
PERMIT LA LIBERATION
DE LA FRANCE

Today, the horrors are commemorated by this plaque on the outside wall of the Ecole de Santé Militaire. "Here, in 1943 and 1944, the Nazi Gestapo, aided by traitors, tortured thousands of resistants and hostages before their death or deportation. Their sacrifice allowed for the liberation of France." *Author photo*

Motor Gun Boat 502, the ship that carried Virginia and Aramis from Portsmouth, England, to the coast of Brittany in occupied France. *Photo courtesy of Norman Hine and Mike Kemble*

A self-portrait sketched by Aramis (Henry Laussucq) in the field in 1944. *Photo courtesy of National Archives*

Virginia's Type 3, Mark II suitcase radio. She used this radio to maintain contact with London during her second trip to occupied France. *Photo courtesy of the International Spy Museum*

Virginia's safe house in the town of Cosne at 18 rue Donzy. *Author photo*

Parachute container that arrived near Le Chambon sur Lignon. The name "Williams" was added after the war. *Author photo*

Désiré Zurbach, or Dédé as he was known to his compatriots, was Virginia's second in command in the Yssingeaux Plateau. Photo circa 1946. *Photo courtesy of Pierre Fayol*

Lt. Raoul Le Boulicaut, known to Virginia and the others as 'Lt. Bob.' Here, in 1939 at the age of eighteen, he's about to ship out with the French Navy. *Photo courtesy of Pierre Fayol*

Virginia with members of her parachute reception committee. Second from the right is Gabriel Eyraud, the young guard of the group's weapons depot. To his right is Dédé. *Photo courtesy of Gabriel Eyraud*

This demolition is typical of the sort Virginia's group inflicted on the Nazis. This train was in the midst of crossing the Pont de Chamalières on August 2, 1944, when detonation occurred. *Photos courtesy of Pierre Fayol*

The building owned by the Salvation Army, located near Le Chambon. Virginia lived here, as well as sent her radio messages and organized sabotages from here. It was also here that the members of JED team Jeremy stayed. *Author photo*

Virginia with the two Americans who parachuted onto the Yssingeaux Plateau. Lieutenant Henry Riley is on the left and Lieutenant Paul Goillot is on the right. Between them is French Lieutenant Aimart. Goillot later became her husband. *Photo courtesy of Gabriel Eyraud*

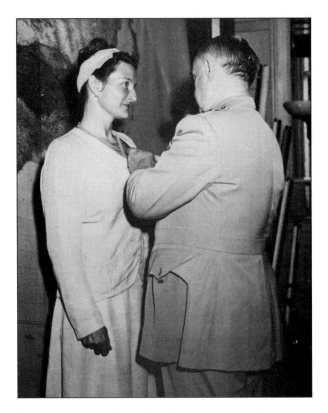

Virginia receives the Distinguished Service Cross from General William Donovan in his office in Washington on September 23, 1945. Her mother was the only other person in attendance. *Photos courtesy of Lorna Catling*

Virginia's Member of the British Empire ribbon. *Photo courtesy of the International Spy Museum*

Virginia's Distinguished Service Cross.
Courtesy of the CIA Museum

Virginia, back home at Box Horn after the war, circa 1946. *Photo courtesy of Lorna Catling*

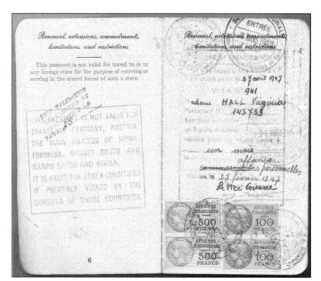

One of Virginia's many passports, circa 1946. *Photo courtesy of the CIA Museum*

Virginia and friends, both human and canine. These were two of the five French poodles she and Paul had. *Photo courtesy of Lorna Catling*

Virginia, left, and Paul with an unknown friend, touring their yard at their Maryland home, circa 1982. *Photo courtesy of Lorna Catling*

Virginia shortly after the war and her return to the U.S. *Photo courtesy of Lorna Catling*

about the German intelligence agency Abwehr, for which she had worked, as well as the radio code they had given her to communicate with them.

PETER CHURCHILL, MEANWHILE, had returned to London via Spain on February 13. Together with Pierre de Vomécourt, he had set up several more groups around Lyon and provided the necessary security and contacts for them. The SOE now had a permanent framework in the zone libre headed by Virginia.

During his debriefing, Churchill made numerous suggestions that he felt would augment SOE's effectiveness. This included the suggestion that Virginia leave the hotel and move to her own flat. The gravest problem the réseaux faced however, Churchill told Buckmaster, was the lack of radio operators and the danger they faced in practicing their trade.

While Buckmaster could do little about the danger, he arranged for three more radio operators to go to France. Churchill was to take them via submarine just as he had done the month previously. It was a dangerous way to travel. Once the sub had closed in on the drop target, it had to cruise back and forth waiting for darkness to surface so that the passengers could disembark. Whether submerged or surfaced, an ever-vigilant crew kept watch for German ships.

On February 25, Churchill shepherded the "piano players" on board a submarine in London. Churchill and the three radio operators were sitting ducks paddling to shore in their canoes. They could be picked off by Vichy police from the shore or by German ships or collaborators' fishing boats from the sea. Absolute silence was of the essence, as was moving slowly. Paddling too rapidly created a phosphorescent wake that was easily spotted. So despite the urge to get to the protection of solid ground as quickly as possible, one had to move at a snail's pace.

They and their equipment landed at nearly the same spot Churchill had dropped to on the twenty-sixth. He escorted them to his contact and returned to the sub the same night with an agent bound for London in tow. The entire operation had come off without a hitch.

THE EVENING OF MARCH 2, there was a knock on Virginia's door. Knocks after dark had become synonymous with a house call from the Gestapo. She had nothing incriminating in the flat, though, and she opened the door confidently. A very pale man, hunched over, supported himself on the doorframe. He told her he was looking for Brigitte LeContre. Wary, Virginia told him that he had found her. "*C'est le docteur qui m'envoie,*" he said. "The doctor sent me" was HECKLER's new pass phrase. Virginia's response was, "*Cela fait longtemps qu'il est venu*"(It's been a long time since he's come).

The man told her his name was Gerard—actually Gerry—Morel and that he had come as a friend of Antoine's, which Virginia knew was Philippe de Vomécourt's code name. Virginia helped him in, led him to a chair, and asked him how she could help.

He had arrived the previous September. All was going well until he was burned (betrayed) in November. In retrospect, he said he was sure it was one of the contacts he had established. The gendarmes arrested him and threw him in solitary in Limoges for three weeks, and then transferred him to Beleyme sometime in December. It didn't take him long to figure out he was about to be put on trial as an "enemy of the state" and that he would die there if he didn't take action.

His solution was to go on a hunger strike, which made him sick and got him the transfer to a hospital in Limoges he was hoping for. That's when the plan backfired. The doctor decided the only way to save his life was to operate and Gerard was in no condition to argue with him. When he came to, the doctor told him he had performed a gastrectomy and taken out part of his stomach.

By this time it was the middle of January. He told his constant nurse, a Sister of Mercy, that as soon as the stitches came out, he was going to escape. One night while the guard was sleeping, the nun helped him walk out of the room and climb over the wall. Despite a horrible blizzard, they made it to a house he knew about that belonged to de Vomécourt. He had been there recuperating ever since, and de Vomécourt had told him when he was well enough, he should move to Lyon and look up Virginia for help back to England.

Virginia was amazed at his story, and at the fact that he hadn't broken open his incision and bled to death. She insisted he stay in her flat that night. In the morning they'd move him to a safe place and have Pep check him over. Gerard was anxious to get out of France; he was sure those responsible for him at the hospital were probably combing the country. But Virginia explained that the best way out of France was across the Pyrénées, which would require quite a bit of stamina. He certainly wasn't up to it. Instead, she promised to sequester him away in one of her safe houses, where he could stay unseen until he was strong enough to leave the country.

The next day, Virginia contacted Mme Guérin, who, the month before, had begun to accumulate flats for such emergencies. There was one near Place Ollier that Gerard could use, she said. Virginia deposited him there and contacted Pep to come have a look at him. Then it was off to Le Provost's; Gerard would need a carte d'identité, a ration book with the appropriate months torn out for authenticity, and other papers to make him appear legal.

A week later, Gerard's health was much improved and he was ready to make his exodus from France. Virginia would accompany him initially, as his cover. Traveling together they looked like any other couple on their way to a holiday. Before they left, she presented him with a tattered and grayed piece of paper: his demobilization certificate from the French army. It stated that he had suffered an injury in defense of the country and that he was fit only for the least taxing labor, thereby explaining why he wasn't working.

Their plan was to leave on the first morning train south for Marseille, where they'd spend the night with Virginia's good friend Mme Landry in the Vieux-Port, the old part of town. Next they would take the train west to Toulouse where Virginia would put him in the capable hands of the men she knew there who would get him across the Pyrénées into Spain. From there it was on to Portugal for a ship home to England.

It took them until 2:00 PM to get to Marseille where Mme Landry welcomed them with open arms and had seen to it that her son had shopped the black market to provide a hearty dinner. Their trip to Toulouse the next day was even longer. After an early morning start, they arrived at 4:30 in the afternoon. They took two rooms at a hotel that Virginia understood to be run by a Resistance sympathizer. The proprietor was very amiable and happily suggested a restaurant for their dinner that night. When they questioned him about a guide for passage into Spain, he told them to be in the lobby the next morning at 10:00 to meet a man who might be willing to discuss such business with them.

The following day, the agent was in the lobby when Virginia and Gerard arrived. He said the guide he represented was on his way back from a crossing and would be happy to take Gerard. The price for him to arrange Gerard's meeting with the guide was four thousand francs, to be collected in advance. The agent would turn the money over to an uninvolved third party, the hotel proprietor for example. If the meeting failed to take place for some reason, the agent continued, the four thousand francs would be returned to Gerard in full. The fee for the crossing itself was twelve thousand francs, which Gerard would pay directly to the guide. Virginia figured an arrangement like that would probably ensure the hotel proprietor a cut in the action as well. But she couldn't fault the man, as tough times required one to do anything possible to guarantee food on the dinner table.

The whole process went off without a hitch. The guide met with them the next day as the agent had promised. Payment was arranged and Gerard was set to leave for Spain that night. As Virginia prepared to return to Lyon, Gerard thanked her profusely, telling her he owed her his life. He asked her if there was anything he could do for her when he returned to London. She laughed and asked him to send her a new pair of shoes.

Five days after her return from Toulouse, on March 14, Virginia received the telegram she'd been waiting for from Ambassador Leahy in Vichy. The Corsicans were to be moved to a Vichy concentration camp in Mauzac the next day, forty miles from Beleyme on the Dordogne River. Virginia knew the place. It was still a prison, but the conditions were much improved over Beleyme. She got the news to Marie Bloch. The Corsicans were one step closer to freedom.

A little over a month after that, however, her nerves were jangled when she received news that Pierre de Vomécourt had been picked up and sent to Fresnes Prison outside Paris. He had parachuted back into France on April 1. Furthermore, his brother Jean had also been arrested. It was a stark reminder to Virginia, as well as to every other agent in France, of what a tenuous wire they were walking and how close they were each day to falling victim to the same fate.

THE GERMANS HAD AN ALMOST neurotic necessity for organization, which permeated all aspects of their government, including their human repositories. The unwanted masses they were collecting were interned in one of three types of camps: concentration, whose internees were used either as slave labor or summarily exterminated; internment, where Jews, foreigners, prisoners of war, and those considered "enemies of the state" were confined; and transit, which functioned as collection centers, most often for Jews, bound for the concentration camps.

The camp system was set up in all of the Nazis' conquered territories, including France. The most notable were Gurs, a transit camp near the Pyrénées, about fifty miles from the Spanish border, and Les Milles, an internment camp located in Provence in southern France. Jews, both French and foreign, as well as other groups of "undesirables" lived and died in the camps. Food was scarce, as was clean water. Disease ran rampant with so many individuals living in such confined spaces. Torture and cruelty of every type imaginable were inflicted on men, women, and children.

There were camps in occupied France too, primarily of the transit variety. Drancy was a camp just outside Paris. It was an unfinished housing complex that the Germans took over, and became an infamous stopping-off point for Jews before they were shipped to the nightmares awaiting them at German death camps like Auschwitz or Majdanek. Conditions in Drancy were even worse than in the other camps. In October 1941, in an effort to save resources, the Germans had released nine hundred sick and dying interns, figuring they it would be more cost effective for them to expire on the streets. Shortly after the prisoners' release, an observer noted in a Paris underground newspaper: "I have met several living skeletons who can hardly stand. They are the Jews freed from Drancy."

THE FIRST TIME VIRGINIA SAW the yellow Star of David on a child's jacket, it appalled her. The exploitation of adults was bad enough, but including children gave her new loathing for the enemy. On June 1, 1942, on behalf of Vichy, René Bousquet ordered French Jews to wear the stars, just as the rest of Europe's Jews did. "There would be no problem if they had blue skins," Bousquet was quoted as saying. "But they don't and we need to know who they are."

Jews' cartes d'identité were also stamped "Juif." Virginia found the whole notion of branding people disgusting. A sense of urgency now accompanied her work. They had to rid the country of the Nazis and their ilk. There just never seemed to be enough time to do it all.

Virginia's flat on Place Ollier was a veritable Grand Central Station, with RAF pilots, agents, and Resistance friends needing assistance or a place to catch a quick nap before moving on to the next event. This left her with very little time to do anything of a personal nature. Not that there was much she could do. War-torn France was no place to afford the extravagancies of bubble bath or toilet water. Most of her bathing was done out in the sink in her flat, with cold water, one body part at a time. That is, when the flat was hers alone. She washed her hair in the sink as well and wore it pulled back in a bun at the nape of her neck. Its natural wave gave her the luxury of not having to pin it up at night.

Virginia had never worn much makeup, even during the prewar years. But she did have the remnants of a lipstick tube and a little pot of rouge that she applied for special occasions. For the most part, though, her job was to blend in with the struggling French and not draw attention to herself. The more bland and ordinary she appeared, the better.

The one bright spot on the personal front in the spring of 1942 was the arrival of a new pair of shoes, thanks to the message Gerard took back to London. They arrived in a parachute drop that Labourier had gone to fetch in late May. They weren't really new—just new to Virginia. Sporting a pair of spanking fresh oxfords when most French were having a hard time finding enough food would have caught the attention of too many people. Rather they were a pair that had been procured from some refugee newly arrived from France. Baker Street gave all incoming expatriates new clothing in exchange for their old ones, which were then issued to outbound agents. It was crucial that all agents appear no different from any other Frenchmen, right down to the label in their skivvies.

The days seemed to move by at an incredible pace. Virginia rarely had time to reflect on her mother or her brother and his family back home in Baltimore. But she was certain that Vera was keeping them informed of her safety. The letters the SOE sent to the families of agents were identical, just the names were changed. And they all carried Vera's signature as secretary of the fictitious organization, The Inter-Service Research Bureau. Virginia hoped they were of some comfort to her mother.

Dear Mrs. Hall,

We continue to receive excellent news of your daughter, Virginia. We are very proud of her and hope you are as well.

Sincerely,
Vera Atkins, Secretary, Inter-Service Research Bureau

11

AND THE WALLS CLOSE IN

VIRGINIA HAD BEEN IN FRANCE almost a year. During that time a great many radio transmissions and messages had been sent with the names of Brigitte LeContre and Germaine in them. Now, in early June of 1942, Virginia was of the opinion that perhaps it was time to take on new names. London concurred and Marie Monin became her new nom de guerre, with Philomène her new code name. Those in Lyon who knew her as Brigitte LeContre and Germaine continued to address her as such. She had already been living a lie for months—what were two more names? She wondered if she would remember to respond to Virginia Hall when she finally returned to the United States.

On a bright June day in 1942, "Mlle Monin" left her flat on Place Ollier to meet with the current HECKLER circuit radio operator. His name was Pierre Le Chêne, code-named Gregoire. He had arrived from London on May 1 and had bounced from one safe house to another to make his broadcasts, staying just steps ahead of the Gestapo. Their direction finders were becoming ever more sophisticated and deadly.

One of Le Chêne's preferred locations was the home of M. and Mme Joseph Marchand, who lived above one of Lyon's newsstands along the Rhône River. It was there that Virginia was to meet him. But when she arrived at their home at number 2 quai Perrache, the newsstand owner was standing in front of his shop, ostensibly sweeping the sidewalk.

As soon as he saw her, the shop owner greeted her and ushered her in. He had become a good friend of the HECKLER circuit, acting as a letter box and keeping his eyes and ears open for news that would be of interest to the Resistance.

Once inside he told her that the Gestapo were tossing the Marchands' apartment as they spoke. He didn't know who else was up there, but he thought it wise for her to leave via the exit at the back of his shop and wait at the Café de la République. He promised that as soon as he had news, he would send word to her. Virginia thanked him for his keen attention and followed his suggestion to wait at the café. Thirty minutes later, Le Chêne himself came in and sat down with her, visibly shaken and telling her that he had been closer to arrest than he ever hoped to come again.

He had been transmitting, he explained, thinking that one of the Marchands was playing lookout. Each of them thought the other was doing the job and it turned out no one was. Mme Marchand's ability to talk saved them all. She kept the Gestapo busy at the door, insisting that they wipe their shoes before coming into her house. It was a long enough delay for Le Chêne to stash his radio beneath a sideboard with a partial false front. The Gestapo had torn the place apart, he said, but never found a thing.

Virginia asked about the Marchands. Le Chêne laughed and told her that as he left, Mme Marchand was giving Monsieur an earful for not doing what he was supposed to. Le Chêne said Monsieur really wasn't to blame, but he wasn't about to get between them. The good news was that Le Chêne had managed to get out all of the messages he was to send, including the most important one asking for additional funds.

Virginia needed cash, a lot of it, to pave the way for the Corsicans' escape. Pierre had told his wife that George Bégué—code-named Georges, the most senior agent in their group and the first to arrive in France from SOE—thought he could duplicate the key to the hut where they were being kept. He had done some metalworking in his youth and said if ever there was a time to turn a hobby into something useful, this was it. All he needed was materials and tools.

With the additional funds brought to Virginia by an incoming agent, she and Marie had plenty of capital for the plan they had put together. Marie was still allowed to bring her husband food packages, but now she would include clean linens and books, removing the soiled linen when she left. Virginia would supply her with the money to make whatever purchases she needed on the black market.

Marie followed Virginia's directions. At first, the guards tore through the packages to make sure they didn't contain any contraband, but after about a month they became accustomed to the arrangement. They stopped their searches and just waved Marie through. Once that happened, Marie began to include tins of sardines in tomato sauce with the food, also purchased on the black market. The tin was the material Bégué would use to fashion his key. And folded among the linens or stashed in the books were files, pliers, and tin snips. Any materials they no longer needed were wrapped up in the soiled linens. Once the work began, Marie told Virginia that the group sang obscene songs at the top of their lungs to drown out the noise of Bégué's work.

As that part of the scheme slowly unfolded, Marie and Virginia had to identify guards who would be willing to look away while the men escaped. They found their marks among the exterior guards who patrolled the perimeter fence. These men had nothing to do with the prison. They were poorly paid refugees from Alsace who had come to the interior of France after the Germans invaded their province. And, as Marie learned, their love of the Vichy government was not absolute. They were willing to take bribes.

Each time Marie went to visit her husband, she spent the night in the only hotel in the nearby town of Mauzac and passed the time in the hotel's café before retiring. As it happened, the off-duty guards also spent time there and Marie became familiar with them. She got to know one of them especially well and discovered he augmented his guard's salary by running a bar not far from the camp. He was interested in earning additional francs to supplement his other two jobs and listened carefully to Marie's proposal.

Near the end of June, Marie visited Virginia to bring her up to speed on the progress. Georges had each member of their group study the door key they saw on the guard's belt. Taking into consideration each one's observation, he had finally made a key. The next step was to test it. The men had observed the guards' patrols and timed their test accordingly. But to Georges' dismay, the lock did not open.

Marie had also conveyed to her husband how to communicate with the inside guard she had bribed. He would transport messages from the Corsicans to the guard on the outside in tubes of aspirin tablets. Of course if either of these guards decided they would simply take the money already given them and inform the gendarmes of the pending escape plot, all hell would break loose. The guards, the Corsicans, and Marie would be tortured to gain additional information. And if any of them were unable to hold up, Virginia could be implicated as well. Then they would all face a firing squad.

As June slid into July, Marie kept in very close contact with Virginia. The importance of freeing these men was huge to the Resistance effort, and the pressure the women were operating under was enormous. Finally in early July, Marie came to Lyon with the news that a successful key had finally been produced. But they had also had a very close call.

As he'd been directed, Pierre had passed the aspirin tube to the inside guard named Welton. When Welton didn't see his friend outside the prison fence, he decided to put the tube in the fellow's coat pocket in the cloakroom. Unfortunately, he got it in the wrong coat, one belonging to the mess sergeant. When Marie arrived at the prison, there was a message from the sergeant waiting for her. When he questioned her, she denied any knowledge of what he was talking about until he convinced her he was willing to help as well. For a price, of course.

The fifty-thousand-franc price was not a deterrent. The man had told Marie he would stand guard for them at the hollow outside the prison fence where the Corsicans were to meet the car. If the coast was clear, the mess sergeant would flick on his cigarette lighter. They were to inform him of the day when they delivered the cash.

Adding an additional guard made Marie and Virginia nervous. It was one more person who might double-cross them to worry about. On top of that, another change from their original plan had occurred. Two of the Corsicans decided not to try the escape. Their lawyers had convinced them that the risk was too great and it would not be long before the charges against them were dropped. Everyone else knew this was unlikely, but the two insisted. Virginia hated changes in plans so late in the game, but she didn't have any choice. The escape was set for the night of July 16.

The night of the escape was illuminated with a brilliant moon. Each Corsican had prepared a dummy to fill his bed so that the guards wouldn't become suspicious until the light of day. When those who made the night patrol returned to their guardroom at about 3:00 AM, the men crawled out of their hut, one by one. Welton whistled and tapped his stick on the ground to make as much noise as possible, covering any noise coming from the escapees. Once they'd crept under the prison's barbed wire fence, the eleven Corsicans, plus the outside guard and the mess sergeant, ran three kilometers to the awaiting car.

They drove about fifteen kilometers farther and then hid in an abandoned farmhouse. Virginia and Antoine (Philippe de Vomécourt) had seen to it that the house was equipped with soap and razors, fresh clothing, and biscuits and jam, and they continued to provide for the men throughout the next week. Once their false papers arrived, the men made the trip to Lyon two or three at a time, where they met Virginia. She had arranged for their exodus from France via Spain. But each of them vowed that once he had given Baker Street his report, he would be returning to continue the work he had only gotten the chance to begin.

Virginia was enthused and relieved at the same time. This was quite a victory for London and the Resistance. Like her, these men were SOE pioneers. Their knowledge and expertise was of great importance, augmented by the fact that they now had intimate knowledge of the Gestapo and two Vichy prisons.

IT WOULD BE MONTHS BEFORE Virginia learned of the horror that was taking place in Paris at the same time the Corsicans escaped. While other countries in Europe had fallen to the Germans, France was the only one that also rounded up Jews to hand over to them. Members of Pétain's government told one another that if they aided the Nazis in this way, the Germans might be inclined to keep Vichy's sovereignty intact. The collaborating French even exceeded the human quotas requested by the Nazis, using collection methods as horrific as the occupiers.

During the days of July 16 and 17, 1942, a *rafle* occurred in Paris. Gendarmes arrested twelve thousand Jewish men, women, and children. This mass of humanity was deposited in a sports stadium known as the Vélodrome d'Hiver, where nothing had been prepared for them. They had not been allowed to bring much with them, and were given only minimal food and no water by their captives. There was nothing available to protect them from the scorching summer sun or the chilly nights. As there were only a few WCs, they filled up immediately and were never emptied.

There were pregnant women among them who delivered their babies, aided by a charitable few near them. There were the infirm who suffered from tuberculosis, dysentery, and other maladies, and who terrified the rest.

This crowd contained only three doctors and a handful of nurses. And not one German was anywhere to be seen. All of the guards were French.

After existing for five days in unspeakable squalor, their sojourn in this hell came to an end. The adults were separated from the children and shipped to transit camps for deportation to Auschwitz. The Germans had only been interested in the French gathering Jews over the age of sixteen, which left the French with 4,051 motherless children. The children were terrified, some so young they were unable even to give their names to the ever-present government record keeper. At the request of the Vichy president, a day later the children were also bound for Auschwitz.

The man who gave the order for this heartless roundup was Vichy President Pierre Laval. Back in 1940, after using his media empire to support the Vichy government and Pétain as its dictator, Laval had been made president. He developed such close ties to the Nazis, that other Vichy officials requested his removal. Pétain complied in December 1941, but in April 1942 Pétain recalled him to the presidency. Ruthlessly rounding up the Jews and treating them in the most appalling manner would only be his first act of inhumanity.

VIRGINIA KEPT LONDON on top of things by sending off long, coded reports with outgoing agents. It was important that London know every detail of life in the zone libre. In one report she wrote:

> People take a pretty sour view of the British these days, but they are still hoping for their victory and many, many of them are willing to help, but they would appreciate seeing something concrete besides retreating. They acknowledge the vastness of the task the British have taken on, but are not able to take the really broad view. However, a good part of the army is ready and the 153rd regiment here, whose officers are almost all Alsatians and Lorrainers, is ready to march tomorrow—with pleasure.

Virginia was driven to make everything she touched a success, but being a perfectionist had its downside. It was discouraging to see what was needed but not be able to force others into action. To be sure, she was gratified with the number of Resistance recruits who kept surfacing. There just wasn't enough time to organize them properly.

May I urge again that a good executive and organizer be sent here. Talk to Olivier—he understands somewhat the situation. Actually we could use about six clever chaps in various centers this side. It's a snowball, but you do need a certain number of perfectly and utterly reliable persons—persons from "home."

A few weeks later, Virginia reported on the French mentality. This kind of information was vital for London. It allowed them to project what kind of support they might expect should the Allies ever be able to mount a landing on the continent of Europe.

The unrest in the south amongst the peasantry is growing. Continued interference by the government in their private affairs is getting them down. The fact that they cannot keep seed for plantings but must ask the *ravataillement* [sic] [Food Control Office)]for seed, and in order to get it, must promise from 50 to 99 percent of the harvest to the *ravataillement*, again has soured them considerably. Many are not planting wheat this year because they have to give it all back. The country folk are turning more and more against the government and more and more toward the English whom they don't like, fundamentally. And of course, the wine situation is unbearable, the latest aggravation being that no wine can be served in the south, Marseille and Avignon, etc., with dinner in the evening. It is all flowing north.

THE PREVIOUS MONTH, a colorful SOE agent by the name of Dennis Rake arrived in Lyon. Justin, as he was code-named, was completely open and honest with Virginia at their first meeting, telling her that he had joined SOE primarily because he was without family obligations. But he had a personal reason as well. He wanted to prove to himself and the world that just because he preferred romance with another man, it didn't mean he wasn't brave. He was as good a "piano player" as the next fellow, Rake told her. And if he died as a result, that was his fate. But it wouldn't be for lack of bravery.

The direction of Rake's preferences didn't matter to Virginia and she told him so. Le Chêne had moved on to another réseau and HECKLER desperately needed another radio operator. She was grateful that he had come. Furthermore, embracing individuals' differences had been part of her upbringing.

Virginia had been the victim of prejudices at the hands of the Foreign Service. Sitting in war-torn France five years later, she presumed Rake had survived his share of rejection as well.

Her first message for him to send to London was of a personal nature. She needed some parts for Cuthbert, she told him, parts that weren't available in Lyon. She asked him to include the message on his next "sked," short for "schedule," which was the radio operator's scheduled transmissions. Rake told her he would be contacting London later that day and Virginia wrote up the message.

Cuthbert was in need of some new bearings at the articulation where the wooden leg met the foot. She didn't know if there was a prosthetist in Lyon, but it didn't matter. She wouldn't risk going to a stranger. A woman with a strong accent and a wooden leg would become quite a topic of conversation and result in the kind of attention she had tried to avoid for about a year. Nor was she sure a London prosthetist could help her. Individuals who made them did so very precisely, and they didn't share their techniques with others. Since hers had come from the United States, she was fairly certain that's where the bearings would have to come from.

Virginia pared down all of this information as best she could and Rake sent off the message, never knowing who or what Cuthbert was. A few days later he received word back that she was correct in assuming that help would be needed from America.

Vera, again on behalf of the Inter-Service Research Bureau, had contacted Virginia's mother, who was happy to procure the necessary parts. They were sent to London and from there, traveled to the zone libre in the rucksack of an incoming agent.

One morning in August, Le Provost informed Virginia that he learned that the Gestapo wanted to question a Canadian woman. At the time, there were only a couple of women agents in unoccupied France that Virginia was aware of. None of them were Canadian and none of them were in Lyon. Since this discussion occurred between local Gestapo agents, she assumed they were looking for a local woman. There was only one they could be referring to: her.

To make matters worse, Le Provost told her he had just heard from Labourier that Rake had been arrested. That would be an enormous blow for all of the area réseaux. Rake's work was essential and with him imprisoned a vital link was removed from their chain. Of course that was only the half of it, the selfish half. His detention most certainly meant his enduring rough treatment at the hands of the gendarmes and the Gestapo.

Le Provost gave her arrest details, which he'd gotten fourthhand from Labourier who had heard from a contact who had gotten the information from the owner of the café in Montceau-les-Mines where Rake had been arrested. Evidently Rake was waiting to meet two other agents and appeared agitated that they had not yet shown up. A police inspector became suspicious and walked over to question him. He asked Rake what his profession was. A *chemisier*, shirtmaker, in Lyon was Rake's answer. The inspector then asked how much he made and Rake told him eight thousand francs a month.

It was a ludicrously high amount and made the inspector even more suspicious. He ordered Rake to empty his pockets, which contained a great deal of money, all brand new, in numerical series, and not pinned. When the two agents he had been waiting for arrived, Le Provost continued, they were also told to empty their pockets. One of them had a large amount of cash, and like Rake's, it was unpinned and in a series. Furthermore, when the inspector looked at their cartes d'identité, the handwriting on them was identical, although the two men supposedly came from different towns.

The carelessness astounded and angered Virginia. London knew better than to send such suspect currency. And agents traveling together should have known to examine one another's *cartes*, if only to make sure they could support each other's stories if they were ever stopped and separated. It was a waste. There weren't enough agents as it was. And now they'd lost another radio operator.

Le Provost told her that Rake was being held in a camp at Vernet, not far from Toulouse. The other two had been taken to Castres, another eighty kilometers farther east. Virginia and Le Provost commiserated over the loss of Rake and the others, and then discussed the normal procedures following the arrest of an agent or one of the Resistance members. First and foremost was to gather information. It was like gold, and cost almost as much. But its purchase would determine if, when, and how an escape could be planned.

Virginia had observed the different agents who passed through Lyon. Each was responsible for his own security, and how he approached it depended on a variety of things, such as his cover story, mission and, of course, his personality. Rake's arrest had been partially his fault and partially London's. But she had met other agents who were downright cavalier about safety measures. They pooh-poohed London's admonitions about not making rash decisions and avoiding Resistance candidates who talked too much. They ignored the rule never to talk about work unless discussing it with others would further its progress. These were basic rules they had all learned in their training at Wanborough.

Now that they were in the field and everything was authentic, including the bullets, some agents still couldn't adhere to the rules. It was beyond Virginia's comprehension. She was discreet to a fault. Several times over the past year, the feelings of one or another of her Resistance members were hurt. They felt they were being excluded from a discussion or a mission because she saw them as untrustworthy. That was not at all the case. Rather, it was because almost all work was done on a "need to know" basis.

Virginia felt responsible for the safety of every man and woman who had agreed to work with her. If the Gestapo picked them up, she didn't know how she would react. But she hoped their capture would never be as a result of indiscretion on her part.

Since early 1942, a French courier by the code name of Étienne had come each week from Paris with information to transmit to London. He collected the news from reliable sources and occasionally brought microfilms to be sent as well. Virginia supplied him with money to pay his sources and the situation worked seamlessly until late July. Étienne told Virginia he wouldn't be able to make the trip to Lyon any longer, but another man would take his place. It was someone she could have complete confidence in, he said. He told her not to worry about giving him the 150,000 francs needed for payment to their sources. The new man would see that they get it. And he would take care of reprinting and distributing the documents in the *zone occupée* as well.

As Etienne had promised, on the fourth of August a new courier did indeed arrive from Paris. He followed his predecessor's custom and went to Dr. Rousset's office to leave his package, giving the doctor the appropriate pass phrase. But Virginia had not yet left the money and documents for pickup, as Dr. Rousset hadn't wanted her to leave such a large sum of money lying around. The new man said he was in a hurry and returned to Paris empty-handed. Virginia and the doctor discussed the situation and decided that when the courier returned, Dr. Rousset would notify her and she would bring the cash to his office.

It wasn't until August 25 that the courier reappeared at Dr. Rousset's door and asked to see "Marie." When Virginia arrived, she scrutinized the man carefully. He was about five foot seven, the same height as she was, and just as slender. He had a receding hairline and bright blue eyes. But his hands were what she found most interesting. They were very delicate, the skin on the backs looked thin and soft, almost like the hands of a woman.

He was very cordial and introduced himself as Abbé Ackuin, code-named Bishop. The abbé's French was perfect, but his accent was decidedly German. He apologized for his delay in returning, saying he had been very concerned, as one of his best aides, Pierre, had been arrested. The abbé was afraid that Pierre had had an incriminating document with him at the time of his detention, so he thought it best not to risk the capture of himself or anyone else. He had therefore stayed home.

Virginia commented on his interesting accent, and the abbé explained that he had grown up in Alsace, near the German border. He went on to tell her that now he felt there would be no repercussions from the arrest of his aide and that he would continue collecting information from his "young men." These were scouts, boys on the street, and members of the organization for adolescent boys that the French had founded to match that of the German Hitlerjugend.

The abbé told Virginia he was anxious to return to Paris and asked her for the money that would go to his contacts as well as the film he needed for the microphotographs. He promised to return the following Tuesday with more information.

Virginia's instincts told her there was something not quite right about the abbé and she shared her thoughts with Rousset. She would ask London about him, perhaps they would have some useful information.

But Rousset thought her concerns were unfounded. He had heard that the abbé preached anti-Nazi sermons and he had seen him handing out pictures of de Gaulle after he left Rousset's office on his previous visit. A German sympathizer would never do that, Rousset told her.

But Virginia wasn't convinced. She contacted the circuit's new piano player and had a message sent to London on his next sked. London replied the following day. The abbé's bona fides checked out. She was told to continue working with him and supplying him with money, film for micro-filming documents, and a radio.

Virginia's concerns were heightened when she learned four days later that others in the Parisian group had been arrested. The arrests had occurred on August 15 and 16, ten days before the abbé's visit. He couldn't possibly have been unaware of them. But why hadn't he said anything? What was he up to?

On September 1, the day of the abbé's scheduled return, a man arrived at Rousset's office looking for asylum. The Gestapo wanted him, he told the doctor, who in turn explained to the man that he had come to the wrong place. But the man insisted, saying that he had been sent by the abbé.

When the abbé arrived the next day, Virginia had a long list of questions she wanted answers to. Her cordial demeanor from the previous visit was replaced with one of cool intensity. She demanded to know why he had sent a man to Rousset's office. The abbé explained that he had needed help, but Virginia ordered him not to send anyone to them without discussing it with her first. He was to act as a courier for the réseau not a nursemaid. Then she confronted him about the other arrests in Paris and asked why he hadn't told her about them. His response sounded plausible. He hadn't been sure if the people had actually been arrested or had just gone underground. He didn't want to bring her any more bad news on their first meeting. Furthermore, when he got back to Paris, he had given her money to a Resistance member by the name of Janine, who in turn gave it to the group's banker. Now Janine was nowhere to be found and he didn't know who the banker was. He was completely adrift, he complained. He insisted that he needed the names of other contacts in Lyon in case Virginia should disappear overnight like the others had.

The abbé looked genuinely upset, wringing his soft hands and biting his lip. Or was he nervous because he was not being truthful? Virginia's gut told her that there was something not right in this scenario. She told him to go back to Paris and trace the people who had disappeared. He was to try to reorganize the group and return to Lyon on September 20 with his report. He would receive further instructions then.

Abbé Ackuin did not return to Lyon, however. Instead, he went to Puy-de-Dôme where he was able to work his way into GREEN HEART, the local SOE réseau that included the Newton brothers. Everyone in SOE referred to them as "the twins," even though Alfred was nine years older than Henry. The abbé put them completely at ease with all he knew about the Resistance. They believed him to be a loyal French patriot who was familiar with other SOE agents. Through the relationship the abbé formed with the GREEN HEART members, he learned Virginia's radio code name, as well as the code names of others in the HECKLER circuit.

★ ★ ★

ABBÉ ACKUIN WAS THE PSEUDONYM used by Robert Alesh. Born in Luxembourg in 1906, his studies took him from there to Fribourg in Switzerland. After finishing at the university, he completed seminary training and worked in a variety of parishes in the area surrounding Paris. When the Nazis occupied northern France, a group within his current parish organized themselves into a Resistance group. Alesh aided them in their anti-Nazi activities. He handed out literature and photos of General de Gaulle, and helped in spiriting away local Jews.

In 1941, Alesh learned of a vacancy within the French diocese. He applied for the position and was told by the German priest in Paris, who was in charge of making diocese decisions, that the job could be his if he swore an oath to Germany. Alesh had no problem with this since one of his family members was a parish priest in Berlin and his native country of Luxembourg was a part of the Third Reich.

Shortly afterward, Alesh was summoned to the office of the second in command of the Abwehr, the German military intelligence organization. It was known he had Resistance ties, he was told. Now, as a German, he was in a position to aid his country by acting as a double agent. The alternative was deportment to a concentration camp. Alesh quickly agreed to the new line of work.

It wasn't long before he became a quick success at exposing Resistance members. To many, it was unbelievable that the clergy would stoop to such despicable actions. But Alesh felt no remorse and became very adept at espionage. Early on in the imprisonment of Pierre de Vomécourt, an escape was planned. Alesh, visiting the prison to listen to the confessions of the prisoners, heard about the plan and reported it to his superiors. The escape was foiled and de Vomécourt was put into solitary confinement. Alesh's next target, the Abwehr told him, was in Lyon.

WHILE THE WORK THAT VIRGINIA'S GROUP was doing in Lyon was applauded in London, the Gestapo in the zone libre noted it as well. Condemned agents escaped from prison, pilots disappeared after parachuting to earth, acts of sabotage occurred in factories and on rail lines. The trail that the Gestapo was following in their investigations led to Lyon. And its number one goal became the capture of whoever was in charge there.

Several months earlier, in June of 1942, a new man arrived in the city of Dijon and went to work at the Sicherheitsdienst, the intelligence service of the SS. Dijon was one hundred miles due north of Lyon, about twenty-five miles into the occupied zone. The new arrival, Klaus Barbie, had been an ardent Nazi for nine years, dedicated to all the party stood for, including contempt for those who didn't meet the racial standards. Barbie was stationed in Holland after the Germans arrived and it was there that his gruesome appetite for torture developed.

When he appeared in Dijon, he had already cultivated a range of sadistic treatments that served his purposes. For gathering information, if promises of money or immunity didn't entice his prisoners to talk, he frequently stripped them, men and women alike, and beat them into unconsciousness. He used handcuffs lined with metal spikes. The more resistant the prisoner, the tighter he had the cuffs pulled until the spikes tore into flesh. He hung victims on metal hooks or plunged them into tubs of ice-cold water, forcing them down to the point of drowning. If the prisoner fainted, he was dragged out of the water and revived, and if he still refused to talk he was plunged into the water again. All of this was interspersed with beatings.

Regardless of the fact that a prisoner had no information or had given him all he knew, Barbie continued to employ his vile treatments for his own pleasure. Occasionally he stroked his favorite cat during an episode of torture, or accompanied a prisoner's cries for mercy by playing a love song on a piano.

Barbie overheard talk one day in late August about the Gestapo's efforts in Lyon against the local Resistance. They had heard about a woman there, a Canadian they thought. This woman had been seen frequenting cafés and restaurants, usually in the company of one or two men, rarely the same ones. Capturing such an important pawn in the game of chess being played with the Resistance would certainly further his career, Barbie reflected. And the more he thought about it, the more resolute he became in playing a part in her detention.

"I would give anything to lay my hands on that Canadian bitch," he told his staff. Without being aware of it, Virginia had suddenly become one of the Gestapo's most wanted.

12

FLIGHT

AS EARLY AS 1938, President Roosevelt realized that the United States would have to become involved in the crises that were unfolding around the world. To that end, in 1939, he asked for, and Congress approved, an increase in military spending. The British were purchasing an enormous amount of American war implements and materials needed to fight the Germans, and the president recruited civilian manufacturers and engineers to build up military supplies. The American motor industry began manufacturing tanks, naval vessels, and landing craft. It was clear that the U.S. economy would be vital to the Allied war efforts.

When Britain could no longer afford to buy what it needed, Congress passed the Lend-Lease Act on March 11, 1941. It gave Roosevelt the power to sell, transfer, exchange, or lend equipment, up to an appropriated amount of $50 billion, to any country to help it defend itself against the Axis powers.

The desperately needed equipment was sent to Britain aboard ships traveling in convoys. The Allies had learned during the First World War that a group of ships moving together was the best defense against the menacing German submarines, the *Unterseeboots*, commonly referred to as U-boats. But the Nazis were not deterred, creating the "wolf pack" tactic. Rather than U-boats haunting the seas singly, a number of them would lie in wait. When one spotted a convoy, it signaled the others, and they all went in for the kill. Unable to fend off attacks from all sides, the convoys suffered heavy losses. Still the ships continued to stream across the Atlantic, manned by brave seamen dedicated to the cause.

When the United States entered the war, the U-boats began cruising American waters. In the first four months of 1942, eighty-seven ships leaving East Coast shipyards were sunk in the Atlantic, including one just fifteen miles off the New Jersey shore. The U-boats then moved to the Gulf of Mexico to attack ships coming out of the yards there. In May 1942 alone they sank another forty-one.

Despite a promise to defeat Germany first, American military powers were heavily engaged in the war in the Pacific through mid-1942. Battles in the Philippines, the Coral Sea, Midway, and Guadalcanal required enormous resources, and they cost the United States dearly in men and matériel. Although a number of bombers arrived in Great Britain that year, they saw only a limited number of campaigns. Their crews weren't idle, however. The bomber commanders and their men learned tactics and the Allies built up a strong ground organization.

Also at work in Britain at the close of summer 1942 was an unfamiliar American lieutenant general by the name of Dwight D. Eisenhower. He was to assume command of the daring Allied attack in North Africa, code-named Operation Torch, that was in the planning stages. Torch was aimed at German-held African countries along the Mediterranean and would be a three-pronged attack. Thirty-five thousand American soldiers would leave the United States to disembark in French Morocco. Another thirty-nine thousand would leave from Britain to take western Algeria at Oran. The third prong was made up of ten thousand Americans and twenty-three thousand Brits who would also leave England to attack at Algiers in Algeria.

Eisenhower's opinion on Torch during its planning was one of awe: "The venture was new. . . . Up to [this] moment no government [has] ever attempted to carry out an overseas expedition involving a journey of thousands of miles from its bases and terminating in a major attack."

ONE EARLY OCTOBER MORNING, Virginia received news that infuriated her. French citizens had handed over yet another British flyer to the Gestapo, which was paying well for them. That made three in the last month. These collaborating French had no idea, of course, what fate awaited the flyers. Many assumed it was a prison sentence until the termination of the war. Others simply didn't care. A bundle of francs at a time when a great many were going to bed hungry more than made up for guilt.

Not to be outdone, Virginia told Rousset that if the Germans were paying for flyers, they would too. They would spread the word that each man turned over to them was worth ten thousand francs, plus any expenses the citizens were out for food.

Radio operator Le Chêne was back in Lyon and had stopped by Rousset's office that morning to say he was in desperate need of some new radio tubes. In an effort to stay off the streets as much as possible, he had asked Rousset to see about them for him. Tubes had arrived in the parachute drop Labourier had picked up the previous night and were now stashed at the home of M. and Mme Catin. The Catins had been recruited to join HECKLER four months earlier. Both Monsieur and Madame were willing to assume any and all risks, acting as couriers between Lyon and Avignon, carrying messages to be sent to London or between Resistance members. Even their teenaged children had volunteered, independently of their parents' involvement. It was only at a meeting in Rousset's wine cellar that the four of them realized they were all engaged in the cause.

Virginia told Rousset that she'd be happy to pick them up, as she was headed in that direction to sign the papers for her new flat. The search for new living quarters had been difficult. The only suitable location she could find was on the sixth floor of a building with no elevator. But it was better than the alternative, which was to stay in her current flat and have people popping in all the time. Some dope, she said, had given her name and address away. Suddenly, she had begun to get an astounding number of people at her door who wanted to go to England.

The previous night it had been an old man who supposedly just got out of the camp at Vienne. He had told her that Mr. Lanlo of Nice sent him. Virginia told Rousset she didn't know anyone by that name, nor did she know anyone named Bondy, who was still in the camp and also gave the old man her name. He had brought her ten eggs and told her that he could get her four more if she wanted. Evidently he had been informed that her services could be bought with hen fruit.

Rousset asked her if she had given the man their usual instructions, which Virginia said she had. Whenever anyone approached a member of the HECKLER réseau, the member first disavowed any knowledge of the subject the stranger wanted to discuss. It was commonly known that everyone gathered at Place Bellecour to discuss news, so the stranger was directed to go there for a couple of days, with the possibility of receiving the information he was seeking. Then, another member of HECKLER would observe the stranger to see if he was approached by anyone else and to determine if he was genuine.

Rousset turned the subject to one Virginia had avoided for months: her return to London. It was an unwritten SOE rule that agents remained in the field for no more than six months and then went back to England to "cool off." Virginia had been operating for thirteen months straight and London was strongly suggesting she return. She had agreed to go home later that month, but was now having second thoughts.

In a recent report to SOE headquarters, she had written:

> I have asked you to arrange my clipper passage for the end of October, but I may postpone my departure.. . . . I just want to have it all in order to be able to get my visas so that I can leave promptly if it seems advisable to do so.

Virginia remained unconcerned about her own safety. There was no reason for her to think otherwise. Why should she? *She* was in charge of her fate, not the Gestapo. *She* was directing the action in Lyon and unoccupied France, not the collaborators. *She* was conquering territory, not the Germans, even if only figuratively for the time being.

Still she had heard stories about incarcerated agents and Resistance members who were dragged into the prison yard, and, within full view of the other inmates' windows, were stood against the wall and executed for their "crimes against the state" or for giving "aid and succor to the enemy." The jailers hoped witnessing executions would encourage the other prisoners to divulge information, and some did. But others, far greater in number, remained silent to the end.

Resistance members were publicly tortured as well, and some were even executed in plain view. Virginia stumbled across one such display on a late October afternoon. The day was warm and the sun an autumn gold. She was on her way back to her flat and came around the corner to see four men and a woman chained together and being hauled behind a police vehicle. Two of the men were on their feet running, but the other man and the woman must have fallen and were being dragged. Their bodies were bloody, their clothing shredded. The gendarmes in the back of the truck were laughing, encouraging those on their feet to keep running. The scene nauseated Virginia. She didn't know any of the people, but it didn't matter. She knew their destination and their fate, if they survived the present ordeal.

Every story she heard about the death of someone fighting for a free Europe knifed into her. And for those who were tortured first, death did not come easily. The training the SOE agents had received in England might have made them aware of torture, but Virginia was quite certain it could never truly prepare them for the genuine article. She assumed she was no different from her compatriots in wondering how much she would be able to take if her turn ever came. How would she hold up?

By this time, the new Gestapo chief, Heinrich Müller, had authorized "sharpened interrogation" for terrorists, namely the Resistance and British agents. He approved exhaustion exercises, regulated beatings, sleep deprivation, starvation, and confinement in dark cells. The treatments were used to gather intelligence against those who had "plans hostile to the state," or for confessions of guilt.

And there were other tortures even more demented. Some victims were subjected to having larger and larger stones pressed upon their chests until they confessed, or, as the weight of the stones became too great for them to breathe, they suffocated to death. Others were subjected to the funnel. It allowed the torturers to force-feed them fluids, from salt water to whatever the depraved mind could imagine, including vinegar, urine, and diarrhea.

Slowly tearing out fingernails and toenails was a common method for seeking confessions. Pliers, sometimes heated until they were red hot, were routinely used. But nail extraction could be accomplished even more slowly and cruelly by driving needles or wooden wedges and splinters under the nails to pry them loose. Worse still, sometimes the wood was dipped in boiling sulfur.

News of these atrocities and others reached Virginia via escaping agents and Resistance members. Some of them had only witnessed the tortures, others had been victims. The stories sickened and fretted her, to be sure. But they did nothing to deter her. It was vital to achieve a Nazi-free Europe. Anything else was just not acceptable.

ON SATURDAY, NOVEMBER 7, 1942, Virginia received word from Lyon's American Consulate, at the request of the embassy in Vichy, that an invasion of North Africa was imminent. She was told she had better make plans to leave Lyon if she didn't want to stay in "forced residence" for the duration of the war. Taking all of the papers she had hidden in her flat, she sped to Rousset's office to begin liquidating everything they had stored in his wine cellar.

The circuit rule was to have people there at all times should uninvited Gestapo callers arrive at the doctor's office. In that event, the doctor would signal a warning to those in the cellar by feigning a cramp and stomping on the floor. He would delay the callers, while below, any evidence of Resistance work would be scooped up and the cellar returned to its former identity as a storage facility of wine-soaked barrels and dusty bottles.

Virginia instructed those in the cellar to put items that could be destroyed into a washtub and burned. Those that were vital were piled up and sorted. She gave one réseau member, Nicola, the official seals, blank government documents, and the two hundred thousand francs she had brought from her flat. From now on, Nicola would handle the finances for the group, she told them. If a German occupation occurred, which was looking more likely, she would have to leave immediately. There wouldn't be time for good-byes, so she bid them a collective, albeit premature, *au revoir.*

During the flurry of activity that continued over the next hour, each member wished Virginia well in the event they didn't see her again. She and Rousset had agreed to meet for lunch after they had finished. They left separately and took different circuitous routes, ending up at a café not far from his office.

Waiting for their food, Virginia told him she had no intention of leaving until she was able to get Rake out of prison and on his way back to England. And there were other loose ends she wanted to get tied up. But Rousset disagreed. She would be of no use to anyone if she was arrested. Virginia was still not convinced she could leave. All of them would need her help and her contacts in the gendarmerie if they were picked up. Again Rousset overrode her. She had taken extreme security measures and they had all learned from her. Their arrests were unlikely.

Virginia said nothing more, but she wasn't convinced. The following morning, she left her flat to pick up a newspaper. As she rounded the corner, she ran into a fellow she knew from the Deuxième Bureau, France's Secret Service allied with the Resistance. He told her that the Allies had begun the invasion of North Africa at three o'clock that morning. They were all under orders to leave, and he heartily advised her to do the same, and the sooner the better.

The Germans would not take the North African assault lightly. In fact, they would see it as an immediate threat to their holdings on the European continent. And rightly so. North Africa would be the perfect place for the Allies to assemble an invasion into southern France. To counter any possibility of that, Virginia would have bet the farm that the Nazis would be occupying all of France within days.

She thanked the Deuxième Bureau man for the information and continued on to the café, now out of curiosity. Would Lyon's citizens or the local gendarmes have any inkling of the changes certain to take place in the very near future?

The paper she picked up had no news of the invasion. It was printed under the watchful eyes of the Vichy government. Any news adverse to France's current situation, or that of Germany, was always cleverly couched. The staff journalists, even if they knew about the North African invasion, had probably not yet been given the fanciful version of the event; the version that would portray the military of the Third Reich swatting away the invaders as if they were flies. By early evening, though, Virginia had other worries on her mind.

One of her réseau members, Artus, had gone to a nearby village to confer with a friendly gendarme who could help Virginia get out of Lyon the following Wednesday. Virginia was to meet Artus at 6:00 PM, but he didn't materialize. Neither did Nicola, who was expected later that evening. Perhaps they were nervous about coming to the flat, or maybe they thought she had already left. Worse still, maybe they'd been picked up.

At nine, she was hungry and headed out to get some food at the Café de la République. Her friend from the Deuxième Bureau had the same idea and was just leaving as she arrived. They exchanged greetings and then he said softly in her ear that the Germans were expected in Lyon sometime between midnight and dawn. To keep up appearances for the others in the café, she laughed as if he had just told her a joke, linked her arm with his, and walked back outside with him to the corner. She thanked him and wished him good luck. He tipped his hat and walked away.

Virginia went straight to her flat where she began packing a bag. She hated leaving Lyon with so many loose ends, so many people depending on her. On the other hand, Rousset was right: when the Nazis came storming into the zone libre, their first act would be to clear it of Resistance people.

The Gestapo was already looking for a Canadian woman, so because of her accent and gender, she would be quickly singled out. And there was nothing she could do from a jail cell. The last train to Perpignon, one of the jumping-off points for those crossing into Spain, left Lyon at 11:00 PM. She figured she'd better be on it. She took one last look around her flat and went back out into the cold night.

THE TRAIN ARRIVED IN PERPIGNON just as the sun was peeking over the mountains. Virginia had slept lightly and little, as was her habit. An extravagance such as lounging in bed till noon had never been her style anyway, and it seemed an even sillier waste of time in the midst of all there was to do.

Perpignon appeared to be a quaint town, with the mighty Pyrénées Mountains as a backdrop, far from the sounds of guns and marching feet. But it was actually a hive of activity. Agents for guides who led the expeditions across the mountains hung around every corner looking for a financial opportunity. Meanwhile, informers and Gestapo agents prowled the streets and cafés in search of victims.

Virginia walked to the Hôtel de la Cloche and requested a room. She had gotten word that the proprietor was a Resistance sympathizer, and although she didn't discuss politics with him, he appeared to be quite amiable. She signed in as Mlle Marie Monin and climbed the stairs to her room.

Exits out of France began by hiking to Spain across the snow-covered Pyrénées, a trip of thirty miles or more. From there one took a train south to Barcelona and another west to Lisbon, Portugal, then a ship to England. Virginia's first chore in Perpignon would be to go to the city square in search of Gilbert, a contact who could arrange mountain guides if the price was right. But since he could only be found there between two and three in the afternoon, she decided a couple of hours of sleep would be a good use of her extra time.

She awoke at noon, hungry. After freshening up with cold water from the sink in her room, Virginia walked out into the brisk November air to a café for lunch. Then she strolled over to the square in search of Gilbert. Having met him once in Lyon, she recognized him immediately. Gilbert's fee for arranging guides was twenty thousand francs, out of which he would pay the guide. Virginia was to pay him on the day of departure, which, he said, would probably be two days hence. He would send word to her hotel once he had the details organized.

Several hours later, Gilbert called the hotel and asked Virginia to meet him at a café a few streets over. She saw him when she arrived, sitting with three other men, whom she assumed were guides. But when introductions were made, Gilbert explained that the men, two Frenchman named Antoine and Henri, and a Belgian army captain named Jean, were also in need of passage. They had been involved in the Resistance, but were now hunted men. They believed they had information that would be useful to London, after which they hoped to be sent back to France to continue the fight.

Virginia asked them why she needed to be involved. Jean explained they had no money, to which Gilbert just shrugged. Although he was rabidly anti-German, he was a businessman first, with an opportunity to sweeten his agreement with Virginia. He seemed to trust these three men, however, and Virginia trusted him. She negotiated a fee of fifty-five thousand francs for the four of them. Usually escapees were passed from one guide to another during the course of their journey. But in this case, they would have just one to take them all the way to Spain, a man who was on his way home to visit family. He was the best guide in all of the Pyrénées, Gilbert assured them. Virginia hoped he was right.

AT 7:00 AM ON WEDNESDAY, November 11, 1942, German troops crossed the demarcation line. There was no longer any zone libre in France, as the Axis powers now controlled the entire country. And the date was symbolic since it was the date the First World War armistice had forced Germany to her knees. Hitler never failed to incorporate irony into his strategic planning.

In Vichy, Pétain became a virtual prisoner, while Laval continued to work toward a place for himself within the Nazi organization. He had, in fact, been summoned to Hitler's presence in Munich two days earlier. Laval had hoped that the meeting was to discuss his future, but Hitler was interested in securing the bases in French Tunisia where he could mount his counterattack to the Allied invasion. Laval returned to France empty-handed only to discover that Vichy was now in German hands.

With Pétain out of the picture, General Eisenhower, who had led the Allied troops in Operation TORCH, appointed Jean-François Darlan as civil and military chief of French North Africa. A naval admiral, Darlan had previously served under Pétain as commander in chief of French armed forces and as high commissioner in North Africa. Both Churchill and Roosevelt approved of the appointment on the grounds that it would assist military operations in the area. But de Gaulle was incensed by the snub. The French Resistance was none too happy either, as Darlan, next to Pétain, was the longest-serving and highest-ranking official in Vichy, and had been labeled a collaborator.

THE EVENING OF THE ELEVENTH, Virginia left her hotel in Perpignon, carrying her valise, and walked to a street corner several blocks away. A car arrived a few minutes later, driven by Gilbert. Virginia climbed in, joining Antoine, Henri, and Jean. The two-hour drive to the town of Lavelanet was fairly quiet, with only an occasional utterance from one of them, to which the rest would reply *oui* or *non*. Around 8:00 PM, they arrived at the safe house in Lavelanet, about twenty-eight miles from the border. There they met their mountain guide, Juan. Virginia told him that she spoke Spanish and would be translating for the group. He was not a man of many words but he did inform them that occasionally the snows on the mountain summits delayed departures. They were in luck, however. Based on the next day's report, Juan told them, the weather would be favorable and they could leave as soon as they were dressed.

Virginia had brought her heaviest clothes with her, and she was issued a pair of used boots, apparently included in the price. Her real concern was her amputation stump. She only had a single woolen "stump sock" to absorb perspiration and prevent blisters and sores from developing. But given the kind of exertion she was sure they would endure, she needed an additional sock to alternate with the one she had. That way, she'd always have a dry one.

She didn't want to appear greedy by asking for an additional pair of socks, nor did she want to go into detail about her leg. Juan was already grumbling because she was a woman. If he found out she was an amputee, he really wouldn't want to take her. She pulled aside the owner of the house, a woman who had thus far tended to the group as if she were a mother hen. Virginia asked her if she had an "widow" sock, one that had lost its mate. The woman smiled and scurried off, returning with one, no questions asked.

Virginia and each of the men, along with the guide, were given rucksacks already supplied with enough food for their journey. To that they added what few personal belongings would fit. Then they piled back into the car and were driven another ten miles, arriving at their embarkation spot around midnight.

The night was clear and cold. A heavy blanket of snow covered the ground. Virginia looked up at the imposing mountains in front of her, a luminous bluish white in the moonlight. The Pyrénées' highest peak was around eleven thousand feet. She guessed they were already at four or five thousand. The last line of Robert Frost's "Stopping by Woods on a Snowy Evening" came to mind: "and miles to go before I sleep."

Their climb began to the east of the ski town of Ax-les-Thermes through the Orgeix Valley. Those first several hours were hiking straight uphill and had to be walked in absolute silence. The French customs guards, along with guards from myriad German organizations, patrolled the area, known as the *zone interdite*, the forbidden zone. Anyone caught in it would be taken directly to the authorities in Perpignon. They sneaked past the towns of Orgeix, Orlu, the ironworks at Orlu, and the Bisp Bridge. The dark silence was punctuated only by the occasional bark of a dog. Each time the climbers froze in their tracks, but never saw another human.

When dawn broke, Juan stopped them to have a snack, although they weren't terribly hungry. Courtesy of the SOE, Virginia had supplied each of her fellow travelers with a tablet of Benzedrine, an amphetamine that suppresses the appetite and fatigue. But their guide insisted that they eat something and they all complied, like children under the watch of a stern nanny. Conversation remained at a minimum, but Virginia glanced at each of the men's faces. Juan appeared completely indifferent to the whole affair. This was his job, no different to him than if he was a merchant or a bar owner. The three Resistance refugees had grim expressions. Virginia couldn't tell if it was fear or fatigue, or both, etched into their faces. But no one complained and after they passed around the flask of *eau-de-vie*, they continued on.

The rising sun cast its rays over the diamond-studded snow. However, by 10:00 AM, the wind had turned glacial and an icy fog enveloped them. The drifts on the ground were now knee-deep and Virginia was exerting an enormous effort to make her prosthetic leg function. With the majority of Cuthbert buried in the snow, walking normally was almost impossible. She was forced to take every step with her good right leg, using it as a snowplow, after which she dragged Cuthbert. On top of that, they were continually going either uphill or downhill, always on an uneven surface. She redoubled her efforts, determined to keep up with her companions.

To distract herself, Virginia took in her surroundings. On one side was a deep ravine, descending hundreds of feet. On the other side was a magnificent glacier. Under different circumstances, what fun it would have been to climb up the glacier and slide down into the ravine, just like she and her brother had on the hills surrounding Box Horn Farm. The snow in Maryland was never as deep, of course, nor was the air as bone chilling, but those gleeful winter hours building snowmen and snow forts along with the rousing snowball fights, were wonderful memories. Never would she have imagined she would one day be running for her life, zigzagging up the side of a mountain.

Juan appeared to be following a stream, although there was no real path. It hit home that she and her companions were really at this man's mercy. He had already collected half of his money. He could have easily led them into a trap, or left them to freeze in the dark of night. But desperate as they were, they had no choice but to trust blindly. Virginia hoped that Juan was worthy of that trust.

Her rucksack weighed heavily, the straps cutting into her shoulders despite her many layers of clothing. Her traveling companions kept shifting their packs as well. When they finally arrived at a pass between the mountains, Juan wrote "2,460 metres" in the snow. Virginia assumed it was their altitude. She did some quick math and guessed they were somewhere around 7,900 feet.

No wonder they were all struggling. At an altitude like that, breathing is difficult. In addition, the wind had picked up. Several times she thought it might lift her up, had her feet not been packed so far down in the snow. The terrain was growing trickier. The gradient was now steeper and there were very few handholds to help them along. For the first time, Virginia labored to suppress her fears. No longer was being arrested her primary concern. Now it was survival.

They began to descend a little from the pass and less than an hour later, Virginia could see the outline of an ice-covered lake in the distance.

It was the Lac des Bouillouses, Juan told them. Evidently he played tour guide as well as mountain guide. They struggled on until, directly in front of them, a mirage arose from the snow: a rough cabin with no windows and a chimney rising out of the top like the stem on an apple. Reaching to the roof on one side was a large pile of wood.

Juan told his weary flock in broken French that they would stop here to rest. He dug the snow away from the door, pulled it open, and ushered them in. It was cold inside, but there were six wooden cots slung with canvas. Each had an old blanket lying on it. Juan disappeared and then reappeared with an armful of wood he deposited on the floor in front of the crude stone fireplace.

Henri was concerned that the smoke would attract attention. But Juan assured him that he would only be making a small fire and the wind would dissipate it. He made a blowing sound imitating the wind to make sure they understood his meaning. Each of them chose a cot and lay down. Virginia was certain they all had hypothermia. How could they not after hiking almost twelve hours through snowdrifts in freezing temperatures? Antoine complained from his cot that his left foot was so cold he couldn't feel it. Virginia smiled at the irony. If only her companions knew that she could *never* feel her left foot.

They slept four hours or so before the cabin's cold awoke them. Juan was crouched at the edge of the fireplace, spreading out the coals to extinguish the fire.

Virginia wondered if he had slept at all.

Still under the blanket, she unlaced the leather corset holding her prosthetic leg to her thigh. She wanted a dry stump sock before they resumed their trek. As she feared, blisters had developed from the pressure and friction. They had opened and were oozing, sticking to the wool. There was nothing she could do about it until she arrived in Barcelona.

The men all complained that their legs were stiff, the result of going from extreme exertion to complete lack of motion. But at least the chill had worn off. They ate some of the food from their packs, drank a bit of the hot tea Juan had made with melted snow, and each took another pull from the bottle of *eau-de-vie*. Benzedrine tablets were passed around and the group trooped silently back outside to begin their journey again.

Virginia guessed it was about four in the afternoon on Thursday, November 12. It seemed like weeks since she'd left Lyon. She wondered if the Germans had arrived in the city yet. More important, she wondered what her friends were doing and if they were safe.

The group was climbing again, and arrived a short while later at another mountain pass. In the waning daylight, Juan again wrote the altitude in the snow, 2,392 metres, 7,650 feet. They began another descent, but mercifully the wind died down, as going downhill was much more treacherous than going up. The clouds parted and so many stars appeared in the sky that it seemed as though there were more of them than the velvety dark. They arrived at the shore of another frozen lake and followed the stream that fed it.

When Virginia first saw them, she thought the lights ahead of her were stars at the edge of the horizon. But when Juan turned to his group and put his finger to his lips, she realized it was a village. The stream widened into a river and a second village also appeared on the other side of it. It must have been almost eight o'clock and no one was moving on the streets when they entered the village on their side of the river.

Juan led them to the back of a house at the edge of town and rapped rhythmically on the door. It opened slowly revealing a young man. Behind him stood a young woman holding a baby. Juan entered and motioned the rest to do so as well.

The young man introduced himself as Philippe and his wife as Anne-Marie. A fire crackled cheerily behind him and Virginia could see mats of straw laid out in front of it. She and the men sat down on them, which felt terrific. Juan had kept them moving at a rapid pace, but he was really a superior guide. He'd gotten them to cover a great deal of terrain at a good clip. He sensed when their exhaustion was about to do them in, and timed their rests to perfection.

The two Frenchmen fell asleep on their mats as soon as their heads were down. Anne-Marie retrieved blankets from the other room and covered them, then brought blankets for Virginia, Jean, and Juan. Virginia didn't remember much after that until the baby's cry awakened her before dawn. She stretched and again changed her stump sock beneath the blanket. Her situation had become worse as the sores had grown larger.

Philippe and Anne-Marie bustled around preparing a breakfast for the voyagers of coffee, bread, and jam. When they'd finished eating Philippe lifted the bottom panel from a bench against the wall and pulled out a suitcase. Virginia recognized it immediately: a radio transmitter. And he assured her that it worked, explaining that several months earlier someone who had passed through had left it behind in case it was needed.

Virginia was elated. She'd left Lyon in such a hurry, London had no idea when or if she was coming. Nothing had been arranged in the way of passage for her from Barcelona. On top of that, she was bringing three additional people. She had been trying to figure out how she was going to make it all work. The sight of the radio felt like Christmas morning.

She had often watched Gregoire at the Marchands' and knew the necessary frequencies. And she remembered enough of her Morse code training to be able to tap out a crude message. She was able to raise London and send off her message. They radioed back that they were glad to hear from her and would make the necessary arrangements for all four of them from Barcelona to London. Were there any other pressing issues? they asked.

"Cuthbert is being tiresome, but I can cope," she radioed back. After several minutes of silence, she assumed that the communication had been terminated. Suddenly the radio came back to life with the message, "If Cuthbert tiresome, have him eliminated." She smiled.

Once she'd finished with the radio, the group reassembled for what Juan had told them would be the final leg of their expedition. They thanked Philippe and Anne-Marie for their hospitality and left the house in pairs, slipping into the woods behind it, to a prearranged meeting place. They headed south and when they reached the next summit, Juan stopped and turned to the group explaining that the land that lay below them was España.

In the far distance, the snow disappeared. Spain was warmer, and the green valley was inviting and promising. Virginia looked behind her, comparing the Spanish vista to what they had spent the last forty hours crossing. The tall, imposing snow-covered peaks of the French side were quite a contrast. They had almost made it.

But they still weren't out of danger. Even Spain was honeycombed with German agents. Plus, Spain's head of state, General Franco, had a police force that was vigilant in watching for clandestine travelers. And almost as dangerous as those two groups, Philippe had told them they also had to be on the lookout for the former Spanish Republicans. Exiled from their country and condemned to death by Franco after the insurrection, they lived in the wild. They were hungry, desperate, and bored. If they couldn't steal food or money, they were just as easily inclined to torture victims for entertainment. On top of that, the Spanish border guards patrolled the area on skis.

When they twice saw ski patrols coming down from the summit, Virginia's party fell to the snow-covered ground at Juan's signal. Otherwise, they trod lightly and quietly, picking their way past the village of Meranges and into the Serge River valley. Still on Benzedrine, they needed to stop only a few times for a bite to eat, before they moved on, arriving at their goal, San Juan de las Abadesas, by early evening on November 13. Juan wasted no time with long good-byes. At the outskirts of town, he collected the rest of his money from Virginia, tipped his hat, and was gone.

The group had been prepared for their arrival before they left France. Virginia and Jean each had the name of a safe house for that night, and Antoine and Henri would share a third. They were to clean up, eat whatever the homes' owners could provide, and not leave the houses. Being housebound was not a problem since they were all so worn out.

The foursome agreed to meet at the train station the next morning and take the earliest train to Barcelona, scheduled to depart at 5:45. They had been told it was never patrolled by any police agency and they would avoid any passport searches.

They agreed to meet before 5:45, in case the train schedule had changed, and then entered San Juan separately so as not to arouse the suspicion a group of bedraggled strangers would draw. After arriving at her safe house, Virginia was so exhausted she mumbled a few words of thanks to the homeowners for the food, clean clothes, and warm water in the washbasin. She then fell into a dead sleep in the bed they provided. The next morning she awoke with the señora gently patting on her shoulder.

Virginia asked her if she had any salve. She told the señora she had blisters from the hike. She just didn't go into any detail about where the blisters were. The woman returned with the salve and told Virginia to keep it for the rest of her journey. The donation was truly generous and one from the heart; medical treatments were precious in these hard times. After cleaning and medicating her blisters, Virginia tore up the leg of her long johns to fashion a new stump sock and packed its remains and the salve in her bag.

It was 4:30 AM when Virginia arrived at the practically empty station. Henri, Antoine, and Jean arrived shortly after and they all settled separately on wooden benches to wait for the train. Just minutes after they had sat down, four Spanish civil guards appeared and rounded them up into a group at gunpoint.

One of them demanded their *pasaportes.* Their passports, of course, did not have the *entrada* stamps required for a legal entry into Spain. The plan was that they would get them from a contact in Barcelona, avoiding authorities until then. That was the whole purpose of going on this early train.

Virginia smiled at the guards and began digging through her pockets and rucksack, stalling for time, and hoping for a plan to come to her. The three men did the same thing. But the guards were not patient men, and the one who had demanded their passports took Virginia's arm. The three men were shoved roughly into place behind her, surrounded by the other guards still brandishing their weapons. They were marched the few blocks to the police station and deposited in jail cells.

13

BIDING TIME

ON FRIDAY THE THIRTEENTH OF NOVEMBER, the same day that Virginia was thrown into a jail cell in San Juan de las Abadesas, the Gestapo appeared at Dr. Rousset's office and took him to their headquarters. Two days earlier, the Nazis had swept into all of unoccupied France. The armistice army was disarmed and Pétain pleaded with his countrymen to obey the new government. When the Nazis arrived in Lyon, with them came a new Gestapo chief, SS Obersturmführer Klaus Barbie, whose job it was to ferret out Resistance members, suck out as much information as possible from them, and have them eliminated.

Dr. Rousset was shown a poster with a sketch of Virginia. Directly beneath it were the words, "*La Dame qui Boite*" (the Limping Lady). The poster continued with information about Virginia and ended by stating, "She is the most dangerous of all Allied spies. We must find her and destroy her." Rousset had seen other wanted posters hung around the city. He assumed Virginia's image would now join the others. When asked, he acknowledged that he knew the woman on the poster. Anyone with half an eye for observation would have seen her coming and going from his office, he said. She was a patient who suffered from a variety of maladies so she saw him frequently for treatment. But he had no idea that she was an enemy of the state. Had he known so, he assured the agents, he would have gotten in touch with them immediately. The questioning continued in this vein for hours.

Meanwhile, Alesh was questioning the doctor's maid, Eugénie. The abbé had just returned to Lyon and arrived at the doctor's home shortly after the

Gestapo had been there. Eugénie was close to hysterical about the doctor's arrest, and Alesh attempted to calm her by telling her they needed to find the woman named Marie Monin. She could fix the whole mess, he told her. Eugénie blubbered through her tears that she hadn't seen the "English-woman" for over a week; that she had just disappeared.

Still attempting to calm her, Alesh suggested that perhaps visiting some of Marie's other friends would shed light on her whereabouts. The sooner they found Mlle Monin, the sooner they could help Dr. Rousset. Eugénie brightened at this idea and told him what she knew: the addresses of the Joulians and Mme Guérin. Alesh told the maid not to worry, that he would undertake to resolve this whole issue himself, and made an immediate visit to the Joulians and then to Mme Guérin. All of them were very distressed to hear about Rousset's arrest. Although they'd never met Alesh, he seemed to know so much about Virginia and the doctor, they assumed he could be trusted. Over the next several days, they gradually allowed him into their circle of confidence. They agreed that finding Virginia would be useful, although they had no idea where she was. Alesh encouraged them to speak with all of their contacts and to introduce them to him. Together, the abbé told them earnestly, they might be able to arrange for Rousset's release.

AFTER SEVERAL HOURS IN THE JAIL CELLS of the Seguridad General in San Juan de las Abadesas, a group of officers came in and took Virginia and her three companions to an office. Sitting behind a tall desk was another member of the Spanish Guard. Virginia told him she wanted to speak to the American consul in Barcelona. "*Silencio!*" he told her and shoved a register at her. She and the others signed their names and the guards took them out of the station to a waiting horse and wagon. Under the curious stares of the passersby, the wagon creaked out of town, heading east.

Virginia had no idea where they were going and her questions were ignored by the guards on the wagon. Three hours later they arrived at the town of Figueras and were taken to the train station. When the train arrived, a new group of Civil Guards got off and collected Virginia and the three men.

"I want to see the American consul in Barcelona," Virginia told the new group.

"*Si, mañana,*" one of them said, and the rest laughed.

Two hours later she was sitting in a cell in the wretched Miranda del Ebro prison outside Figueras. She had been separated from the men upon arrival, taken to a wooden barracks, given a thin, filthy blanket, and ignored when she again requested contact with the American consul. Her cellmate was a pitiful-looking young woman named Elena, who had a wracking cough. Elena said she'd been there for five months, with one month remaining on her sentence. Virginia asked what her crime had been.

Elena explained that she was a *punta* in Barcelona, a prostitute.

Virginia's rucksack had been gone through multiple times since her initial arrest. The end result was that while all of her papers and money were gone, the guards had allowed her to keep her few personal belongings, including the salve. She had continued to apply it and since she wasn't walking much anyway, the blisters were beginning to heal. Elena was amazed when she first saw Virginia take off her wooden leg.

She told Virginia shyly that she had never known anyone missing a limb. This admission was followed by a dozen questions about how and when the accident had happened. Virginia never talked about it to anyone, but for some reason, locked in the godforsaken Spanish prison, discussing it with a complete stranger was not the least bit uncomfortable.

Their cell was damp and cold. A winter rain fell every day, interspersed with gloomy gray skies. They slept on the ground like animals, huddled under their threadbare blankets and ate pale, mustard-colored soup, with an occasional green glob floating in it. She asked to see the American consul every time a guard came to the cell.

After she'd been in prison for a week, Virginia awoke one morning to find Elena trembling from chills and burning with fever, complaining about a knifelike pain in her chest. Virginia got the attention of the guards and demanded that they send in the doctor. A dirty little man who called himself a physician arrived an hour later. He identified Elena's problem as pleurisy, and began to leave the cell. Virginia was horrified, and insisted, as Elena's illness was obviously serious, even life threatening, that the doctor not leave before giving her something.

The doctor was not moved, saying that Spain was a poor country without enough medicine for the citizens, let alone enough to share with the prisoners. Elena would either survive or not. By the sheer will of both Virginia and Elena, the young woman survived to her release day three weeks later. The first thing she would do, she swore to Virginia, would be to mail the letter Virginia had written to the American consul in Barcelona.

On December 2, after twenty days of incarceration, Virginia was finally released to a representative of the American consulate. And twenty-three days after that, she was having Christmas dinner with Vera Atkins and a group of friends in London.

Conversation was kept light; there was no discussion of missions or Germans, scarcely a mention of the war. When the others left, Vera toasted Virginia's success in France.

Virginia thanked her politely, but explained that her return was merely a stopover. Her real interest was getting back into the fray. Vera tried to discourage her impatience. She'd only returned and was still much too hot to go back to France. *My New Year's resolution for 1943 then,* Virginia thought, *is to cool off in a hurry.*

AT THE SAME TIME VIRGINIA was sharing the holidays with her friends, a great deal of turmoil was boiling in France. Darlan, Eisenhower's pick for civil and military chief of French North Africa was assassinated on Christmas Eve. Henri Giraud was his successor and immediately alienated the Allies by arresting several Frenchmen who had aided Eisenhower in TORCH.

Giraud met Churchill, Roosevelt, and de Gaulle in Casablanca at a war conference, which took place between January 14 and 29, 1943. It was decided that de Gaulle and Giraud would become copresidents of the French Committee of National Liberation.

In Lyon, despite his promises to the contrary, Alesh, of course, had made no headway in securing the release of Dr. Rousset from the Lyon Gestapo. It was now April and he had been in regular contact with the remnants of Virginia's HECKLER circuit for four and a half months. He knew their code names and the roads they traveled to the neighboring cities to conduct their sabotage. He knew how they spirited away downed pilots. He was beginning to understand how they ushered in arriving aircraft loaded with supplies. And he told them daily that if only Marie Monin could be found, Dr. Rousset's fate would surely have a different outcome. Then, mysteriously, the abbé disappeared and those in the circuit never saw him again.

By this time, Gestapo chief Barbie had moved his office from the Hôtel Terminus to the École de Santé Militaire, where construction on his specially ordered torture chambers was now completed. The posters with Virginia's likeness, shown months earlier to Dr. Rousset, had been his idea, and it infuriated him that he had not yet captured her or even received any useful information about her. The doctor had been of no help and had been sent to Fresnes prison, outside Paris, where he was kept in solitary confinement. From there he had been shipped to Buchenwald. Barbie's patience had worn thin and he felt it was time to round up the rest of the "Limping Lady's" rebels.

The Joulians were arrested on April 6. They were taken to the École de Santé Militaire and tortured. Mme Joulian's teeth were knocked out and her arm was broken. Mme Guérin was the next to be picked up on April 8 at one of her flats, which also housed two Canadian airmen. Before answering the door, she helped the airmen escape out a back window. Then, in her inimitable style, she managed to delay the Gestapo long enough for the airmen to get away.

Mme Catin was arrested as well, although M. Catin was able to escape to the mountains. Mme Guérin's friend, M. Genet, was arrested on April 10, and Labourier, Le Provost, and the Marchands were picked up in the ensuing days. Only Maggy (Andrée Michel) evaded immediate capture, although the Gestapo eventually caught up with her, too. None of them acknowledged being a part of any Resistance organization or of knowing an individual by the name of Marie Monin. Enraging the Gestapo with their silence, they were all sent to prison camps.

In the south of France, more trouble erupted for the SOE. Peter Churchill had made another submarine trip to the Mediterranean coast, this time bringing in Victor Gerson, who went on to establish the "VIC" escape line across the Pyrénées. Churchill then moved on to Montpellier where he organized the SPINDLE réseau. London sent him a very brave, and very lovely, courier by the name of Odette Sansom, code-named Lise.

Without realizing it was happening to them—and as frequently happens when members of the opposite sex are forced together under stressful situations—they fell in love. However, Lise was being trailed by an Abwehr agent, Hugo Bleicher. She and Churchill were arrested in southeastern France on April 16, 1943, and sent to Fresnes Prison.

Life was changing for Pierre de Vomécourt as well. In solitary confinement in Fresnes for ten months, the Nazis announced to him one day that he was being moved to a camp in Germany where hostages were being assembled should they be needed later on to negotiate with the Allies. The Nazis already knew who he was and what he'd been doing before they arrested him. A catch such as he was would be highly valuable. But de Vomécourt announced he wasn't leaving Fresnes without the other members of his réseau who'd also been arrested with him.

To make his point, de Vomécourt threatened suicide rather than accepting preferential treatment. The Nazi guards were not about to risk such an important prisoner and agreed to move his cohorts along with him to Colditz Castle, a prison near Leipzig in Germany.

IN MAY OF 1943, Spain was a boiling cauldron of espionage and intrigue. To keep an eye on activities there, both Great Britain and the United States had agents in the country. So did Germany and Japan. The SOE placed such importance on the country that they assigned Virginia, one of their most valuable agents, to a post there. She would again go in undercover as a journalist, this time as a foreign correspondent for the *Chicago Times*. After arriving in Madrid, she was instructed to take two or three months to establish her cover and allow the Spanish authorities to become convinced of her bona fides. She would officially work within SOE's Section D, which was responsible for investigating "every possibility of attacking potential enemies by means other than the operations of military forces."

Virginia was briefed ahead of time on her potential nemeses. First, and most disturbing, was American Ambassador Carlton Hayes, who considered espionage in a country friendly to the Allies to be "un-American." Far more threatening were the myriad Gestapo agents lurking everywhere in Madrid. And even more prevalent were the members of General Franco's Seguridad General. Virginia had already encountered them during her arrest and imprisonment.

Spain was under the leadership of the Fascist Generalissimo Francisco Franco, who had come to power in 1936 during Spain's Civil War by squelching the Republicans who had earlier exiled him. He had been approached by Hitler to join the Axis on several occasions, but refused. In meetings with the Nazi leader, Franco frequently rambled with self-importance. But his underlying reason for refusal was that his country was still recovering from its own war. Plus he was not anxious to elicit bomber attacks from Great Britain. Their joint meetings were so unproductive that when Hitler finally stormed out of the last one, he said he would rather visit the dentist to have his teeth removed than have another meeting with Franco.

The fact that these tête-à-têtes did not go smoothly boded well for the Allies. If Franco decided to throw in with Hitler, it could mean the closure of the Straits of Gibraltar to Allied ships. Furthermore, using Spain as a new base, German bombers would be able to fly farther south and west in their attacks against those ships. And with Spain as an Axis country, dreams of an Allied invasion of southern France would fade.

When Virginia arrived in Madrid in the early afternoon of May 17, it was a bright spring day. She had not seen the capital city since her European tour with her family years earlier as a child. She took a cab to her hotel, freshened up, and asked the hotel desk clerk for directions to the restaurant where she was to have lunch with her superior, Hugh Quennell, head of SOE's Iberian Section.

Quennell told Virginia it was his understanding that they were to meet socially through a member of the press department at the British Embassy. Tom Burns, John Stordy, or John Walter were his contacts. Virginia said she didn't know them as yet but had planned to drop in on them to make their acquaintances. She found the mention that they were to meet socially odd, after the struggle she'd left in France and asked Quennell if there many social events.

He laughed at her naïveté. Social events were the only sanity they had. Life in Spain was a game of hurry up and wait. A message would arrive from London stating that they needed something immediately. His team would leap into action at the order and then would hear nothing more for another week, leaving them completely unoccupied.

The whole setup sounded completely foreign to Virginia, so she changed the subject and asked Quennell if he had any contacts that she could approach to find out about her friends in Lyon. Quennell took on a genuinely solicitous air. He'd heard that she'd just come off a rather event-filled year and a half and he promised to see what he can do about information from Lyon. Work in Spain was different from that in France. Agents were forbidden from any involvement in direct action or sabotage. But they did have some interesting things in the works concerning wolfram.

Virginia had never heard of it. Quennell explained that it was a Portuguese ore that yielded tungsten. And tungsten was the most valuable strategic war metal. From it, tough, heat-resistant steel and high-speed cutting tools could be manufactured, implements that could increase the production of military equipment ten times over. Steel hardened by tungsten was a vital war commodity. The Germans were the first to use it in their armor plate and for their high-velocity, armor-piercing projectiles.

Virginia was almost afraid to ask him what SOE's part was in the project. London had told her to be ready to undertake any jobs that Quennell considered appropriate for her. Surely mining wouldn't be one of them. It wasn't, of course. The Germans wanted to get wolfram out of Portugal for their use. The Allies wanted to divert it for their use, which at the same time deprived Hitler of it. SOE's part was to gather intelligence to help with diversions.

This still did not sound like the kind of work Virginia was accustomed to. Nor did the next job Hugh talked about: locating safe houses for SOE's use in Madrid and the surrounding area. But a week after her arrival, Virginia got the idea that being a wireless operator might bring her the excitement she foresaw lacking in her current assignment. Plus it would be of great use to the agency.

Hugh, however, discouraged that idea, saying they were pretty well covered in the peninsula in that department. But they could use indigenous people, Spaniards who might come in handy for one reason or another. But he cautioned her that she should only approach men who had fought on General Franco's side in the war. No Republicans, as serious diplomatic complications would ensue if the Spanish government found out SOE was employing men with the wrong sympathies.

Shortly after that discussion, Virginia came up with another idea. What about doing some joint work with the American agents in Spain. Again Hugh vetoed the idea, begging her not to take offense. The Brits preferred to remain independent of the Yanks. The previous week, two of them were arrested for buying foreign currency on the black market for the purpose of passing it on to incoming agents. It was a good idea, Quennell said, but bad execution.

LONG BEFORE VIRGINIA TRIED to settle into a new life after fleeing France, General Charles de Gaulle had been forced to do the same thing. The general was a difficult man. Some said it was his extreme shyness that caused him to appear aloof. Others said it was his six-foot-five-inch height that made him ill at ease. Still others proclaimed the forty-nine-year-old general was simply unapproachable. Whatever the cause, his exile in England had been particularly difficult after the fall of France.

When Winston Churchill first met de Gaulle, he asked Major General Sir Louis Spears, who had accompanied de Gaulle out of France, "Why have you brought this lanky, gloomy Brigadier?" Spears said, "Because no one else would come." There was a gradual warming between Churchill and de Gaulle, particularly in light of their common interests in theater and history. On June 28, 1940, the British officially backed the general as "leader of all the Free French, wherever they are to be found." They agreed to supply his movement in exchange for his acceptance of their directives.

De Gaulle was resolute on many issues regarding his plans for freeing his country from the Nazi stranglehold. He had an absolute belief in his mission, and his devotion to France was clear. He was convinced that he possessed the qualities necessary for leadership and believed that he alone knew the best course of action to take in fighting for French interests as he saw them. His obstinacy become so well known that a Frenchman living in London during the war remarked that de Gaulle "ought to remember that the enemy is Germany, not the British."

From the start, de Gaulle did not want to appear as though he were a puppet of the British government, so he created what would become the Bureau central de renseignements et d'action (BCRA). The bureau's purpose was to organize, direct, and supply the Resistance, but it was the British who carried out the mission. However, the British were expressly forbidden from recruiting any Resistance members into the SOE.

De Gaulle's relationship with the United States was on far rockier ground than his British one because Roosevelt's government had officially recognized Vichy France, a move that incensed de Gaulle. Vichy had, after all, branded the general and his Free French supporters as traitors, and had passed down two death sentences with de Gaulle's name on them.

Then on October 25, 1941, Frenchman Jean Moulin arrived in London and a new chapter in de Gaulle's Free French movement was begun. Moulin came with detailed information about Resistance groups, lots of them, all over France. These loyal citizens were ready to fight the Germans on all levels, and Moulin believed the next step was to organize them into one unit. De Gaulle and his aides had already infiltrated France with agents with success, and the general believed that such agents, combined with the organized Resistance Moulin was describing, would become the foundation of a France free from the Nazis.

Despite the British work with the Resistance, de Gaulle's mind-set was still that he alone knew what was best for France. He sent Moulin back as official delegate of the French National Committee to the unoccupied zone.

Moulin's job was to persuade the southern movements to recognize the general and coordinate their work under the Free French authority.

Moulin worked tirelessly to this end. He returned to London numerous times with reports on the headway they were making. Then, on June 21, 1943, the Gestapo arrested Moulin in Lyon. Someone in his own Resistance circle had betrayed him. He was taken to the École de Santé Militaire, where the notorious Butcher of Lyon—Klaus Barbie—personally tortured him. So brutal was Barbie's treatment of him, that after three weeks of abuse, Moulin died, never having divulged a word about his work. Killing Moulin was stupid on Barbie's part, as he gained nothing. And it was both a shock and an energizer for the Resistance. They had lost a great leader, but they had gained a martyr and symbol of their cause.

THE SPANISH SUMMER slid by with Virginia still doing what she characterized as "a waste of time and money." She hadn't been able to get any definitive information about HECKLER. She held out hope that all was well, but she feared the worst. And she hated not being able to do anything about it. In September she laid her cards on the table in a letter to Buckmaster:

> I've given it a good four months. Anyhow, I always did want to go back to France, and now I have had the luck to find two of my very own boys here and send them on to you.

In an amazing story of survival, two Frenchmen Virginia had worked with in the Lyon area, Lieutenant Marcel Leccia and Lieutenant Élisée Albert Allard, had escaped from a prison camp in Kaiserslautern, Germany. They returned to France and crossed the Pyrénées when the Germans invaded the unoccupied zone. The SOE was alerted of their arrival in Madrid and they were reunited with Virginia.

Her letter continued:

> They want me to go back with them because we worked together before and our teamwork is good. Besides, we have a lot of contacts that—well they will explain it to you. I suggest that I go back as their radio, or else as aider and abetter, as before. I can learn the radio quickly enough in spite of skeptics in some quarters.

When I came out here I thought that I would be able to help F section people, but I don't and can't. I am not doing a job. I am simply living pleasantly and wasting time. It isn't worthwhile and after all, my neck is my own, and if I'm willing to get a crick in it because there is a war on, I do think . . . Well, anyhow, I put it up to you. I think I can do a job for you along with my two boys. They think I can too and I trust that you will let us try, because we are all three very much in earnest about this bloody war.

My best regards to you and the office and to Mrs. Colonel B.—I was pleased to hear that—and I hope she gets some of the lemons I asked the boys to drape themselves in upon departure.

It wasn't long before a response arrived from Buckmaster on October 6. In it, he referred to Virginia using a code name he'd come up with on the spot.

Dearest Doodles,

What a wonder you are! I knew you could learn radio in no time; I know the boys would love to have you in the field; I know all about all the things you could do, and it is only because I honestly believe that the Gestapo would also know it in about a fortnight that I say no, dearest Doodles, no. You are really too well-known in the country and it would be wishful thinking believing that you could escape detention for more than a few days.

You do realise, don't you, that what was previously a picnic, comparatively speaking, is now real war, and that the Gestapo are pulling in everything they can? You will object, I know, that it is your own neck—I agree, but we all know that it is not *only* your own neck, it is the necks of all with whom you come into contact because the Bosch is good at patiently following trails, and sooner or later he will unravel the whole skein if he has a chance. We do not want to give him even half a chance by sending in anyone as remarkable as yourself at the moment.

Now that I have got the above off my chest, and I am sure you will realise that I am right "*au fond,*" let me make what I hope is a constructive proposal to you. I know your heart is in F Section, and I know that F Section has missed you greatly. If you are feeling that you are not pulling your weight where you are, why not come back to London and join us as a briefing officer for the boys? Your duties would [be]:

- To meet them when they come back from the field, to hear what they have to say, to analyse it, and to see that they get their questions answered.
- To see that they are properly looked after from the point of view of material things—i.e. clothes, equipment, etc. In other words, see that the clothing and equipment officers of F Section produce the jobs in time and correctly.
- To brief the new boys with the fruits of what you have yourself learned and what you have picked up from the latest arrivals.
- This, I know, sounds like a sit-down job of the same type as you are doing now, but it has this possible, repeat possible, advantage. If and when officers from here go into the field round about D-day, you will be in the right place to start from. I obviously can make no promises as to this at the moment, but it is a possibility.

This was not the response Virginia wanted to hear. As far as she was concerned, the really important work needed to be done before D-Day, and who knew when it would even occur anyway. She did not want to be sitting in some silly office in London, doing what anyone else could do, when she knew her talents could make a difference in the field. But before she could go back to France, she had to return to London. She agreed with Buckmaster that her current identity would be a problem, but who was to say that the reflection she looked at in the mirror was the only one she might have.

DURING HER SOE TRAINING, Virginia and the rest of the recruits had been warned that those who were willing to work undercover should not do so with the hope of receiving accolades. Any agent should understand that drawing notice to oneself threatened to defeat the purpose of the elaborate cover stories they had developed. Virginia liked the anonymity, in fact she preferred it to overt attention. But all of that seemed to be overlooked shortly after she returned to London in November of 1943.

Britain's King George VI had approved a list of individuals to be honored with the Most Excellent Order of the British Empire. Virginia's name was on that list in the Member division. The MBE, as it was known, had been created by the king's father, George V, in 1917 to honor the thousands of people who served in numerous noncombatant capacities during the First World War. It was awarded "for service in the field, or before the enemy, or for services to the Empire," and it was one of the few orders that included women or noncitizens of the British Commonwealth.

Virginia declined the customary audience with the king, given the fact that she was, and intended to be again, an undercover agent. Rather, she received the prestigious medal in private at SOE headquarters, and then wasted no time in meeting with Buckmaster to take him up on his offer of a position in F Section.

But Virginia extracted a promise from him: he was to allow her to take wireless training. She would do it around whatever work schedule Buckmaster set for her. She maintained that the biggest mistake they were making in France was not seeing to it that all agents were trained in wireless. By only sending one operator for every six or eight or dozen agents, the operations were being hamstrung. The operator wasn't able to keep up with the workload, she told Buckmaster, which made him more liable to be picked up, which in turn left entire circuits without any contact with HQ. If there was a chance that she could go back to France, she wanted to make sure she could play any role.

Buckmaster, enthused at having Virginia working for F Section again, had no complaints about her request for wireless training, and the next phase of her SOE career began. She had one more request of him. Could he gather any information about her friends in Lyon? He came back to her a week later with the news she feared. He had it on good authority that the Gestapo had rounded up a good many of her Resistance contacts in Lyon.

The news sickened Virginia. The wonderful French patriots she had recruited were so brave, so dedicated. And they were strong, too. She refused to believe that the entire group had perished. In thinking over the events of her last months in Lyon, she was convinced that Abbé Ackuin had been up to no good. She should have had him followed all the way back to Paris and found out exactly what he was doing. And she should have taken care to protect the circuit before leaving in such haste. But hindsight, as they said, was twenty-twenty. She had to look forward to the new possibilities in front of her.

Not long after beginning work at Baker Street, Virginia heard about a relatively new American organization, the Office of Strategic Services, set up at Grosvenor Square, not far from the American Embassy. The word she got from a friend was that the organization's head man, a charismatic former army colonel by the name of William Donovan, happened to be in town, staying at the fashionable Claridge's Hotel on Brook Street. Virginia's friend had all the details about the OSS.

FRANKLIN ROOSEVELT FIRST MET William Joseph Donovan when they opposed one another in the 1928 New York gubernatorial election. Despite the fact that Roosevelt won the election, a lifelong friendship developed between the two men.

Donovan was a stocky Irishman with piercing blue eyes. A whir of activity, he had been the commander of the sixty-ninth "Fighting Irish" regiment of New York in the First World War. His fearless charges earned him the nickname "Wild Bill." In one such attack against an overwhelming number of Germans, he reportedly shouted to his troops, "What's the matter? You want to live forever?" He was the only individual from that war to receive the Distinguished Service Medal, the Distinguished Service Cross, and the Congressional Medal of Honor, miraculously surviving the war to receive them all personally. After his service, he became a successful and wealthy New York lawyer, and a dabbler in Republican politics.

Shortly after the French signed their armistice with Germany in the summer of 1940, President Roosevelt sent his friend Donovan to London to determine how the Brits would stand up against German attacks. While he was there, Donovan developed a relationship with the British Secret Intelligence Service, MI-6. When Donovan returned to Washington, it was with two messages for the president. First, he believed Britain would hold her own against the Nazis, provided the United States supplied additional resources. Second, he strongly suggested that America develop an organization to control foreign intelligence and covert operations.

Putting Donovan's suggestion into action, Roosevelt launched the Coordinator of Information (COI) on July 11, 1941. Donovan, then fifty-eight, would be at its helm. All was not smooth sailing, however. America's existing intelligence agencies, including the FBI and Army Intelligence, thought the COI was a waste of time and resources. And they objected to this upstart agency's encroachment into their domains. But Donovan was never deterred. In the words of one OSS staff psychologist, "Wild Bill" possessed "the power to visualize an oak when he saw an acorn. . . . For him the day was never sufficient unto itself; it was always teeming with seeds of a boundless future. . . . Every completed project bred a host of new ones."

A year after the inception of COI, on June 13, 1942, a reorganization occurred. The propaganda division became part of the newly created Office of War Information. The rest of the agency remained under Donovan's control and became known as the Office of Strategic Services (OSS). According to President Roosevelt, its purpose was to take "all measures . . . to enforce our will upon the enemy by means other than military action, as may be applied in support of actual or planned military operations; or in furtherance of the war effort; unorthodox warfare, guerrilla activities behind enemy lines; contact with resistance groups; subversion, sabotage, and unorthodox or 'black' psychological warfare."

With a direct line to the president, Donovan procured large amounts of money for OSS, most of it undocumented through proper governmental channels and hidden in various budget appropriations. Roosevelt reportedly told Donovan, "If I'm going to trust you with the secrets of the country, I can trust you with the money, too."

Initially, Donovan manned the OSS with people from his circle of friends and acquaintances—Ivy league graduates and other wealthy individuals with well-known names like Mellon, Morgan, Vanderbilt, and Du Pont. He recruited actors and writers and even a major league baseball player. This cast of characters quickly earned the OSS nicknames from its detractors, names like "Oh, So Secret," "Oh, So Silly," and "Oh, So Social."

Future James Bond creator, Ian Fleming, then a ranking officer in British Naval Intelligence, suggested to Donovan that he seek out men of "absolute discretion, sobriety, devotion to duty, languages, and wide experience," who were aged somewhere between forty and fifty. Donovan's preference lay in the opposite direction—180 degrees. He sought out young people who were "calculatingly reckless" with "disciplined daring" and who were "trained for aggressive action." And he began adding new members to his cast of characters: former thieves, safecrackers, forgers, circus performers, and Communists.

The OSS's first mission was to gather intelligence for the invasion of Vichy-controlled North Africa, Operation TORCH. The agency's future depended on the success of this initial foray into espionage. OSS agents arrived in North Africa to enlist the help of French resisters there. In addition, they were able to coerce assistance from ten thousand Arab tribal leaders for the sum of fifty thousand francs. A false plan was leaked to the Germans, alluding to the fact that the invasion would occur at Dakar in Senegal. Once the invasion fleet was under way and the code phrase "*Robert arrive*" was broadcast on French radio, the Nazis were caught by complete surprise when the Allies landed at Morocco and Algeria, fifteen hundred miles from Dakar.

As the battles raged after the initial landings, the OSS next involved its newly created Research and Development Department. Word had come from the field that something was needed to stop the seesaw battles and deter the Nazi advances into territory already fought over and won by the Allies. OSS agents found the answer in camel dung: it was everywhere in the desert. They launched the idea of developing explosive camel dung to be scattered by the Americans as they vacated an area. When Nazi Field Marshall Erwin Rommel's unsuspecting tanks drove over it, they would be left severely damaged, thereby critically slowing his advance. The invention was a booming success.

With these achievements under his belt, Donovan silenced the concerns of many of his naysayers. The OSS had proven its merit and was ready to take on the rest of the war.

OVER THE COURSE OF HER FIRST several weeks in the F Section office, Virginia gleaned more information about the OSS. During the summer of 1942, she learned that a forty-four-year-old multimillionaire by the name of David Bruce had been appointed to head the London office of the OSS. The following January, the American and British intelligence organizations struck a working agreement between them, with the Americans insisting that the two be equal worldwide partners, despite the fact that the British had a two-and-a-half-year head start in the field.

A new idea took seed in Virginia's mind and began to grow. Since the Americans were still relative novices in undercover work in France, her expertise would be of great value to them. She had almost completed her wireless training, giving her yet one more skill to add to her repertoire. Since the OSS and the SOE were working closely together, transferring to the American organization would be more like changing sections within SOE than changing entire entities. And as far as her being known by the Gestapo, she could avail herself of the many advances that had been made in disguises.

Once she had fitted all the pieces into place, Virginia approached Buck-master with the idea. He hated to see her leave his F Section, and he was cer-tainly concerned for her safety. But he had learned during their three-year relationship that once she set her mind to something, very little would deter her. He begrudgingly gave his blessing for her to contact the OSS, and after several meetings her transfer became the subject of missives around Grosvenor Square. In a March 1944 memo, an OSS officer signed off on her request:

> I have interviewed the above mentioned lady and I feel confi-dent that the main reason she wishes to transfer from SOE to OSS is for national reasons. . . . She has been briefed to go in the field as [a] radio operator with an organiser belong to OSS and she has again expressed a desire to go as an American body.
>
> The financial side, that is to say the salary she might earn with OSS, has never been discussed and does not seem to worry her in any way. She merely stated that all money she might earn she would like to be sent to her mother, Mrs. E. L. Hall, Box-horn Farm, Parkton, Maryland.

On March 10, 1944, Virginia signed an agreement with the OSS. The term of employment was for one year, for which she would receive $336 per month, payable directly to her mother. The well-written contract was evi-dence of the number of lawyers on the OSS payroll and covered all points that might be of issue in the future. These included Virginia's agreement "to proceed to any place to which she may be directed, whether within or out-side the continental limits of the United States"; "to keep forever secret this employment and all information which she may obtain . . . unless she shall be released from such obligation"; and "that she assume absolutely, all risks incident to this employment."

With Army Major Paul van der Strict's signature on behalf of the OSS, Virginia was accepted as a member of the Special Operations group. *La dame qui boite* was once again bound for Nazi-occupied France.

14

RETURN TO WAR

WHEN BUCKMASTER HAD TOLD VIRGINIA in his letter to her in Spain that "the Gestapo are pulling in everything they can," he had hard evidence to back his statement. The Nazis were furious about the acts of French Resistance, and carried out reprisals in every part of the country. In Paris, the Nazis murdered fifty people a day for five days after German government officials were gunned down. The murders stopped only after the Nazis were satisfied they had the culprits in custody, the latter having been ratted out by "helpful" collaborators. In Nantes, two hundred and fifty miles southwest of Paris, forty-eight citizens were executed for killing a German colonel. And in Tours, two hundred miles south of Paris, a grenade was tossed into a column of German soldiers on their way to a movie. More than half the city was burned to the ground, and a great many of the young men were taken away, never to be seen again.

A great deal more had changed since Virginia left France. The Resistance found themselves no longer fighting just against the German army and the Gestapo. A new organization had entered the picture. It was called the Milice.

Shortly after France had fallen to the Germans, World War I veteran Joseph Darnand was made head of the Légion française des combattants, the Legion of French Veterans. The organization consisted of chivalrous gentlemen hoping to recoup honor for the defeated French army. But the group was too staid for Darnand's taste and a year later he developed a faction within the legion called the Service de l'ordre légionnaire, which supported

Pétain's Vichy France. In January 1943, he reorganized once again, and the Milice was the result.

This Vichy secret police force was a paramilitary organization that swore an oath against "Jewish leprosy," democracy, and individualism. The Milice was really a Fascist gang, half fanatics, half thugs. Their ranks swelled to thirty-five thousand and included the dregs of French society: former criminals, gangsters, and the depraved. The Milice worked in the areas where they lived, familiar areas, making them much more effective than the Gestapo in that regard. And unlike the Police Nationale, which sought out "enemies of the state," the Milice hunted, tortured, and killed for personal gain and satisfaction. Those with grudges against former lovers or business associates found the Milice the perfect outlet for their revenge. The populace hated its members and it quickly became the most dangerous enemy of the Resistance.

Buckmaster had also been right when he told Virginia, "What was previously a picnic, comparatively speaking, is now real war." The France she was about to reenter in March 1944 was more starving, more dangerous, and more desperate.

AS ITS ARCHITECTS SAW IT, the OSS was charged with three functions: intelligence, which included research and analysis, secret intelligence, counterespionage, and collateral offices; operations, which included sabotage, guerrilla warfare, psychological warfare, and related activities; and the self-explanatory schools and training.

Within those functions were the seven branches, organized in a similar fashion to those of the SOE. Each branch had a director who reported to another director, who ultimately reported to General Donovan. The branches included the Secret Intelligence (SI), which gathered on-the-spot information from within neutral and enemy territory; Special Operations (SO), which conducted sabotage and worked with Resistance forces; Morale Operations (MO), which created and disseminated "black propaganda"; Operation Groups (OG), which trained, supplied, and led guerrilla forces in enemy territory, sort of a combination SI and SO; Counterespionage (X-2), which protected Allied intelligence operations and identified enemy agents overseas; the Maritime Unit (MU), which conducted maritime sabotage; and finally Research and Analysis (R&A), which produced the economic, military, social, and political studies and estimates for every strategic area from Europe to the Far East.

Within R&A was the research and development unit, sometimes referred to as the "department of dirty tricks." It was run by Dr. Stanley Lovell, the happy and bespectacled rebel responsible for the exploding camel dung used in Operation TORCH. He and his team never tired of creating new products with an eye on destroying the enemy. "Aunt Jemima" was a powdered form of TNT that looked like any other wheat flour. When detonated it was a powerful explosive, but to avoid suspicion, it could also be kneaded, baked, and eaten with no harm to the consumer.

Likewise, Lovell's group also invented an exploding lump of coal that could be tossed onto a coal truck and would eventually find its way into the firebox of a Nazi locomotive. And then there was the "firefly," a little plastic cylinder that could be dropped into the fuel tank of a Nazi vehicle. Once the tank's gasoline had expanded the rubber retaining ring, it would explode. The "firefly" would be as successful in a Nazi staff car as in a Panzer tank.

MONDAY, MARCH 20, was a gray day in London. The city's trees and flowers had no confidence that spring was coming anytime soon. Consequently, new growth and buds were nowhere to be found on any of them. Virginia took a noon train out of Victoria Station, heading south for the English Channel. She lugged two suitcases. One was soft-sided and bulging like a cow about to calve. It carried the items she would use to change her identity. The other suitcase was smaller, about two feet long, but at thirty pounds, heavier than the first. It contained a Type 3 Mark II transceiver, a combination radio transmitter and receiver.

While many OSS agents were infiltrating France by parachute, Virginia's wooden leg would prevent her from jumping. Rather, she was returning to France by sea. Two hours and sixty-six miles from London, Virginia's train arrived at the port city of Portsmouth. She took a cab from the station to a pub, where she met a young British naval officer. After a quick lunch, he took her to the Devonshire Royal Navy Base, a blur of British and American naval uniforms, and dropped her off at a small building set apart from the others.

Inside, Lieutenant Paul Williams welcomed Virginia and immediately offered her a cup of tea. Her companion hadn't arrived yet, Lieutenant Williams told her, so in the meantime, he would give her a quick rundown on their operation. She would be crossing on a Motor Gun Boat, officially MGB 502, under the lieutenant's command. The mahogany-skinned vessel was 117 feet long, fast, and safe. The trip to the French coast would probably take no more than six hours.

And Lieutenant Williams told Virginia she shouldn't worry about the Germans. MGB 502 was fitted with a two-pounder Vickers antiaircraft gun, a couple of twin-mount .50-caliber machine guns, and a semiautomatic two-pounder gun.

Virginia wasn't really interested in the details of the armaments; only that the boat had them.

Although strong tides formed along the Breton coast, Lieutenant Williams continued, there were plenty of deserted beaches that suited the operation perfectly. She and her companion would be landing at a point called Beg an Fry. His crew was familiar with the waters there, no shoals or offshore reefs. When they were close to shore, the boat would slow down considerably, running quieter and with less wake. Virginia and her companion would go ashore in a camouflaged rubber dinghy.

This is it, Virginia thought. I'm finally going back to France. Lieutenant Williams told her they'd be leaving at twenty-two hundred hours. A knock at the door ended their conversation. The door opened at his command and Virginia turned to see a stocky, balding man with spectacles. He announced that his name was Aramis and offered Virginia his hand. He had a slight French accent, which Virginia took as a good sign. It meant he was probably of French parentage and could compensate for her decidedly Anglo accent.

She introduced herself as Diane, the code name she and Major van der Strict had decided upon before she left London. Lieutenant Williams had some other business to attend to and suggested that perhaps Aramis and Virginia would like a private office to discuss business. After that, they would all meet again in the officer's mess for dinner and make their final preparations for departure.

As soon as they were alone, Aramis was very anxious to get to know his new working companion and began by telling Virginia all about himself. In no time at all, he had told her that he was a commercial artist from Pittsburgh, was sixty-two years old and was a civilian. This would be his first mission in the field, but he felt confident that he was up to any challenge that came their way.

Virginia was concerned about Aramis immediately. It wasn't his age or his inexperience; it was his willingness to open up so completely with a relative stranger. Never mind the fact that they would be partners. The number one rule for agents at the OSS and the SOE was never to tell the truth about themselves. New recruits were taught they could only abandon their cover if they were in a closed room with a staff member who took the initiative to say, "We are now talking under X conditions." Then, and only then, could an agent divulge the truth about himself.

Failure to adhere to that rule had gotten recruits thrown out. They were cleverly tested on it. Regardless of their performance on a particularly grueling day of physical trials, intelligence tests, and "Gestapo-style" questioning, the hopeful students were told one by one that they had failed. They were then sent individually to a room where a sympathetic staff member would offer them a cigarette and ask what had happened, hinting that perhaps something could be done about it. Recruits were often so relieved at a friendly face that they forgot the basic requirement of secrecy and divulged everything that had happened to them that day, without the staff member telling them they were talking under "X conditions." And that became their demise.

Virginia was not willing to put herself or their mission in jeopardy by saying anything more than was absolutely necessary. She told Aramis that she had done a significant amount of wireless training at the SOE classes in London, avoiding any mention that she, herself, had been an SOE agent. Their circuit would be a joint operation with the Brits, who would call it SAINT. The Americans would refer to their circuit as HECKLER. She would be the wireless operator. It was her understanding, she said, that their objective was to gather as much information as possible about German troop installations and movements in central France, and to locate potential reception fields for parachute drops. In addition, she had been told that Aramis would spend most of his time working in Paris, developing safe houses there, and that he should have any necessary outgoing messages couriered to her. She would transmit them along with her own findings.

Finally, Virginia disclosed that she would be disguising herself as much older for their mission and would don her costume after dinner. Once they'd covered those topics, Virginia had very little more to say to Aramis and their conversation dwindled to a discussion of weather and how it might affect their trip that night.

Their dinner with Lieutenant Williams was a much brighter event, as he regaled them with stories about his experiences in the Navy. At eight o'clock, Virginia excused herself to begin preparations for her disguise. She returned to a small room where she had dropped off her belongings earlier. The room had a sink and running water, necessary for the first part of her disguise. Pulling the hairpins from the carefully formed bun at the nape of her neck, she wet her hair in the sink and applied the dye she'd brought with her from London. By the time she'd finished, her soft brown hair was a dull gray color that she would eventually pull into a severe bun and cover with a large babushka.

Next, Virginia remade herself into a plump, elderly woman. First she donned a starched peplum to make her hips appear broader, and over it she pulled on two heavy woolen skirts. To increase the bulk on her torso, she put on a man's shirt and sweater, and stuffed all of that under a ratty woman's pullover. Brown woolen stockings and scuffed sabots completed the look.

The entire outfit had been provided courtesy of agents and refugees coming out of France. Both the British and American governments wanted to make sure everything about the people they infiltrated into occupied territories was authentic, so they developed a wardrobe department that would rival any in Hollywood. And as other agents had done, Virginia had also spent several days the previous week in a dentist's chair, having her fillings changed to resemble those done by French dentists.

The final part of her transformation was to change the way she moved. The "Limping Lady" nickname the Gestapo had given her was insulting. Virginia had assumed all along she walked in a fairly normal manner. Evidently she had not concealed her limp over the years as well as she thought she had. Under the present circumstances, it was vital that she master a new gait. In keeping with her disguise, a shuffle was appropriate, combined with the kind of stoop brought on by old age. She had practiced and perfected this demeanor over the past months. It had to pass muster.

THE OSS WAS A STICKLER for authenticity. Virginia's clothing and new dental work were evidence of that. But in addition to agents changing their appearances, they also had to change their life histories by creating entirely new identities. The process had been honed to a science. The agent first filled out two questionnaires, in French of course, building a past of complete fiction. They answered precise questions about fabricated family members, phony education and work experience, and mock travels they'd taken within France and her colonies. Most important for the men were the details of their military experience during the war.

Next the agent and his supervisor went over the particulars required for the myriad papers all French citizens were now required to carry. The Germans were obsessed with organization and categorizing. Consequently, they had instituted separate cards for every facet of life. There was a carte d'identité, *carte d'alimentation* (food ration card), *fiches de mobilisation* (military papers), *carte de textiles* (clothing ration card), *permis de conduire* (driver's license), *certifcat de recensement* (census card), *carte de tabac* (tobacco ration card), *extrait de naissance* (birth certificate), *certificat médical* (medical certificate), *certificat de travail* (work permit), and *certificat de domicile* (proof of residence).

After proofreading all of the cards, the agent wrote out his new life story again to make sure there were no omissions or contradictions. At a second meeting, the cover was discussed once more and the agent was asked to sign an official document that he was satisfied with it.

Next came a final draft of the cover story. The agent's fingerprints were affixed to his papers and cards, and he was given detailed maps of the areas he was supposed to know intimately. He was sent off to memorize the cover story thoroughly, told to "put himself in the skin of the fictitious person" he was now to become. A rigorous interrogation took place next, by an officer other than the one who helped the agent prepare the cover story. Once that officer was satisfied, the agent was ready to be blended in to his new country. The entire process normally took about three weeks.

Virginia's entry into the OSS had been slightly out of the norm. As she had already been trained in undercover work and had already been in the field, she was exempted from the usual agent training. Furthermore, her cover story was constructed more quickly, using elements she had already created for her work with SOE. The Americans were eager to have such an experienced agent back in France, and she had gone out of her way to let them know how eager she was to go.

WHEN VIRGINIA REAPPEARED in Lieutenant Williams's office after her transformation, neither Aramis nor the lieutenant recognized her at first. Williams said afterward that his immediate thought was the chewing out he was going to give the guard post for allowing civilians on the base. Once they realized it was Virginia, the men assured her that she in no way resembled the woman they had just dined with.

The next hour or so, the lieutenant and several sailors gave Virginia and Aramis lessons on how to get out of the dinghy that would put them on the

French shore. It was essential that they do it quickly and quietly. Their lesson came to an abrupt end when a sailor appeared to tell them it was time to board the boat. Virginia and Aramis were seated inside the cabin area, where they were protected from the wind and the spray. They faced a strong head wind, but the speed at which the boat was traveling compensated for it and the ride was not quite as bumpy as Virginia had expected. About five hours later, she felt the engine slow, which of course increased the effect the waves had on the vessel. The crew got the dinghy ready, and with a hearty handshake from Lieutenant Williams, Virginia and Aramis set off for the Breton coast.

OSS INSTRUCTIONS FOR VIRGINIA and Aramis 's mission were divided into three parts. First, they were to establish themselves in an "accessible place not more than 100 kilometers to the south or southeast of Paris." Second, they were to "proceed to find three safe houses, one in Paris, the second in a small town within easy reach of Paris, and the third somewhere in the country." The final stage of their mission was to consist of "setting up in each of these three houses one large and one small wireless set, ready to operate as quickly as possible should a wireless operator arrive."

They were also both carrying cash. Virginia had five hundred thousand francs and Aramis had a million francs. The London office expected them to be in contact for any other needs as soon as possible.

BRITTANY IS THE FRENCH PROVINCE that juts out into the channel and is frequently referred to as the "*nez rouge de France*," the red nose of France. The double entendre refers to the shape of the province, similar to that of a nose, and the fact that the frequent harsh winds cause some elder inhabitants' noses to be permanently reddened from broken blood vessels. The coastline is unfriendly, craggy, and often very steep. But the independent Breton people were the antithesis of their harsh homeland: cordial, loyal to the Allied cause, and eager to organize into Resistance groups.

Aramis and Virginia's landing was less than ideal. Aramis stumbled getting out of the dinghy and fell onto the rocks. He tore his pants, cut his leg, and was drenched. They were to walk to a small barn just a mile inland, which was owned by a member of the local Resistance. A cold rain had started to fall and with Aramis limping badly, a walk that should have taken them fifteen minutes, took almost an hour. It was about 4:00 AM when they arrived at the barn and settled against some straw bales for a quick nap. When the farmer woke them an hour later, Virginia asked him for a bandage for Aramis 's leg and a needle and thread to patch his trousers. When the man left, she told Aramis that since his disguise was that of an elderly man, his new limp was a great asset. He was not amused, however.

They left the farmer's barn an hour later, looking like any other elderly couple, and walked along the rutted road that led to the town of Morlaix. Aramis 's identity papers showed that his name was Henri Lassot. Virginia's read Mlle Marcelle Montagne. In Morlaix, they went to the train station and bought two second-class tickets for Paris. They hobbled up into the car and sat in near silence the entire four-hour trip. Aramis even dozed on and off. But Virginia's eyes were glued to the French countryside. It had been eighteen months since she'd left, and the country now appeared even more chained to the Nazi boot. German soldiers with dogs often patrolled the passing train platforms. Bomb damage was evident in the fields and pastures from craters and upheaved earth. In the towns, it could be seen in the rubble of burned-out buildings.

When they arrived at the Montparnasse station in Paris and walked out into the city, what Virginia saw devastated her and she struggled to maintain her composure. The once beautiful City of Lights was now a wretched-looking ghost town. While it had not been heavily bombed, as had London and other French cities, it had received its share. Virginia saw half-destroyed buildings and piles of rubble and burned-out automobiles.

Fortunately none of the city's treasures had been touched: the Eiffel Tower, the Arc de Triomphe, and Notre-Dame still stood proudly. But they now wore flags of the Third Reich. German street signs had been posted everywhere directing drivers and pedestrians to Nazi military establishments. And to keep the Parisians up to date on news, the German-controlled newspapers posted clippings on buildings for those passing by on the sidewalks of major thoroughfares.

The French men and women Virginia saw were a sorry lot. Their hollow eyes stared straight ahead, yet didn't seem to see. They especially avoided eye contact with the Germans, who had begun calling Paris "*la ville sans regard*" (the city that never looks at you). Some Parisians sat dejectedly on the sidewalk, begging for food with outstretched hands, but not speaking. Others tried to sell anything they could find for a few francs, from broken pieces of furniture to shoelaces. Aramis and Virginia proceeded at their slow pace, not saying a word to anyone they passed, nor to one another. When they finally arrived at their destination, 59 rue de Babylone, to their great relief the door opened after the first knock. The owner of the home, Mme Long, was someone Virginia knew from her prewar days in Paris, and whose activities in the Resistance she had learned about from Philippe Vomécourt when she was still in Lyon.

Mme Long's welcome of the two weary travelers was genuine. She told them she had secured a room for Aramis at a nearby boarding house whose owner was an avid Gaullist. Then she sat them down in her kitchen and boiled water for tea.

Again Aramis chatted about himself and gave hints about their mission and his clumsy landing on the coast the night before. His candor irked Virginia, not because she didn't trust Mme Long with the information, but because he was so willing to divulge it. When he limped off toward the boarding house two doors down, Mme Long expressed concern to Virginia. She said her home was open to Virginia, but that she didn't want Aramis to return. Virginia told her she understood completely and promised Mme Long that since they were leaving first thing in the morning, he wouldn't have to come back. She said she would tell him that Mme Long thought she was being watched and that he'd better not contact her when he came back to Paris.

The next morning, March 22, Virginia and Aramis left Paris by train for Châteauroux, and then changed trains, arriving in the town of Crozant in the midafternoon. They walked to a little village just down the road called Maidou, where Virginia found M. Eugène Lopinat, a farmer she had orders to contact. Lopinat wasn't terribly active in the Resistance, but could be counted on to find lodging for those who needed it. He took Virginia to a one-room cottage he owned at the opposite end of the village from his little farm. The cottage had no electricity and no running water.

Virginia would work for Lopinat, tending to his cows, cleaning his house, and preparing meals for him, his elderly mother, and their hired hand. The arrangement was that she would eat her meals with them as well.

Shortly after they had arrived, Aramis said he was tired and wanted to get started for Paris. But before he left, Virginia brought up the subject of his talking too much. She insisted that he tell only those he had taken into his confidence *exactly* as much as they needed to know, and no more. And she was particularly insistent that he not tell anyone about her. Furthermore, he was to send a courier when he needed to communicate with her, and the same one each time. They had already agreed on a code phrase for the courier to identify himself to Virginia.

Aramis was insulted by the reproach and huffed off down the road toward Crozant. Virginia wasn't worried that she had hurt his feelings, only that he wouldn't take her words to heart. But there was work to do. She wanted to explore her surroundings before she had to go make dinner for the Lopinats.

The whole setup appeared to be perfect. The cottage was at the end of an isolated dirt path that no one would travel without the distinct purpose of coming to see her. The house had a loft with a window, accessed by a ladder. She could make her radio transmissions from there, spreading her antennae out the window and down the backside of the house without fear of it being seen.

As the days passed, Virginia decided cooking meals at Lopinat's house was an adventure. There was no stove, so she had to cook on an open fire. The country-dwelling French had fared better in the area of food thus far in the occupation than had their city-dwelling counterparts. And the Lopinats were no exception. There was always an ample supply of vegetables to make soups and stews, and even an occasional slab of meat. There were eggs from the Lopinat's chickens, when they weren't stolen, and usually ingredients to make bread.

Lopinat's mother assumed Virginia was near her own age, and often tried to engage her in conversation. Virginia would nod and smile and say, "*Oui*," but tried to avoid her as much as possible. The time she spent with Lopinat's livestock, however, was a different matter. The cows needed to be taken to pasture every day, which gave Virginia the perfect excuse to take in the countryside in search of fields for the receptions of landings and parachute drops. There were precious few areas that would work, but for those she thought had possibilities, she made note of the coordinates.

It was all going well except for Aramis. He was proving to be a disappointment. Rather than using couriers, he insisted on coming to Virginia in Maidou himself with his news. Having him around made her nervous, and she was never confident that he hadn't talked too much in Paris or on his journey. Furthermore, he could easily be followed. Her brief sojourn in the Spanish prison was more than enough of a taste for Virginia. The last thing she wanted was to spend any time under German guard. Furthermore, despite his robust appearance, Aramis wasn't very hardy. On each trip, he would tell her how exhausted he was and how he'd had to go to bed for several days when he'd returned to Paris after the previous journey.

He did bring good news on occasion, however. He reported that he had located several safe houses in Paris. They could be used as stopovers for agents or hiding places for pilots in need. In fact, he told her, one of the houses was already harboring seven Allied airmen, five of them American. The safe houses needed code phrases for entry, so the two of them devised phrases and Virginia radioed the information to London. Herein lay her second disappointment in the mission thus far: radio contact was spotty at best.

It had all started out well. Her first message to London had been on April 4, letting them know that she was temporarily installed and that Aramis was in Paris. When she radioed the message about the safe houses, London replied, asking the number they could accommodate. She told them on her next "sked" and gave them the pass phrases for each house. But then things began to go south. She would send a message, only to have them reply they weren't able to copy her.

They suggested she extend the aerial, which she did. They suggested perhaps the weather was bad, but it wasn't. They suggested that it was the Germans, scrambling the signals and wondered if they were honing in on her with their direction finder. This, she agreed, was a distinct possibility, making Aramis's unnecessary trips to her house even more nerve-racking. An old woman would not be receiving visitors and suspicions could easily be aroused.

But Virginia was determined to make the most of her situation and gather as much intelligence as she could. The Allies needed to know the location of German troops and their movements. How could a little old lady who tended cows get information from the German army? The answer was right in front of her: cheese.

Lopinat's mother made cheese for their own use. Why not make more of it to sell? Virginia had learned to make cheese on Box Horn Farm, and whether the cows were American or French didn't matter, the process was still the same. She was fluent in German from her days at the academy in Vienna, so when she came into close proximity to sell her cheese to the Germans, she might be able to eavesdrop on their conversations. She'd then relay the useful information back to London, presuming, of course, it was a day when the radio was working properly.

Lopinat and his mother thought the idea of making a little extra money from the Nazis was a good idea, and loaded Virginia up with a basket of cheese the next day. Once she had taken the cows to the field, she started walking toward Crozant. It wasn't long before she came across a small German convoy on the road. She took a deep breath and hobbled up to one of the officers. He asked her what she was peddling, to which she responded in an old crone's voice. He wanted to know the price. She had figured this out ahead of time, thinking ten francs was reasonable. Another officer walked up then to add his opinion. They discussed the worth of the cheese in German and the first officer finally gave Virginia the money, took his cheese, and waved her off.

It had worked! Although she'd not gleaned any information on her first foray, it was a perfect dress rehearsal. She had multiple performances over the next several weeks. And although her radio was still not functioning perfectly, it was good enough for her to pass on overheard information about troop movements and weapons depots to OSS in London. She had just finished her "sked" one day and was putting her radio away in the loft when she heard the sound of a truck engine. Her first thought was that Aramis was now driving to see her. She closed the radio's suitcase and slid it among the crates and disused furniture stored in the loft. Once she'd descended the ladder, she resumed her character and shuffled to the door. Standing in front of her cottage was a truck full of Germans.

The ranking officer in the group asked her what she was doing in the middle of nowhere by herself. Virginia explained in a raspy voice that she took care of M. Lopinat's cows and cooked for him and his mother.

The officer wasn't satisfied with her response and ordered three soldiers to go into the cottage. She stood frozen, her mind racing. Had she sufficiently hidden the radio? She heard her few pieces of furniture crash to the floor. Simultaneous ripping sounds told her that her bed was being torn apart. And then she heard the ladder being set up against the loft. Tense seconds ticked past. Not a sound came from the cottage interior. She began to think about how far she could get on foot before the Germans fired at her. No, she decided, running wouldn't be the answer. It would be better to talk her way out of trouble, declaring she had no idea what was in the loft. She was an old woman and couldn't climb the ladder. As long as she could plead her case here, she had a chance. But if this truckload of Boches turned her over to the Gestapo, they'd soon find out she wasn't who she was pretending to be.

Virginia leaned against a post supporting the porch roof. It was something an old woman would do, but she needed steadying as well. She was certain the German officer could see her heart pounding beneath her clothing. The soldiers finally came out and marched directly to their officer. One of them carried something, although Virginia could not see what it was. The officer looked over the soldier's shoulder at Virginia and walked slowly toward her. He stopped and peered at her.

The officer recognized her as the old woman who peddled cheese up and down the road. And it was cheese that his men had found, good cheese they told him. Certainly she wouldn't mind if soldiers of the Third Reich helped themselves to some. The officer looked hard at her for a few seconds and then reached into his pocket and threw some coins on the ground in front of her.

The men piled in and the truck turned around and rumbled away. Virginia tottered back into the cottage, but her unsteadiness was not feigned. That encounter had been too close. A week later, the Germans picked up four citizens of Maidou and shot them. Their bodies were spiked through the neck on an iron fence in the center of town as a warning to those who might think about joining the Resistance. Two days later, Aramis came back with a message for Virginia. A newly arrived OSS agent had not made his radio checks. The London office feared that he had been arrested. That was enough for Virginia. At her appointed sked, she radioed London, WOLVES ARE AT THE DOOR. STOP. WILL BE IN CONTACT SOON. STOP.

Virginia and Aramis left for Paris immediately. The next day, he invited her to meet two old family friends of his, Mme Rabut and her grown son, Pierre. Theirs was one of the safe houses he had procured. Virginia liked Mme Rabut immediately and felt at ease with her and confident in her. Three days later, when Virginia was ready to depart for her new location, she asked Mme Rabut to accompany her. She envied those agents whose accents were as perfect as native French people. But she couldn't take chances. She had decided never to travel without a French chaperone, someone who would reduce her need to speak.

The two women took the morning train to Cosne, a city about five hours southeast of Paris. Virginia went directly to the home of Colonel Vessereau, chief of police for the department of Creuse. His position made him a valuable member of the Resistance, and Virginia had been apprised of his work by OSS in London. The colonel and his wife were expecting Virginia and couldn't have been more accommodating. They had a room for her and told her that their attic would be perfect for transmitting. Mme Rabut stayed the night and before she left the next day, Virginia asked her to keep her new location in Cosne a secret. And if Aramis had any messages for her, Virginia suggested, perhaps Mme Rabut could bring them to her. Mme Rabut was thrilled to play an even greater role in the Resistance.

Colonel Vessereau was anxious to introduce Virginia to the Resistance group he'd been building. He had developed ties with several local gendarmes who were military men, seen action before the armistice, and hated the Nazis. They, in turn, knew of a group of about a hundred men who were ready for action. The men were members of the Maquis.

IN FEBRUARY OF 1943, the Third Reich had instituted the Service du travail obligatoire in France. Since the earlier program that exchanged workers for POWs had not been successful, this new law decreed that all young men between the ages of twenty and thirty-four must go to Germany for obligatory work service. They were to replace Germany's workforce, which was made up either of casualty figures or those embroiled in the fight. Hitler's goal was to import 1.5 million Frenchmen. In response, thousands fled to the country, living in the woods and hiding among the hills. They organized into militia groups, and borrowed an expression from Corsican bandits, calling themselves "men of the underbrush," the Maquis. It was only natural that as the Resistance sabotage became known, they would try to offer their services.

The theme of the Maquis was a reflection of the refrain from the French national anthem, "La Marseillaise." Written in 1792, the refrain begins with the lines *"Aux armes, citoyens! Formez vos bataillons"* (To arms, citizens, form your battalions). And that was exactly what they did. They were the perfect fighting force: strapping young men, albeit undernourished, with an ax to grind against the Nazis.

Over time, the Maquis grew to include a variety of refugees from justice, including German deserters, anti-Franco Spaniards, and urban resisters. Whenever possible, the peasantry provided the Maquis with food, shelter, and clothing. Their guerrilla tactics against the German military became widely known, and the citizens of occupied France silently applauded these anonymous freedom fighters. But what they lacked was arms. An Allied spy like Virginia was someone they were anxious to meet.

IN A TOP-SECRET DOCUMENT prepared on May 19, 1944, by American Military Intelligence, the Cosne area Resistance was described as "fairly well organised. Big possibilities, guerilla experience." The document concluded that the area had "very good potential strategic and morale value, subject to further development in outlying districts."

Virginia knew all about the area's potential. She and Colonel Vessereau had decided the best route to take was to split the Maquis in Cosne into four groups of twenty-five men each. These men had dreamed about resistance, but hadn't had sufficient means to carry it out. Getting someone from London who was arranging to arm them was a dream come true. And it was a clear indication that the world had not forgotten them.

Virginia arranged a parachute drop for the night of May 15. To facilitate agents' requests for supplies, OSS had created groups of like items that agents could order by code name, depending on their need. "Dough" contained general demolition items, "maggots" included magnets and explosive supplies, and "yeast" was a container full of incendiary materials.

For the Cosne Maquis, Virginia requested "dough" and "maggot" containers, plus additional containers of "sten" guns, weapons that were cheap to manufacture, easy to assemble and disassemble, and tough enough to endure the drops. Best of all, they could be fired with German 9 mm ammunition, a plus for anyone who could capture any. Virginia had already trained the colonel, his wife, and several others on how to signal arriving planes, and they recruited half a dozen Maquis to help them haul away and conceal the supplies. The eleven of them arrived at the designated field at 11 o'clock to wait for the plane and its twelve containers. As soon as they heard the plane, Virginia flashed an M, the night's code letter, in Morse with a white light. The plane signaled back and Virginia reilluminated her light. The colonel, his wife, and another Resistance member then lit their red lights. The four of them made a diamond shape with Virginia nearest to the incoming plane. If the flight crew drew lines from one light to another, the point where the lines crossed would be the desired point of the drop. Of course to figure out their positions, Virginia had to take into account the wind speed, which could cause the containers to drift. Looking for wayward containers in the dark was like searching for the proverbial needle. Not to mention the pressure of trying not to arouse suspicions of neighbors and passersby.

This night's drop came off without a hitch. The containers floated to almost the exact spot Virginia had envisioned. With difficulty, the Maquis members concealed their excitement at the array of supplies now at their fingertips. Of course there was still work to do, since the parachutes had to be disconnected and buried in holes they had to dig, and the containers had to be loaded onto the waiting hay wagon and carted back to town. Once they had accomplished that, the group split up with only two men riding on the hay wagon. The other eight left in pairs, taking separate routes back to their homes.

By this time, Virginia had actually left the home of the colonel and was living in the nearby town of Sury-près-Léré, in the garret of a farmhouse owned by Jules Juttry. It was best for her to move around so as not to jeopardize herself, or her hosts, by transmitting from the same location all the time. M. Juttry was elderly; Virginia guessed him to be in his mideighties. He was not at all pleased to have Virginia living in his house, and suspected she was a German spy. His widowed daughter, Estelle Bertrand, had made the arrangements.

Estelle was nearing fifty and had come to live with her father after her husband was killed during the fighting in 1940. She had been a part of the Resistance for several years and was inspired by the fact that an American would give up so much for the cause of France. She had accompanied Virginia to that night's parachute drop, having learned the reception procedures, and would be setting them up once Virginia moved on to her next destination.

On Tuesday, May 28, Virginia received a radio message from OSS headquarters in London:

> HAPPY TO HAVE RECEIVED YOUR CONTACT OF THE 25TH. STOP. PE-
> RIOD OF ACTIVITY IS COMMENCING. STOP. PLEASE COMMUNICATE
> BEFORE NEXT FRIDAY ALL INFORMATION GATHERED SINCE YOUR
> ARRIVAL CONCERNING LARGE MOVEMENTS BY TRAIN OR ROAD.
> STOP.

Virginia pondered the words "period of activity" and wondered what that might be. But her job was to report, not to question. For whatever reason, headquarters needed this information before Friday, June 2, 1944.

15

LE JOUR J

SPRING OF 1944 WAS ONE OF THE WORST in the history of Europe. Torrential rains, powerful winds, and raging seas pounded the shorelines of both Great Britain and the European continent. The violent weather bolstered the members of the Third Reich. It appeared that even Mother Nature was on their side as she stalled what they were sure was the imminent Allied invasion of Europe.

The Germans knew the Allies were coming because they had been bombarding the western coastline at Calais all spring long, "softening up" the area. It was a likely assault location, as only twenty-seven miles separated France from England at that point. But Hitler believed that when the invasion did come, his Atlantic Wall would hold back the Allies.

Making Europe "an impregnable fortress" had been the Führer's dream since the fall of 1941. It was a ridiculous plan. The coastline he intended to reinforce stretched about three thousand miles, from the Arctic Ocean in the north to the Bay of Biscay in the south. Construction of the wall had been moving at a snail's pace until a commando raid on Dieppe, France, in August of 1942. It was the Allies "test tube" raid, to give them an idea of the strength of the German defenses along the channel. The 5,000 commandos were almost all Canadian, and they suffered heavy casualties—almost 600 killed, 1,900 captured, 590 wounded, and 287 missing. Those surviving were rescued by ships and returned to England.

Despite turning away the invaders, an infuriated Hitler demanded that the work on his wall be redoubled and that it proceed "fanatically." And it did. Thousands of slave laborers from conquered countries worked day and night. The enormous amounts of concrete and steel necessary caused a strain on other war production, so corners were cut on the wall. But even now, in June of 1944, the continuous fortification that Hitler had envisioned, and demanded, did not exist.

The Führer's second problem was how to man what would inevitably become the second front of the war. The majority of his army's strength was directed at the Russians, but his developing Atlantic Wall also required manpower. He was haunted with questions. How many troops should be diverted there? And where to put the greatest concentration?

To handle these critical issues, Hitler put Field Marshall Erwin Rommel in charge of the coastline defenses. Rommel was commander in chief of Army Group B, the most powerful of the German armies in the west. He didn't believe for a minute that Hitler's fortress would hold back the Allies. He had faced them in North Africa, and although he had been defeated there, he knew how they fought. His plan for the defense of France and the rest of Europe was simple. Draw the enemy in, allow them to land, and then attack the beaches. To that end, he had half a million men standing guard on the Atlantic between Holland and Brittany, with the bulk of his Fifteenth Army stationed at Pas de Calais. Millions of mines were laid, both on the shore and in the water. Armaments of all sorts were trained on the beaches. When the Allies arrived, and they certainly would, Rommel's army would mow them down before they got ten meters inland.

When April became May, and May slid into June, Rommel determined that the invasion was being held up so that a simultaneous attack could occur with the Russian Red Army in the east. The summer offensive could not begin there until after the thaw in Poland, sometime in mid-June. And thus, the Third Reich relaxed ever so slightly.

HEARING THAT STRANGERS HAD BEEN asking questions about her in Sury-près-Léré, Virginia knew it was time to move again to another safe house. She relocated to Sury-ès-Bois, nine miles to the west, again finding herself living in a farmhouse.

She had radioed London, as she'd been requested to do, with information about German troop movements. There had been some, but nothing out of the ordinary. The area she was in was just about dead center in France and important rail lines ran throughout it. She reported on the trains too, their times and what they appeared to be carrying. But again, nothing was out of the ordinary.

As she had done for nearly three months, Virginia played the part of an old peasant woman. This time she was moving a herd of goats from field to field, all the while keeping a lookout for those who would work for parachute drops. She delivered goats' milk to members of the Resistance, giving her the perfect cover to pass messages as well. And the donkey cart she borrowed from the farmer provided ideal transportation for moving the goods that floated to earth in cylinders. She arranged for two parachute drops from Sury-ès-Bois. The Resistance needed more arms and supplies, therefore a radio set, battery chargers, soap, and money arrived. These two drops proved to be the highlight of the late spring days, and Virginia became edgy, as there was very little else to do.

Of all the elements that made up her job, this was the most difficult: the tension-filled calm before the next storm. And if an Allied invasion of France was the next storm, it would be of tornadic proportions. A person of action, Virginia craved striding forward to attain a goal. Incessant waiting was unnerving. It gave her too much time to think, and not about the obvious danger her work entailed. Rather, her thoughts meandered across the spectrum. They paused first on her mother. Was she well and did she have enough money? Was she worried about her daughter's safety? Virginia felt, of course, that there was really no need for her to be concerned.

But motherly instincts are deep-seated. Mrs. Hall had written to Captain Grell, a name and London address Virginia had given her before leaving for France. Mrs. Hall wanted to know about the welfare of her daughter. On June 2, Charlotte Norris responded on behalf of the captain and the fictitious First Experimental Detachment:

> From a security point of view there is little I am permitted to tell you about your daughter's work. . . . But this I can tell you: that your daughter is . . . doing an important and time-consuming job which has necessitated a transfer from London. . . . We here are in constant touch with your daughter, and are immediately informed of any change in her status. I shall be happy to communicate whatever news of her to you.

Sometimes Virginia's isolation bothered her. She was a people person who loved being in the center of a crowd. But for about three years, she had lived lies. She could never completely confide in anyone, get close, or let her guard down. That was her only regret about her chosen path. But when she stepped back to consider the whole picture, reflecting on the vital nature of accomplishing her duties, it was a small sacrifice.

A thick tension enveloped the Resistance members in early June 1944 as well. They knew an invasion was imminent, just as the Germans did. And like a great many French people, they had hoped that it would occur months earlier. Thoughts of liberation even permeated the churches as priests prayed from their pulpits, urgently asking God for deliverance from the evil occupiers. They cautioned their parishioners to be patient and not to act out unilaterally against the Germans. These rogue attacks almost always brought severe reprisals by the Nazis.

Some French had become disenchanted, grumbling that the Allies had promised to send help, but hadn't delivered. Virginia took a more pragmatic approach, explaining to those around her that launching an attack before preparations had been finalized would be suicidal. There was no sense in trying to pull off something half baked. It would destroy the element of surprise and could prove lethal to many of those involved. There was no time for complaining, Virginia told them. Far too much work had yet to be done in preparation.

She and the members of HECKLER, like other combined SOE and OSS circuits throughout France, had been directed to follow a well laid-out plan, code-named PLAN VERT. For the last month, while they continued to recruit and train new members, they also gradually increased their acts of sabotage. Armed with the supplies from London, they had made attacks against local Nazi headquarters and vehicles. They had taken out essential roads and telephone stations, and had successfully removed German explosives from bridges the Allies would need in their advance across France.

When the invasion did occur, Virginia told her circuit members, their advance work would prove to be invaluable to the Allies. And she assured them that they were not alone. Groups such as theirs were being trained all over France, all ready to aid the Allies.

THE GREATEST ARMADA THE WORLD had ever known was amassing near the Isle of Wight, just off the coast of the British city of Portsmouth. More than four thousand vessels were loaded with two hundred thousand men, twenty thousand vehicles, twelve hundred planes, and fifteen hundred tanks. They were poised for action. Their destination was the beaches of Normandy.

The men aboard the assault ships had been killing time on the choppy channel waters for three days. Zero hour had been set for the morning of June 5, and the first wave of the armada was dispatched. But the weather forced them to be called back. Like the French, these Allied troops were tired of waiting. They had been trained and prepared. The days of no action were chipping away at their readiness and morale. And listening to Radio Paris, the German propaganda station, was of no help.

"Axis Sally" talked of hearth and home and all they were missing. She suggested that their wives and sweethearts were probably now in the arms of other men, and she aired songs to intensify their homesickness and apprehension. On the morning of June 5, she played a new song, a haunting mockery of a popular tune called "I Double Dare You."

I double dare you to come over here.
I double dare you to venture too near.
Take off your high hat and quit that bragging.
Cut out that claptrap and keep your hair on.
Can't you take a dare on?

I double dare you to venture a raid.
I double dare you to try and invade.
And if your loud propaganda means half of what it says,
I double dare you to come over to me.
I double dare you.

Supreme Allied Commander General Eisenhower and the rest of the Allied military leaders had been delaying the invasion, hoping for a break in the weather. From their secret headquarters, a trailer set in an English field near the coast, they debated the pros and cons of holding off one more day or going for broke. Throughout the day of June 5, the heavy winds and high seas appeared to moderate a bit, and the generals decided this was the break they had sought. Operation OVERLORD, the Allied invasion of France, was on.

ON DAY 1,452 OF THE GERMAN occupation of France, Virginia sat on the floor in her room in the farmhouse, along with M. Juttry's daughter-in-law,

Estelle, and several other members of their circuit. There were only thirty-two other Americans in France on this day. But that was to change soon.

Virginia and her group were listening to the BBC's French broadcast for that evening.

"*Ici Londres. Les français parlent aux français. Veuillez écouter quelques messages personnels*" (This is London. The French speaking to the French. First, please listen to a few personal messages).

The broadcast included, as always, a number of personal messages. From wine cellars to hay barns, Resistance members and Allied agents gathered in secret to listen for the code phrase that would signal the day they had long awaited.

The first half of the code had been broadcast at 9:00 PM on June 1: "*Les sanglots longs des violins de l'automne*" (The long sobs of the violins of autumn), was the first line of poet Paul Verlaine's work "Chanson d'Automne." To those who understood, the words meant that the invasion would begin soon, sometime in the first half of the month. When the second line of the poem was broadcast, those listening would be alerted that the invasion would begin within the next forty-eight hours.

That had been four days ago, and this group of five had listened intently every night since. The room was small, with only a tiny window to let in fresh air. Virginia's bed and washstand took up most of the space. The small table where the radio sat was rickety, and every time someone bumped it in the process of getting closer to hear more clearly, the signal flickered in and out. The Germans had gotten very adept at scrambling the BBC's transmissions, but could only do so one wave band at a time. The broadcasts were actually made on several bands, so if one was unintelligible, another could be tried. And cutting the electricity, which the Nazis did frequently, was not a deterrent either, as Virginia's radio worked on a battery.

Finally, at 8:15 PM, listening to the 261-meter wave band, they heard the second half of the code: "*Blessent mon coeur d'une langueur monotone*" (Wound my heart with a monotonous languor).

That was it: *le jour J.* D-Day.

GENERAL "WILD BILL" DONOVAN was not to be kept out of the fight. He had been responsible for the training and deployment of brave American agents into hostile territory. He hoped to now have the opportunity to see the fruits of their labor. For obvious reasons, U.S. Secretary of the Navy,

James Forrestal, had forbidden Donovan's personal participation in Operation OVERLORD. But Donovan pulled some of his famous finagling, and D-Day found him and his London chief, David Bruce, a part of the mighty armada, aboard the U.S. cruiser *Tuscaloosa*.

When they landed on the Normandy beach, Bruce dived out of the way of enemy fire. He landed on Donovan and somehow managed to gouge him in the throat with his steel helmet. The wound began to bleed profusely, but the general was not deterred. The two men proceeded, ultimately finding themselves caught behind a hedge, the targets of German machine -gun fire. They threw themselves to the ground.

"David, we mustn't be captured," Donovan said. "We know too much."

"Yes, sir," Bruce said.

"Have you your pill?" Donovan asked, referring to the cyanide pill issued to all agents with the instruction that it was better to end their life than divulge secrets to the Nazis.

Bruce shook his head. "Never mind," Donovan said, "I have two of them." He unloaded the contents of his pockets onto the ground. There were hotel keys, a passport, currency of several nationalities, photographs of his grandchildren, travel orders, and newspaper clippings, but no pills.

"Never mind," Donovan said again, "we can do without them. But if we get out of here, you must send a message to Gibbs, the hall porter at Claridge's in London, telling him on no account to allow the servants in the hotel to touch some dangerous medicines in my bathroom."

Then he looked straight into Bruce's eyes and whispered, "I must shoot first."

"Yes, sir," Bruce replied, "but can we do much against machine guns with our pistols?"

"Oh, you don't understand," Donovan said. "I mean if we are about to be captured I'll shoot you first. After all, I *am* your commanding officer."

AS THE POLICE CHIEF FOR THE department of Creuse, the area in which Virginia was working, Colonel Vessereau wrote a notice to be hung throughout the area on June 7:

> Inhabitants of Creuse! The hour that we have long awaited has arrived and the sacred work of the liberation of our land has entered the last phase. We call on all good French, those who have

only love in their hearts for liberty, to contribute to these efforts.
. . . The armistice has been rescinded, the war continues and
with all of our allies, large and small, our victory will be the cor-
nerstone of the world of tomorrow.

His sentiments were echoed throughout France. Once the second half
of the message signaling the invasion had been broadcast, myriad other
messages were sent to circuits and Resistance groups across France. These
prearranged code phrases notified the groups that it was time to put into action all of their preplanned acts of sabotage. Like other circuit heads, Virginia had been told to attack roads, railways, and telecommunications, and
harass occupation troops by whatever means she and her circuit could. The
Allies were certain that the first thing the Germans would do at the onset
of the invasion would be to flood Normandy with additional men and supplies. The rail lines were the Nazis' lifeline and had to be taken out.

Virginia had organized small groups within HECKLER that would be
ready to leap into action once the invasion was announced. Their job was
to lay the explosives on the rail lines around Cosne. Under cover of darkness, the groups went to work on the night of June 6.

Virginia, accompanied by two young Frenchmen, Robert and Gilles, arrived at their designated location around midnight. She had chosen this
particular spot after carefully surveying the area in daylight a week earlier.
It was a meadow, midway between Cosne and Sury-près-Léré with a nice
hedge nearby they could use for cover if they needed it. It seemed unlikely,
though, since there were no lights and no sign of life anywhere around.

Robert carried the rucksack with their necessary materials: two three-
quarter-pound packs of plastic explosives connected to one another by a
double Cordtex lead, two igniters known as "fog signals," two detonators,
and extra Cordtex, which they'd use for the fuse. Robert was to set up the
fog signals and detonators while Gilles's job was to affix the plastic explosive packs to the rail with their attached webbed straps. Armed with a sten
gun, Virginia would stand guard.

They had only been working a short time when Virginia heard voices
down the track. Peering into the darkness, she saw two German soldiers
walking, or rather weaving, between the rails about fifty meters away,
singing at the top of their lungs. They were obviously drunk. She and the
two men grabbed their materials and dove behind the hedge. The three of

them flattened themselves against the coarse grass. The magazine of Virginia's sten could accommodate thirty-two rounds of ammunition, which was what she had with her. She was not at all apprehensive at the thought of emptying it into the Germans, but the noise might bring more soldiers than she would be able to hold off.

The three of them waited, holding their breath. The noise from the soldiers continued, but didn't come any closer. In fact, it seemed to Virginia that it began to grow more distant, until it was no longer audible. Cautiously the three crept back to the train track, but saw no one in either direction. Satisfied the threat was gone, they resumed the work.

While Gilles went back to work on the plastic explosive units, Robert labored with the fog signals. He loaded them with detonators, and placed them about two meters from the explosives. Then he taped Cordtex fuse to the adapters on the signals and handed it off to Gilles who attached the other end to the plastic explosive units. The train would crush the fog signals, which would explode, setting off the detonators, whose fire would travel up the Cordtex and ignite the plastic explosive units, all within the space of a few seconds. The end result would be a derailed locomotive engine and a meter of unusable rail, both of which would take days to repair.

Job completed, the three of them hurried back to their homes. The next train wasn't expected for two hours, and it was never wise for saboteurs to hang around after an explosion anyway. But a smile spread across Virginia's face the next morning when she heard that not only had her team been successful, but so had the other four. That meant four different sets of tracks had been rendered useless for several days, delaying matériel vital to the German defense of the Allies' invasion.

Altogether in those first days after the Normandy landings, 571 rail targets were sabotaged. In addition, Resistance members with ties to the Syndicat de la société nationale des chemins de fer, the train workers union, urged their friends to be as uncooperative as possible. The ensuing chaos resulting from the work of the Resistance caused the Nazis disruption, disorganization, and delay.

ON JUNE 8, OSS HEADQUARTERS radioed Virginia asking her to check on a group of reliable and well-disciplined men, ready to take orders, in the province of Auvergne, seventy-five miles southwest of Lyon. It was an area she was somewhat familiar with from her SOE days, but it had yet to be completely developed in terms of assistance to local Resistance cells. A top-secret document dated May 19, 1944, described it as "little organized as yet"; it could prove useful to the Allies. The men in question were centered in a tiny town called Le Chambon-sur-Lignon. Virginia asked Estelle to accompany her and the two women left from the Cosne train station on June 15 around noon.

Their journey took almost six hours. And it was not without its share of tension. Virginia and Estelle knew, of course, that circuits were sabotaging rail lines across France, just as their own circuit had done. The explosives were laid at night and affected trains traveling then or in the early morning hours. By leaving at noon, they hoped to avoid any booby-trapped rails, but there was always the chance that some avid Resistance cell had laid explosives during the day.

The two women arrived safely at the town of Saint-Étienne at 6:00 PM, having had to change trains three times. They would travel the last miles to Le Chambon by wagon. Virginia had learned that farmers usually hung around train stations to profit from the lack of gasoline. They were there with their horses and hay wagons and acted as local taxis, provided the price was right.

Virginia and Estelle arrived in Le Chambon around 7:00 PM. They found an old hotel in the center of town, registered for a room, and went to the neighboring café for dinner. Trying to be discreet, Virginia studied the people in the café. They all had the look of hard work, and seemed oblivious to the strange women in their midst.

The message she had received from London before their departure told her that a man by the name of Auguste Bohny, a Swiss national, was in charge of all of the activities of the Swiss Aid in Le Chambon. The organization helped the homeless and orphaned children. At least that was what the group's documents claimed. Bohny would be Virginia's best bet to help locate the Resistance leaders.

Estelle spoke tentatively with their waiter, saying she was looking for someone who might give them news about the invasion. Virginia hadn't wanted to draw attention with her accent so her friend did the talking. The waiter called over a man, telling them his name was Hubert Petiet. Estelle repeated her request.

Petiet spoke up with pride, telling them that the Allies were about to march right across France. The Germans would be surrendering every chance they got. Estelle thanked him and they resumed their dinners.

After they'd finished eating, Estelle approached Petiet and asked him if there were others in town who felt as he did about the Germans. Petiet became cautious and wanted to know why. Estelle told him that she and her friend were looking for a M. Bohny. They had information for him they were sure he would be interested in hearing, Estelle said. They could be found at the hotel next door, but would be leaving the following day. If M. Bohny was interested, he should contact them right away.

An hour later there was a knock at their door. The desk clerk told them there was someone downstairs to see them. Virginia and Estelle descended and found Petiet in the company of another man, who was introduced as Auguste Bohny. To verify his identity, Virginia asked him a number of questions about his organization that only he would be able to answer. Conversely, he quizzed her about the contact in Berne, Switzerland, who had passed his name to London. When each was satisfied that the other was genuine, they relaxed. Virginia told him she wanted to talk to the leader of the area's Resistance group and she asked Bohny if he could contact him. Petiet chimed in at this point, saying that he knew the man in question. Virginia asked him to bring that man to their room as soon as possible. And he was to come alone. By this time it was almost 11:00 PM.

Another hour passed before there was a knock at the door. Estelle opened it to see Petiet and another man, whom she ushered into their tiny, dimly lit room. Petiet introduced the man as Pierre Fayol. Virginia told them simply that her name was Diane and dove into the conversation. Did they have areas that could be used for parachute drops? Fayol told her they did, and that he had researched the area himself. They had even given the areas code names that could be passed on to the pilots. They were in desperate need of arms, which was why he had taken a chance on Virginia really being who she said she was.

Virginia next asked him if he could provide forty men. Forty was no problem, Fayol told her. He could provide ten times that many if they were given some organization and the tools to fight with. The toughest question came next. Would Fayol and his men follow orders? Fayol hesitated. It depended on what kind of orders. Virginia told him it would include sabotage and guerilla attacks, to which Fayol heartily agreed. They would follow any order as long as it wasn't in conflict with the orders from their superiors, and as long as their collective goals were the same.

That was enough to satisfy Virginia. These men were exactly what she and London had hoped for. She told Fayol to come back for them at eight o'clock the following morning to show her the fields they'd picked out. He returned the next morning in a benzene-burning Citroën with Petiet and another man named Désiré Zurbach. Two of them had chosen code names for themselves. Petiet was Petit and Zurbach was Dédé. Fayol would use his own name, Pierre. Virginia and Estelle climbed into the car and they took off to look over the potential reception fields. Virginia was amazed at what an excellent job the men had done in their selection. Any one of the fields they showed her would serve well.

She told Fayol that she couldn't make the final decision about parachute drops without consulting her superiors. She would either come back herself or send them a mission to undertake. But she did have money that she was authorized to give them to buy what they needed to tide them over. She was suggesting the black market, and Fayol understood immediately.

They all piled back into the car and drove to the home of Samuel Lebrat, the designated treasurer for the group. Virginia excused herself, went into another room, and returned carrying a stack of thousand-franc bills. It was 150,000 francs, she told them and asked them to count it to make certain of the amount.

Maurice, Samuel's cousin, counted it and told them there were 152,000 francs. Virginia insisted she had given them 150,000 and asked that they count it again. Samuel counted the second time and came up with the same result. She laughed off the incident as if it were her mistake. And she silently congratulated herself for having found a group of honest men.

THE FIVE THOUSAND RESIDENTS of Le Chambon-sur-Lignon, and those of its surrounding area known as the Yssingeaux Plateau, were not unfamiliar with struggle. They were the descendants of the Huguenots, French Protestants who were members of the Reformed Church, which John Calvin had established in 1555. During the sixteenth and seventeenth centuries, the king persecuted them for their religious beliefs, which were in direct theological contrast with the Catholic Church. The Huguenots bore the label of heretics, and those captured were subjected to horrible tortures and death at the hands of the king and the church. The others managed to flee their homes, and a group settled on the Yssingeaux Plateau.

It was not surprising, then, that when the armistice with Germany was signed in 1940, and France's puppet government in Vichy began cooperating with the Nazi quest to eliminate all Jews, the inhabitants of the Yssingeaux Plateau felt as though history were repeating itself. Le Chambon's two Protestant pastors were very vocal in their thoughts about the armistice. Resist without fear, they told their congregations, but also without pride or hatred.

Deciding to become their brothers' keepers was a moral choice for the people of Le Chambon, and it was one easily made. It began when they offered to hide the few Jews within their own population, then helped them escape to neutral Switzerland, 160 miles away via an underground railway.

Word spread and Jews came from other parts of France, seeking escape or asylum for their children. Run by the Swiss, boarding schools were opened on the Yssingeaux Plateau to serve not only the Jewish children, a quarter of their total residents, but also Gentile children, whose families wanted them to be spared from the food shortages and the dangers of war-torn France. In all, seven schools, over a dozen boarding houses, and a large number of local peasant farmers came to the refugees' aid.

In these homes, the Jewish children were taught side by side with the Gentiles. They learned the Lord's Prayer, Christian songs and traditions, and Bible verses. Le Chambon's inhabitants believed that they were finally getting a chance to put into action what they had been taught all of their lives. One farmer's wife summed it up for all of them. The war was a blessing in disguise, she said. It was making it possible for Christians to become familiar with God's chosen people.

As with the rest of France, however, the bucolic peace of the Yssingeaux Plateau was also threatened by the occupiers. Nazis who ventured through Le Chambon found it the perfect location to set up rehabilitation centers for those who'd spent time on the Russian front. They took over two of the town's hotels for their purposes, one of which was across the street from the headquarters of the armed Resistance. The German presence was a physical reminder of the penalty for hiding Jews: either the hell of the concentration camps or a brutal execution.

Miraculously, the German presence never interfered with the work being carried out by the citizens of Le Chambon. By war's end they would have aided five thousand Jews to escape Nazi horrors. It was almost as many as the plateau's entire population. And in the midst of all these good deeds, Virginia was planning to build a formidable Resistance circuit.

16

AUX ARMES, CITOYENS

THE QUAINT FIELDSTONE FARMHOUSE of Mme Léa Lebrat was near La Suchère, on the road that led from Le Chambon to the nearest town, Villelonge. The house sat at the end of a long drive, nestled among the hills that made up the Yssingeaux Plateau. Mme Lebrat was the same age as Virginia, thirty-eight years old. The Germans had imprisoned her husband in 1943, which left her responsible for their farm and their two sons, aged five and eight.

While she had never formally joined any Resistance organization, her willingness to give anything she had to aid those in need made her a de facto member. And resistance was really a family affair for the Lebrats, since her uncle, Samuel, and her cousins, Pierre and Maurice, had been involved from the beginning of the Nazi occupation.

Men who sought refuge, whether they were French, British, or American, found it at Mme Lebrat's. Those who came for food to take into the forests to feed the Maquis knew that Mme Lebrat would help them. If conspirators needed a meeting place, Mme Lebrat was happy to accommodate. She was an angel to the rescue on many occasions, taking incalculable risks. And she announced to everyone who passed through her doors, "Whatever you need, I'll help get for you. Hide a radio transmitter? No problem. But I won't allow guns in my house."

On July 20, 1944, Virginia Hall became another in the long line of Mme Lebrat's houseguests. Six days earlier, at the request of headquarters, Virginia had returned to Le Chambon. But when she arrived, Virginia discovered that the letter she had sent to the Resistance leaders announcing her return had been disregarded. None of the arrangements she had asked for had been made, including a place for her to live and work. Hopefully this bad beginning wasn't a harbinger for the rest of the mission.

It was crucial that Virginia keep up her radio sked so that London was current on any news of enemy troop movements, as well as her whereabouts and welfare. Pierre Fayol invited her to stay with him, his wife, Marianne, and their children; as Jews who had fled Marseille and settled in the Le Chambon area, they were displaced persons themselves. Their little farmhouse had an extra room that they offered to Virginia, and they made their barn available for her radio transmissions.

It was raining the day Virginia arrived with her few belongings, and she had a scarf draped over her head. It struck Fayol that she looked like the Madonna, and much to Virginia's embarrassment the name stuck. She became known as "la Madonne" in Le Chambon's Resistance circles.

The day after her arrival, Virginia explained to Fayol that planes with radio detectors were ever present, pasting any building suspected of containing a radio with a fearsome bombardment. He set about finding her new quarters right away. Two days later, Virginia moved to a barn owned by a baker in the village of Villelonge, several kilometers from Le Chambon. She was nearer to the Maquis, which had become known officially as the Forces françaises de l'intérieur(FFI). They were to be, in General de Gaulle's words, the army of the new France. But the baker's barn was too far from the areas she needed to survey for parachute drops, so she moved once again, this time to Mme Lebrat's.

Housing wasn't Virginia's only issue on her return to Le Chambon. Some of the members of the Maquis found it unnerving to take orders from a woman. Having her in charge was completely foreign in their world, and they mumbled under their breath, "Who the hell are you to give orders?" Virginia summoned the various officers and gave them a simple choice. If they wanted arms and equipment, she would provide them. But in return, she insisted they follow her orders. Groups all over France would be undertaking the same tasks they were going to. It was essential to have a unified effort against the Germans.

She told them that if they or their men were uncomfortable following her orders, they needed to speak up immediately. They would be released from duty and be free to go elsewhere. As an aside, she let them know she wouldn't tolerate any double crosses. She had men, she told them, who were looking out for the interest of the group. Any untoward actions directly to her would be reported straightaway.

On the other end of the spectrum, a handful of men would have followed Virginia into hell if she had asked them. And she would have been hard pressed in her work were in not for three of them.

Désiré Zurbach, Dédé, was born in Alsace, a province on the German border. He was eighteen when the Nazis marched into France in 1940, and by 1941 had lost his entire family. His father died when he was a child, and the Germans had deported his mother and sisters. A year later, in 1942, he arrived in Le Chambon and was taken in by Mme Lebrat.

Dédé headed up a group of about thirty *maquisards* when Virginia met him. She liked him immediately. He was young and ambitious and serious about his work. She had the kind of confidence in him she had had in Pep in Lyon. Dédé became her second in command on the Yssingeaux Plateau and she affectionately referred to him as her "man Friday."

While she was living in the baker's barn in Villelonge, she became acquainted with a twenty-four-year-old Frenchman, whom everyone called Lieutenant Bob. His real name, he confided to her, was Lieutenant Raoul Le Boulicaut. Virginia sensed from her first meeting with him that he was steady, sincere, and hard working.

Bob had wanted to be in the military from the time he was thirteen, and he joined the French navy in 1939. His ship, the *Paris*, was in England when France fell. A month later, he enlisted in the Royal Marines, knowing that was the only way he could help his country. He participated in the Egyptian campaign in 1942, and then entered the Intelligence Service when he returned to England in August of that year. He had a battery of classes in radio, parachuting, and espionage, and because he spoke French, he was sent to Lyon in April of 1943.

A budding career in espionage came to a screeching halt in a car accident in Lyon. Bob had been riding with other Resistance members when they collided with a tree. Gendarmes took him to the hospital half conscious, but not before they found a gun on him. They decided he was dangerous and sent him to a prison hospital where he made the acquaintance of the cleaning lady. The Nazis had killed her son not long before, so one day she brought Bob some wine, a drugged cake, and a twelve-meter length of rope. He plied his guards with the wine and cake, and after they'd fallen asleep, he and several other prisoners exited through a second-story window with the rope. He'd been on the Yssingeaux Plateau for about a year when Virginia met him.

Shortly after Virginia's arrival, she asked Bob if he and some of his men would become her reception committee for the upcoming parachute drops. Bob agreed without hesitation. While she was scouting out new parachute reception fields the next day and reflecting on her good fortune at having discovered such solid gold individuals as Lieutenant Bob and Dédé, a memory from her childhood came to mind. Her father had always said that what a person *was* far outweighed what a person *had.* She had met a number of people over the past several years who proved that adage true, despite the danger and destruction they all faced at every moment. Without a doubt, her friends in Lyon and the group close to her here were worth more than all the world's millionaires.

Virginia also began to rely heavily on Edmond Lebrat, another cousin of Léa's. He, too, led a Maquis group, and in addition to doing courier work for her, he was a man who knew how to find things. Bicycles, pumps, vehicles, fuel, whatever Virginia needed to carry out her mission, Edmond could locate.

Virginia had planned to make her daily radio transmissions from Mme Lebrat's barn. It had no electricity and Edmond came up with an ingenious way of creating power without having to rely on the radio's battery. An old bicycle with pedals but no wheels provided the power. The bicycle's chain was attached to a generator. When someone pedaled, usually Edmond, the electricity created by the generator fed an automobile battery connected to the radio. Virginia had uninterrupted power to make and receive transmissions. From here, she reported to headquarters that she had four hundred Maquis members in five groups and was ready to receive arms for them.

THE FIRST OF MANY LONG-AWAITED parachute drops on the Yssingeaux Plateau took place near Villelonge, on one of the fields that Fayol and the others had shown Virginia on her first visit. As she had done throughout the war, Virginia listened closely to the BBC broadcast for several evenings around the full moon phase in July, sometimes alone, sometimes with others from the group. She was waiting for the code phrase that would give her all the necessary information. She finally heard on July 21: "*Les marguerites fleuriront ce soir*" (The daisies will bloom tonight). This was followed by the phrase "*Je dis trois fois*" (I say three times).

When Virginia heard it, she told Lieutenant Bob, Dédé, and Maurice Lebrat that the drop would be that night, in the field south of Villelonge, reconnaissance letter R. There would be three planes. She had trained Lieutenant Bob's Maquis group of thirty men how to receive parachute drops. The majority of them were with her on that first night when twenty containers arrived, each holding precious cargo. Weapons were the most plentiful: machine guns, rifles, ammunition, daggers, bayonets, detonators, and explosives. Documents came too, with detailed instructions for acts of sabotage, along with hundreds of thousands of freshly printed French francs. The Maquis needed clothing, so London had sent boots, all British army issue. There were vitamin-fortified chocolates and pills of all sorts: some to keep them awake, some to put them to sleep, and cyanide for the obvious usage.

As they were unpacking the cylinders, Lieutenant Bob came across a package marked "DIANE" and he handed it to her. Since the containers were packed by SOE personnel in London, Vera Atkins was still making sure her agents were taken care of. It mattered little to her that Virginia was now with OSS. To Vera, Virginia was still one of her agents and she guessed that a few personal things, like tea and additional stump socks, would be most appreciated. As usual, Vera was right.

There were so many stores that they had to work until about 3:00 AM. But the Nazis had recently decided to advance Greenwich Mean Time two hours throughout France. It meant sunrise was two hours later than it previously had been. The group would be able to load their waiting hay wagons and have everything stowed away before daylight.

Not all receptions progressed without problems, however. Sometimes Virginia and her group would hear their code phrase and then wait for hours for planes that never arrived. Worse still, some drops were so far off course that they had to tear all over the area, trying to account for the number of cylinders they guessed had been dropped. To leave one behind meant it could just as easily be found by the Germans or the Milice and lead to arrests. Incompetence infuriated Virginia, and she would spew out a chain of expletives that shocked her French compatriots. They may not have understood the words, but they certainly understood the meaning.

THE TIMELINE DESIGNED BY THE ALLIES for troop advancements after D-Day showed that by June 15, they would be sixteen miles inland. But the plan had fallen far behind schedule. The Germans were tenacious in holding on to their conquered territory, and in addition to using their armaments to the fullest potential, they also made clever use of the French terrain. Normandy was famous for its *bocages*—thick hedgerows of hawthorn, brambles, vines, and trees that were practically impenetrable. The vegetation was planted on earthen mounds several feet tall, and enclosed small fields, each one resembling a little fort. Defenders who were dug in behind a hedgerow were almost untouchable, and yet were able to position snipers and machine guns that could mow down advancing Allied soldiers. The strain of this kind of fighting on already fragile nerves was enormous.

But the toll on the population of northwest France was just as horrific. In the province of Normandy, those who survived the fighting—many were killed simply because they were in the wrong place at the wrong time—found themselves among the 356,000 who were displaced amid the ruins of their former homes and cities; 135,000 buildings were demolished in the province, with another 187,000 damaged.

Just as they had in 1940, men, women, and children took to the roads, hauling what few belongings they could collect in horse carts, wheelbarrows, or on their backs. And no matter where they went, they faced the constant threat of harm. In addition to flying bullets, the roads and fields were laced with German mines, while Allied planes flew overhead, firing on anything that moved.

There was nowhere for them to stay, so they crammed into wine cellars, caves, tunnels, and cemetery crypts. There was nothing for them to eat, so they butchered the livestock that had been killed by falling shells. Hospitals were filled to overflowing and often had no gas, electricity, or water. Orphaned children wandered aimlessly, as did the elderly. Some of the French were so shell-shocked that when the liberators finally did arrive, they were unable to celebrate the day they had looked forward to for four years.

LIKE PENNIES FROM HEAVEN, containers packed with everything the Maquis and Resistance of the Yssingeaux Plateau needed continued to float to earth. Virginia had realized from the very first moment she saw it that this area would be key in thwarting the Nazis' fight against the Allied advance. The terrain was mountainous and isolated. Very few Germans, save for those at the hotels in Le Chambon, had given it a second look. Unlike Lyon, a city crawling with Gestapo, the plateau had far fewer threats. It was the perfect location to build a Resistance force. But it was not completely secure.

There were several members of the Milice, as well as collaborators, in Le Chambon. And in the city of Le Puy, about thirty-five miles away, plenty of Germans would be only too happy to round up a Resistance group the size of hers. Furthermore, there was still a price on her head, and Klaus Barbie and Lyon were only seventy-five miles away.

Virginia, therefore, took care in her travels. She had moved again, not wanting to put Mme Lebrat at any greater risk than she was already taking. An abandoned house belonging to the Salvation Army was about three kilometers away. It had three bedrooms, two of which Virginia figured could accommodate incoming personnel, and a large barn that could serve as both radio room and meeting place. Mme Lebrat supplied Virginia with food, sending over hot meals when she was too busy to remember to go to the farm to eat.

Virginia's work was grueling. The Yssingeaux Plateau is a part of the Massif Central, known as the "roof of France." It consists of volcanic mountains and plateaus, and is the most rugged and geologically diverse region in the country. Virginia spent her days bicycling up and down the mountains in search of parachute fields, contacting her circuit members, and gathering other intelligence for the sabotage and guerilla attacks. Traveling the rutted dirt roads would have been exhausting for anyone, but Cuthbert made it all the more arduous.

When she wasn't on her bicycle, she was sending or receiving radio transmissions, ever watchful for the German direction-finding trucks. It was vital that Allied commanders receive up-to-the-minute reports on German troop movements, supply depots, and headquarters locations. One day, Virginia and Edmond bicycled into the city of Le Puy to do a little reconnaissance and were amazed at what they saw. Virginia counted eight German trucks parked in the center of town at city hall. Next to them were the flag-bearing limousines she knew carried Nazi officers.

Virginia urged Edmond to find out what was happening. He left and sidled up to a French shopkeeper standing in his doorway. After a few minutes he returned to report that the German General Staff was moving in. Virginia was incredulous. Their headquarters was in Lyon. Could they really be moving to Le Puy permanently?

Edmond said that the shopkeeper had heard they were there to stay, preferring the more central location. Virginia had a different take. It was more likely, she told Edmond, that they couldn't stand the harassment of the Resistance in Lyon. What a feather in their caps this was. They had driven out the General Staff.

As soon as she returned to her barn, she radioed London with the news. It would most certainly call for a change in course of the advancing Allied armies. To capture the German General Staff, the largest field concentration of officers in France, would handicap the Nazi defenses and severely demoralize them.

Virginia's nights were as full as her days. She spent a great many of them out in the fields, waiting for drops. She was very particular about attending every one, to make sure that the supplies were handled properly and arrived at their appropriate destinations.

The Maquis had an arms depot at a nearby farm that was guarded around the clock, not just from the Germans, but from overzealous Frenchmen who might want to increase their own arsenal. Gabriel Eyraud, the young guard on night duty, assured Virginia every time she made a delivery that it would take an army of a hundred men to remove him from his post.

But it was the final destinations of these arms that was the most important to Virginia. As she had done with her men in the Cosne area, Virginia trained explosives crews and sent them on missions almost every night between July 27 and August 12. She had never been formally trained for sabotage, and quite frankly couldn't imagine the need. Planning and organizing these operations was simply a question of using common sense. And the goal was always the same: harass and kill the Germans.

The men under Virginia's command blew up the rail line between the towns of Langogne and Brassac in four places. At Chamalières, they blew up a rail bridge, driving the locomotive into the gulf below. A freight train was derailed in the tunnel at Monistrol d'Allier, and after the repair train and crew had gone into the tunnel to clear the wreckage, they blew up fifteen meters of track behind them. These trains, which all carried men and supplies, were rendered useless against the Allies. And the list went on and on.

One day just after Virginia had finished her daily radio sked, Lieutenant Bob stopped by with a story from the previous night's sabotage activities. Several of his maquisards had gone out to lay explosives at the electrical transformer near Le Puy. They thought they'd have enough time to do their work and get away before the next team of guards came on duty. But the guards showed up early. The men were able to shove their pistols and explosives into their pockets and one of them happened to have a soccer ball with him. Why no one knew, but it appeared to have saved their lives.

They told the guards they were on their way to a practice. The guards never questioned that it was the wee hours of the morning. A game ensued, the guards against the men, and it looked as though the maquisards were going to get away without a problem—until a detonator fell out of one of the men's pockets. A very helpful guard pointed out that he had dropped something. The man scooped it up and the game continued. The guards never bothered to check what it was, they were too interested in continuing the game, which they ultimately lost.

The story greatly amused Virginia. She would have loved to be a part of the sabotage strikes. But after the close call several months earlier with the drunken soldiers, London had told her she was too valuable to risk capture or death. They told her they she could plan the attacks, but not participate. One of those plans included attacking the area's roadways. With rail transportation interrupted, German troops would have to march or be trucked to battlefields. So she trained her "boys" on the guerilla tactics she had learned in her SOE classes.

Armed with their new knowledge, she sent them after a group of nineteen *miliciens* whom they arrested, seizing the valuable documents the traitors carried. Another group of her men, bazookas blazing, attacked a truck carrying German soldiers and their accompanying tank on the Le Puy-Langeac road. Members of the Maquis trapped a German convoy between Chamelix and Pigeyre by blowing up bridges in front of and behind them. After five days of struggling, the Germans lost 150 men. The remaining 500 surrendered, preferring POW status to death.

The attacks that Virginia had coordinated were being mirrored all over the country. Resistance and Maquis groups, fueled with pent-up resentment from the German occupation, took up arms against the invaders. Their work tied down enemy forces, diverting them from the main battles with the Allies. And it hampered Nazi withdrawals.

But these attacks weren't always without costs. A very somber Dédé came to visit Virginia one afternoon in late July to tell her about the ambush of a convoy of twelve trucks near Saint-Paulieu. The setup was sound—the maquisards tipped over a hay wagon in the middle of the road, which forced the convoy to stop. When the Germans dismounted from the trucks, the maquisards hidden in the woods hit them from all sides. But the

Nazis were more heavily armed than others had been and Virginia's group lost twenty men.

This was the sort of news Virginia never wanted to hear. She asked Dédé what had become of the Germans. He told her some were killed and the rest had been taken prisoner. They were being held in the woods and no decision had been made as to their fate. The maquisards had quite a list of suggestions, but they had wanted Dédé to ask Virginia's opinion.

The humane thing to do would be to keep them corralled until the Allies arrive, whenever that may be. But she wasn't running a POW camp, and she didn't much care about being humane after what she'd seen and heard during the past four years. She told Dédé she thought the Nazis' fate should be left up to the men who had watched their families suffer and their friends die.

Virginia felt badly about the deaths of these patriots. They had been energetic, courageous young men with the attitude that they were bulletproof. Over the course of her stay on the Yssingeaux Plateau, she had heard many of them talking about how glorious it was to die for one's country. The fact of the matter is, Virginia thought, dying is still dying, regardless of the crusade. What matters more is how effectively one has lived.

IT HAD BEEN OVER TWO MONTHS since Mrs. Hall had received the letter from Mrs. Norris about Virginia. News from the front arriving in Baltimore was that the Germans were not rolling over in front of the Allies and that fierce battles were being waged in France. Knowing her daring daughter so well, Mrs. Hall's intuition told her that Virginia was somewhere in the melee. She wrote another letter to Mrs. Norris asking for news. On August 23, Mrs. Norris replied: "Virginia is doing a spectacular, man-sized job, and her progress is rapid and sure. You have every reason to be proud of her."

It wasn't exactly an assurance that Virginia wasn't in harm's way, but it did assuage Mrs. Hall's fears somewhat to know that at least her daughter was alive and well.

Four thousand miles away, Virginia had her hands full. Had she known about Mrs. Norris's proclamation that her progress was "rapid and sure," she would have contradicted these words. It seemed as though every facet of her operation were fraught with controversy. Excluding those close to Virginia, the leaders of the various Maquis groups were constantly arguing among themselves about who should answer to whom. The number of Resistance and Maquis groups was as overwhelming as the number of political parties in France. As in politics, each had their own agenda. And all of them were suspicious of the Communists.

Francs-tireurs et partisans was what the Communists called themselves and the numbers were formidable, which was what the rest of the Resistance feared. To many, the thought of a postwar Communist France was almost as great a nightmare to them as the one they were living. Virginia's opinion was that the whole lot of them should forgo their political leanings and fight as a united front. It was a maddening waste of everyone's time and energies. There would be plenty of time to sort it all out once they had driven out the Nazis.

Then there was the issue concerning the Yssingeaux Plateau's JEDBURGH team, or more accurately, the lack thereof. These teams, most often referred to as JEDS, had taken their name from the small town of Jedburgh on the Scottish border. There the Scots had conducted guerrilla warfare against English invaders in the twelfth century. The idea for the JEDS was a joint one of the OSS and the SOE. Each three-man team would include an American, a Brit, and a Frenchman, but very few had this equitable mix.

The JED teams were to provide a general staff for the Resistance groups, encouraging organization. They were also to provide communication links between the FFI command and Supreme Allied Headquarters, always working in the best interest of the Allies' strategy. With limited training, most of them departed from Great Britain. A handful of them, though, arrived in France from Algiers, which had been in Allied hands since the success of Operation TORCH more than a year earlier.

Virginia's group of Maquis had become very large, by this time swelling to numbers nearing fifteen hundred. She could have used the additional organizational assistance, particularly since she had understood that one of the JED team members would be French. There were still some maquisards who were defiant of her authority because she was a woman and not French. Headquarters in London had promised her a team, but as the days ticked by in August, no arrival date was mentioned. It wasn't until the end of the month that she got word that JED team, code-named JEREMY, would be departing from Algiers and arriving on the Yssingeaux Plateau the night of August 25.

Virginia, Lieutenant Bob, Dédé , and Maurice Lebrat made up the welcoming committee for them. The first parachute they saw open belonged to

Captain Geoffrey Hallowes, a member of the Gordon Highlanders and the team's ranking officer. His arrival was as chaotic as it was comical. He got hung up in a tree at the edge of the landing field and when Virginia went to check on him, she discovered he was wearing a kilt with nothing beneath it and cursing loudly. She told him to quiet down and that she'd send someone over to help him.

She went back to the center of the field just in time to see the second man, British Sergeant Roger Leney, and the group's wireless radio man, bounce off a tree on his way down and land face-first in a gully. Only the third member, French Lieutenant Henri Charles Guise, floated gently to earth and disposed of his parachute before seeing about his team members. Maurice aided Leney, who had banged up his knee and was in a great deal of pain. Virginia and the other men went back to see about Hallowes. By this time he had swung himself over to a tree and was busy cutting the cords of the parachute.

When they reunited on the edge of the field Virginia welcomed them and led the way through a small woods to a road and then to the door of the baker whose barn she had used when she'd first arrived. They were the first Allied arrivals on the Yssingeaux Plateau, she explained, and that called for a celebration. The baker hauled out several bottles of brandy and for the next hour, they toasted every subject they could think of. Then the JED team was loaded into the circuit's black Citroën—the same one that was used to haul Virginia around on her first trip—and took off with no lights at breakneck speed. The three newcomers were terrified, which in turn gave Virginia a good laugh. Big tough men, coming to her aid in occupied France, afraid of a little speed in the dark. They arrived at her Salvation Army house and settled in as her first houseguests.

Lunch the next day was at Mme Lebrat's. When she served the first dish of deviled eggs, Sergeant Leney was aghast, saying in England he hadn't seen two eggs together on the same plate in years. That meal and all of those that followed were festivals of food compared to what these men had been enduring across the channel.

THE WAR HAD TAKEN AN INCREDIBLE turn in the Allies' favor during the month of August. They had begun by bombing southern France in July to "soften" it up just as they had done before the Normandy invasion. Then in the early morning hours of August 15, 396 planes of the Provisional Troop

Carrier Air Division dropped more than five thousand American and British paratroopers along the Mediterranean coast. At dawn, while the paratroopers were involved in intense fighting, heavy and medium bombers and fighter-bombers swept over the invasion area and destroyed underwater obstacles, beach defenses, and coastal guns.

Next the American Seventh Army hit the beaches, joined by fifty thousand members of the Maquis. In a matter of a few hours, they had gained a wide beachhead and driven eight miles inland. Cannes and Nice fell, and then Marseille on August 28.

The previous month, the American army had streamed southward to recapture Brittany. When they ran into resistance at port cities like Saint-Malo and Brest, they left them to be harassed by small, but strong, forces from the sea, rather than expending resources to regain them. The cities became isolated outposts, their massive supply garrisons useless to the German army.

Large bodies of the American forces were also thrusting eastward into the heart of France. They freed town after town to the ecstatic screams of the long-oppressed citizens. The forces fanned out in every direction, and the French competed with one another to be among the first to feed and house their liberators.

Parisians knew the Allies were coming. The news had been spreading via SOE and OSS agents and Resistance members since the beginning of August. Enterprising black marketers began selling seats along the probable route of the liberators' entry into the city. The City of Lights was finally going to witness the rout of their invidious captors. Allied flags flew and people dared to sing the "Marseillaise," whose rousing melody hadn't been heard for more than four years.

The German commander in Paris, General Dietrich von Choltitz, had only recently arrived. He had been ordered by Hitler never to surrender the city to the Allies or the Resistance. Rather, Hitler had raged from his headquarters, von Choltitz was to burn Paris to the ground if he was unable to hold it. For his defenses, he had at his disposal more than ten thousand regular troops, forty-nine heavy tanks, and a number of flamethrowers. Just outside the city limits, sixty-nine bombers were ready to drop their payload on Allied forces at his command.

But unbeknownst to von Choltitz or the Allies, the Paris Resistance was putting the finishing touches on its plan for the city to liberate itself. At noon on August 15, a police strike commenced. All but three hundred of the city's twenty thousand officers went off duty. The strikers returned during the night three days later, dressed in civilian clothes and armed. They stormed the Préfecture, Paris police headquarters, on the Île-de-la-Cité in the middle of the Seine.

Shortly afterward, vehicles of all sorts streamed into the city. Tiny sports cars, stolen German staff cars, ancient taxis, trucks, and ambulances were all loaded with armed Resistance members. They attacked the German strongholds all over Paris in a scene reminiscent of the French Revolution of 1789. Their weapon of choice was the bottle grenade, made from emptied wine bottles and an incredible cache of gasoline that had been secreted away in anticipation of this day. Mixing the fuel with sulfuric acid, the Resistance hurled their homemade weapons at the Nazis with blazing revenge.

Following Hitler's orders, von Choltitz had his men lay charges for the destruction of Paris's monuments and bridges. But he had no stomach to obliterate one of the world's most beautiful cities. From his headquarters in the Hôtel Meurice, he silently implored the Allies to hurry. Surrendering was far more preferable to the odious task Hitler had charged him with. At 9:30 AM on August 23, General de Gaulle's troops entered the city, fighting their way to its heart. The Americans entered on the twenty-fifth and by noon the *tricolore* was once again flying over the Eiffel Tower.

Von Choltitz knew that he was powerless to stop the Allies. Fighting was ensuing in the Luxembourg Gardens, in front of Les Invalides, which houses Napoleon's tomb, around the Louvre museum, and the Notre-Dame cathedral. Shortly after 1:00 PM, he surrendered and Paris was once again free.

17

DEATH OF THE WOLF

AUGUST 26, 1944, was a glorious summer day. As dawn broke over the mountains and ridges of the Yssingeaux Plateau, it cast a yellow light on the lavender-colored rocks of the landscape. First on Virginia's agenda was to help JEREMY's radio operator, Sergeant Leney, notify London that they were safe. The other two JED team members, Captains Hallowes and Guise, went to Le Puy, twenty-five miles away, to familiarize themselves with the German strength there. Two members of Lieutenant Bob's Maquis accompanied them.

When they returned to Le Chambon two hours later, Virginia witnessed the most phenomenal sight she had seen yet in the war. Hallowes and one of the maquisards climbed out of the car in the company of Le Puy's German commandant. Hallowes said he wanted to surrender the city. Virginia was incredulous, thinking he meant the entire General Staff. Hallowes told her the General Staff was nowhere to be found, but that the commandant had a sizable number of officers and enlisted men he was surrendering.

A number of these new prisoners were Russian Tartars who had been conscripted into the German army and trained as executioners for terror raids on civilian communities. Hallowes said they had learned that the Nazi command had even discussed a possible massacre in Le Chambon. Now the Tartars were offering to change sides, claiming they'd been forced into the German army.

Captain Guise and the other maquisard were holding the rest of the Nazi officers at their headquarters, Hallowes told Virginia. They had contacted the Maquis in Le Puy for additional help in guarding them. His plan was to put the Germans in the barracks just outside of Le Puy until the Allied forces arrived. And he was impressed with the town's Resistance forces.

Virginia cautioned him about singing the praises of Le Puy's Resistance too quickly, as most of them were majors. Hallowes didn't understand so Virginia explained. They were called "majors" because they were major pains in the ass. Most of them hadn't so much as breathed a word of Resistance since the debacle of 1940. Now that the Allies had made good on their promises, these people were taking their uniforms out of mothballs and claiming they had been part of the Resistance all along.

It was a situation repeating itself all over France. Suddenly the Resistance ranks were swelling to ten times what they had been, and the growth was timed to coincide with the Allies' sweep across the country. Some of these people had actually been overt collaborators. The rest had collaborated in the sense that they had stood by and done nothing as their country was ravaged and their fellow citizens were beaten and killed.

The French were dealing with their traitors without mercy. Those men whose collaboration had been witnessed were being handled by the Maquis, mostly in the form of executions. In addition, the Maquis, along with the townsfolk, spat upon, stoned, and sometimes tarred and feathered the female collaborators. Even moving to another locale where their actions might not have been known was useless, as all of them were publicly sheared of their hair. Their bald heads were a visible testament of their treacherous activities, one that begged for mistreatment by all who had fought against the Nazis, rather than lie down with them.

WITH THE AREA'S MAQUISARDS now numbering over fifteen hundred, Virginia and Hallowes had decided to break them into smaller groups of one hundred and fifty men. These groups would be under commanders who would take orders from Supreme Allied Headquarters via Virginia, Hallowes, and Guise. What they needed now were vehicles and fuel. Since Hallowes and Guise had had such success during their foray to Le Puy on September 1, they decided to see what could be done about the town of Saint-Étienne, fifty miles from Le Chambon and still very much in German hands. When they returned they reported that Saint-Étienne had plenty of fuel, but it was heavily guarded. The group decided a diversion was necessary. They would create a ruckus and when the Germans responded to it, they would steal the gas.

As Virginia was continuing to receive supply drops from London, their arms stores were fairly complete. Two days later, they dispatched a truck to Saint-Étienne armed to the teeth with all manner of weapons and a dozen maquisards. As the truck neared the German garrison there, the men began shooting into the air. The Germans scrambled to their vehicles and the Frenchmen took off, flying down a maze of familiar country roads. Meanwhile, a second heavily armed truck arrived at the garrison in Saint-Étienne. The remaining Germans were held at bay with automatic weapons while the maquisards filled their empty gas cans. It was almost as easy as a prewar trip to the filling station.

That group returned to the Yssingeaux Plateau with their loaded fuel cans, meeting up with the first truck, which was also successful in eluding its pursuers. They hadn't helped themselves to any new vehicles, but it appeared to Hallowes and Guise that small groups could return in the dark to pick up vehicles.

After that, the tasks of the Resistance in the Yssingeaux Plateau would become a little easier. The groups went to work stopping fresh German troops advancing to the western front, as well as those retreating to their homeland. The German retreat was an ironic twist of fate, as the Nazis were now withdrawing in the same manner they had forced the French to flee in 1940. The retreating Germans had no vehicles, so they commandeered bicycles, prams, and carts of all sorts from French citizens to move their supplies. The scene of these retreats was made all the more macabre by the decaying carcasses of German cavalry horses that had either died in the fighting or been ridden to death and were now clogging the Germans' paths. Meanwhile the Resistance continued to take the Germans prisoner wherever it could. For all intents and purposes, the Yssingeaux Plateau, indeed the entire department, was liberated from its vile occupiers.

Virginia was looking ahead as her work in France was drawing to a close. Between July 14 and August 14, she had transmitted thirty-seven messages to London with vital information. She had organized and received twenty-two parachute drops and directed innumerable acts of sabotage. Her group was responsible for killing over 170 Germans and capturing 800 more. And she had laid the groundwork for the JED team, which was now able to take her Maquis to other areas in need of assistance. All in all, it had been a tidy operation.

On the night of September 4, Virginia received instructions to expect two men to parachute to a drop zone near Villelonge. She and her reception committee went to the chosen field, where she tried in vain to signal the incoming plane from her radio. The aircraft sailed over the field. Minutes later, they saw chutes opening against the night sky, about fifteen miles away. Virginia was furious about yet another example of ineptness, this one made worse by the fact it was human life, and not just matériel, which was off target. She later wrote in her report to London, "I find American planes abominable, nonchalant, and careless in their work."

The reception committee scrambled to their vehicles and raced off in the direction they guessed the men might arrive. But driving around in the dark with no lights was dangerous. They risked injury and possibly death either from a leftover German bullet, a wayward cow, or badly placed tree. Despite the area's near-liberation, there was always the possibility of a few Nazis left wandering about. And there were members of the Milice still looking for revenge as well. Virginia determined not to risk the safety of her men or herself, deciding to try to locate the new arrivals in the morning.

Meanwhile, not knowing where they were, the two newcomers were busy burying their chutes and flight suits. Lieutenant Henry Riley from Connecticut, and Lieutenant Paul Goillot from New York, spent the rest of the night searching for the five containers that had been dropped with them. They located three out of the five. During the next two hours, they tried to figure out how best to approach farms for directions, since they weren't convinced that the area was free of the enemy. They certainly didn't want to walk into a trap just hours after their arrival.

As the sun rose, Goillot and Riley cautiously made their way to Mme Roussier's bicycle shop in Le Chambon. They had been told that from here they could contact Virginia. Mme Roussier sent for Dédé, who confirmed their identity. He told the two men that Virginia was currently out, but that they would be able to find her at her house that afternoon. They arrived later in the day, but she was in the middle of her radio sked, so it wasn't until suppertime at Mme Lebrat's that the three of them finally got the chance to meet.

Virginia liked the two men as soon as she met them, especially Lieutenant Goillot. He was inches shorter than she was, but powerfully built and very spry. And his humorous account of the arrival the night before had everyone in hysterics during their meal. They had brought two million francs with them and several messages for Virginia. She brought them up to speed on the situation in the Yssingeaux Plateau with three words: it was over. Everything was over. There were no Germans in the district. They had armed three battalions of Maquis who were now under the tactical supervision of the JED team. Reception fields and committees had been chosen for any further drops. In short, Goillot and Riley were too late.

But Goillot insisted that the war wasn't over. Wherever Virginia was going next, he said, they would volunteer to go with her. Ironically, Virginia had been thinking of heading north to Alsace. Dédé was from there, and she had heard there was still a lot of work to be done in the area.

The next day, the three of them discussed the move with Lieutenant Bob, who put sixteen of his men at their disposal. While Goillot and Riley gave Lieutenant Bob's men advance training in small weapons and guerilla tactics, Virginia took inventory of available vehicles, weapons, and food. By the end of the day they had a completely mobilized, self-contained unit. But the following day, much to their chagrin, they received a cable from London forbidding their self-devised mission. Rather, they were told to remain on the plateau to receive an incoming shipment of arms and a French lieutenant.

They waited the entire night of September 8, but no plane arrived. They received word on September 11 that the drop would occur that night, so again they trooped out to the field. As had happened with Goillot and Riley's arrival, the drop was way off target, infuriating Virginia. When they finally collected the containers, Virginia began to inventory the contents in a thorough and organized manner. She explained that she never wanted anyone to say she wasn't responsible for the money or goods sent to her, especially on her *last* reception.

Cabin fever had reached a peak in Virginia. She was determined to move on to a place where she could be of use. On September 13, she left the Yssingeaux Plateau for the last time with Riley, Goillot, and Lieutenant Bob and his men. They made several stops in an attempt to find a unit that could use them. On the fourth day of what was beginning to feel like a scavenger hunt, they were told to go to the town of Bourges, where they would find an Allied command center and hopefully a new mission.

Upon their arrival, they were subjected to military bureaucracy and chain of command, being sent from one officer to another. After a day of chasing across the region, it became obvious to them that no mission would materialize here either.

But there was a bright spot. During their travels, Riley spotted a château that appeared to be deserted. The group returned there in the late afternoon and found that it was, indeed, uninhabited. Much of the furniture was missing, but the beautiful frescoed walls were intact, as was the sweeping staircase to the second floor. They hauled in their food and gear, and prepared for another night of wartime monotony. But on a tour of the château, Virginia and Goillot found a passageway that led to a hidden wine cellar, untouched by the hatred and death that had raged above.

It might have been considered by some as stealing. But for Virginia and these men, availing themselves of this nectar of the grape was a reward for years of grueling work. They ate and drank and told stories and laughed well into the night. And the fine wine and beautiful surroundings made them all feel normal again, almost as if the war never really happened.

The next morning, along with hangovers, came reality. There was really nothing more for them to do as a group. Lieutenant Bob released his men, with the option of returning home, joining the FFI, or entering the regular army headquartered nearby. He, along with men who wished to enter the army, went with Riley to meet their new commander. The remaining men went in the opposite direction toward Le Chambon, leaving Virginia and Goillot at the château.

Virginia's feelings for Goillot surprised her. He made her laugh, something she hadn't done with such freedom in a long time. And he made her feel as though there were nothing he would rather do than be in her company, with no strings attached. Although she had met many fine men and women during the past four years, her relationship with all of them had always been connected to her missions. She was either a leader or a subordinate, either someone in need, or someone being asked to provide. She had never deviated from the cardinal rule of an undercover agent: keep distance between you and all others, and never get involved.

Throughout the day and into the night they talked about their families and their lives. Goillot had been born in Paris in 1914, making him eight years her junior. He had one sibling, a younger sister named Jacqueline. The family had moved to New York City in 1928, but decided to return to France in 1935. Since Goillot was twenty-one at the time, and had a job and a room in a boarding house, he chose to remain in the United States. He hadn't seen his family in nine years, he told Virginia, although he had heard bits and pieces of news from or about them. He was anxious to get to Paris to see them with his own eyes.

Virginia told Goillot about her past hopes for a position in the Foreign Service, glossed over her accident, and gave him the highlights of her experiences in the war. By the time Riley returned the next morning, she and Goillot had decided that their next destination should be Paris so that he could contact his family. The American headquarters of the European Theater of Operations was now set up in the city and they could all report there for further instructions.

WHEN THEY ARRIVED ON THURSDAY, September 22, Virginia saw that Paris had once again changed. While there was still evidence that the city had been at war, the Parisians had come out of their cocoons like butterflies. The sidewalk cafés were overflowing and people laughed as they strolled the streets. Almost all of the reminders that the Nazis had made the city their own for four years were gone.

Virginia, Goillot, and Riley reported to Supreme Allied Command Headquarters. They were lodged in one of the hotels the Americans were using to house officers in transition, given leave for the next two days, and told to report back the morning of the twenty-fifth.

Virginia suggested that maybe Goillot would like to see his family alone, but he insisted that she and Riley accompany him. They found his mother and sister still living in the apartment they had had before the war. The reunion was joyous, with a great deal of kissing and crying. When Goillot composed himself enough to ask where his father was, the scene turned far more somber. Papa had died the year before, his sister told him. The stress of war and malnutrition caused him to fall ill and he never recovered.

Virginia and Riley made their exit, telling Goillot they would contact him the next day. Virginia struck out on her own, taking in some of the things that made Paris beautiful: the gently flowing Seine, the parks, and the cafés. The next morning, Goillot appeared at the hotel, inviting her to his family's home for lunch. His mother, he said, was anxious to get to know her better. And that first meal turned into several more invitations to spend time with them.

On September 25, Virginia, Goillot, and Riley went together to headquarters. Waiting for them was a memorandum listing nineteen officers, including Goillot and Riley, seven enlisted men and two civilians, including Virginia. They were all ordered back to London, where they would be issued further orders. In light of his family situation, Goillot requested and was granted an additional week's leave. The next morning, Virginia and Riley boarded a military aircraft bound for London. Goillot would join them on October 1.

On September 23, 1944, Mrs. Hall received another of Mrs. Norris's letters from London. The letter informed Virginia's concerned mother, "It is not unreasonable to suppose that Virginia will soon be returning home." Virginia and the OSS, however, had other ideas.

AS SEPTEMBER BECAME OCTOBER, while Virginia was finishing up her operation in France and being debriefed by OSS officials in London, a crack began to develop in the Third Reich's stranglehold on the European continent. And that crack was widening every day. The major ports along the English Channel were vital to the Allies and their supply lines and became priorities for liberation. Shortly after D-Day, Hitler had ordered the major cities to be held as fortresses, to be defended at all costs. He knew that losing them would mean an unlimited supply chain from Britain to feed the Allies' advance. Hitler's fears were realized. On September 12, the Allies took Le Havre, and Boulogne and Calais were won on September 30.

Only Dunkirk remained in Nazi hands, and that was a problem that would affect the Allies' race to the German border. Without the use of the port at Dunkirk, British General Montgomery and American General Patton, each keen to reach Berlin before the other, were forced to rely on a long supply from the Normandy beaches. They had to share the limited provisions, slowing their respective advances.

Montgomery's strategy was to break into Germany through Holland. To that end, the British had already entered the country at Antwerp and Maastricht. Patton, meanwhile, was rushing toward the Siegfried Line. He and his Third Army had chewed up turf across Normandy, played a part in the liberation of Paris, entered Brussels on September 3, and freed Luxembourg on September 15. They went on to cover six hundred more miles of France in two weeks' time.

In the meantime, after one of the bloodiest campaigns of the war, the Russians had pushed the Germans out of their country. In September, the Soviet troops entered Bulgaria and Romania, reached the Yugoslav border, and entered the Warsaw suburbs. And to the south, Allied troops were fighting their way through Italy, liberating Florence and Pisa by the end of September. But from the "Wolf's Lair"—the Third Reich's headquarters buried deep in the east Prussian forests—Hitler could not or would not admit that his cause was lost. Rather he devised a massive counterattack against the Allies. Contrary to the advice of most of his top generals, the Führer's plan was to send Panzer tank divisions and infantry bursting through the Ardennes Forest in Belgium. He reasoned that the surprise attack would cut the Allied forces in two at their weakest point.

Hitler's offensive was launched at five-thirty in the morning on December 16, 1944. The Allies' immediate defense was minimal. The fierce winter weather grounded Allied planes and restricted observation and led to serious losses. But the Allies began to regroup and by the nineteenth, were engaged in a vicious fight. Territories changed hands so frequently that at times no one, including local townspeople, knew which side held what ground.

By the time it ended on January 16, 1945, the Battle of the Bulge had involved more than a million men: 600,000 Germans, 500,000 Americans, and 55,000 British. The casualty list was horrific. Nineteen thousand Americans died, and 81,000 wounded; 200 British were killed, with 1,400 wounded; and 120,000 Germans were either killed, wounded, or captured. The bloody start to 1945 had hardly changed a thing in terms of Allied-held territories. And it made the point that the Nazis were not to be underestimated in what they were willing to risk to reoccupy Europe. Still, the clock was ticking. The last hundred days of the Third Reich had begun.

IT WAS OBVIOUS TO VIRGINIA that there was still a great deal to be done to free the long-suffering Europeans from Adolph Hitler. The job she had undertaken when she joined the SOE in 1941 was not completed, and she wouldn't entertain thoughts about returning to the United States until it was.

From information and conversations at the OSS London headquarters, Virginia was gradually building a picture of what the Allies next expected out of the Germans, particularly the SS and those with an undying allegiance to Hitler. They would most probably relocate to Austria and Bavaria. That would put them geographically closer to the Führer and better enable them to plan their future.

London knew that the terrain was tough. Trying to move men and weapons through it could prove a disaster. The military command believed it was a far better idea to enlist the aid of Resistance members, which had been in contact with the Allies. They would be armed just as the French Resistance had been and could work against the Nazis from within.

The OSS staff saw Virginia as perfect for this operation. She had gone to school in Vienna, and knew the language. She had proven herself to be an excellent organizer and leader on her missions to France. And she was available, anxiously awaiting her next assignment. So, on December 19, 1944, Virginia transferred from the Western European Section of OSS to the Central European Section. Virginia's only request was that Goillot accompany her on the mission. A week later, the two of them left London for Italy, where they would organize their clandestine entrance into Austria.

As soon as she landed at the Naples airport, Virginia could see that war had devastated Italy much as it had France. Many of its beautiful buildings lay in ruin; its bucolic countryside was pocked from falling bombs; its people, although liberated, were still struggling with all they had lost.

The Allies' Italian campaign, conducted at the same time as their sweep through France, had involved some of the hardest fighting in the war, costing the United States forces alone more than 114,000 casualties. But the sacrifice was not in vain. The Allies, with a minimum of strength, had been able to engage German forces in Italy that otherwise might have upset the balance in France.

Virginia and Goillot traveled by jeep from Naples to Caserta, a city seventeen miles to the north. There, at the ancient Palace of the Kings, the Allied Military Forces had established their Italian headquarters. The OSS Mediterranean Theater staff was headquartered there as well, under the command of Colonel Edward Glavin. But Virginia and Goillot reported to the man in charge of Special Operations, former Philadelphia banker William Davis, Jr. He had been on board with the OSS since the beginning, and most recently had done a masterful job in coordinating the conflicting French secret service factions in North Africa.

Davis briefed Virginia and Goillot on their mission, code-named FAIR-MONT. The objective was to organize the Austrian underground. They would be limited in the amount of matériel available, so their goal was to look for individuals of quality, not amassing a quantity. They would be based in the Innsbrück region. Once organized, their first duty would be day-to-day sabotage. No specific targets were given, but OSS did have some priorities in class of targets, namely the German air force, fuel, and oil repositories and enemy communications.

Virginia would be the radio operator for the group. Davis told her he'd heard about her exemplary job in France, but regulations required him to put her through a two-day radio school there nonetheless, followed by a day of practice over in Bari, not far from Caserta. The school would begin on January 19. Her field name would be Camille, cover name Anna Möller. Her story was that she was born in Turkey and was a German citizen, now working for the Sicherheitsdienst. Goillot's field name would be Henri. Since he would remain undercover with the Resistance and didn't speak German, he wouldn't receive a cover story.

WHILE VIRGINIA AND GOILLOT were in Italy preparing for their next mission, unusual bedfellows were being united not far away. Allen Dulles, the senior OSS officer in Switzerland, had been contacted by Nazi General Karl Wolff, a well-connected officer who commanded the SS and Gestapo in Italy. The result of their negotiations became known as Operation SUNRISE.

Wolff and other Nazi leaders were seeking amnesty and escape for themselves and an extensive roster of SS and Gestapo personnel. Furthermore, they were hoping to take along the booty that they had collected during the war: gold, cash, precious jewelry, artwork, and antiques, most of which had belonged to those who had fallen victim to the Final Solution. On the surface, this seemed a preposterous proposal. But in exchange, Wolff had a priceless offer.

Up to this point, Allied leaders had been greatly concerned about Joseph Stalin's postwar plans. They were certain he would continue to foster the spread of Communism across Europe. And they were without a useful deterrent. Enter General Wolff. He and his Nazi cohorts would shift their allegiance to the West and would arrange for an army of some 5,000 anti-Communists of Eastern European and Russian descent. After espionage training at a camp called *Oberammergau*, the army of spies would cover Europe, undertaking a covert battle against Communism. This secret war would come to be known as the "Cold War."

The offer was more than Dulles and the Allied leaders could pass up and Operation SUNRISE commenced. The Nazis, all of whom were war criminals, fled Europe via "ratlines," operated by the Vatican. Thousands escaped, destined for South and Central America. Their numbers included Franz Stangl, commandant of Treblinka, the extermination camp; Gustav Wagner, commandant of the death camp Sobibor; Adolf Eichmann, Holocaust architect; Dr. Joseph Mengele, the "white angel" who performed horrific experiments on inmates at the death camp Auschwitz; and Klaus Barbie, the "Butcher of Lyon."

BY THE TIME VIRGINIA AND GOILLOT were allowed to proceed to the field, it was April 10, 1945. They caught a plane from Caserta to Marseille and then flew to Lyon. There was no time for Virginia to check on her friends, but she promised herself it would be high on her priority list of things to do once the war was over.

From Lyon, a car took them up to Annemasse on the Swiss border. Virginia would cross into Switzerland the next evening and then into Austria the following night. Once she was established, Goillot would parachute in to join her. But as she was preparing to leave the next day, they were told Virginia's border crossing had been delayed. They were sent to the town of Annecy, thirty-four miles away, to wait.

A few days later, word came that their original mission had fallen through, but another opportunity had arisen, to which they agreed without delay. Virginia was already frustrated from having been inactive for so long, but the waiting continued. It wasn't until April 25 that they were finally able to move on to Switzerland, checking into a hotel in Zürich.

During the next six days, they perfected their plans for crossing into Austria, taking shelter in an abandoned mine, and zeroing in on sabotage targets. They collected equipment and arms for the ten men they would take in with them on the night of May 2. To kill time, they even spent two days cleaning their cache of grease-caked automatics and carbines to ensure that the weapons would perform when needed. But at six-thirty on the evening of their planned departure, they received a cable from headquarters in Caserta: "IN VIEW RAPID DEVELOPMENTS MILITARY SITUATION BELIEVED POINTLESS RISK LIVES OF DIANE, HENRI AND GROUP. CANCEL PLANS AND HOLD DIANE AND HENRI PENDING FURTHER WORD."

BY THE SPRING OF 1945, the war had caused millions to lose their lives, some because it was their duty, some because they were persecuted by hatred, and some because an act of fate put them in harm's way. On April 12, the war claimed one of the world's most powerful men. President Roosevelt's health had been in decline for about a year. The stress of his position and the difficult decisions he was forced to make on a daily basis were no doubt contributors to that fact. While visiting Warm Springs, Georgia, the president died of a cerebral hemorrhage. Vice President Harry S. Truman, who had only been inside the White House on two previous occasions, was sworn into office, inheriting a world at war.

Two and a half weeks later, on April 29, Adolf Hitler married his mistress, Eva Braun. He wrote out a will naming Martin Bormann as his deputy and Grand Admiral Karl Doenitz as president of the Reich and commander in chief of the armed forces. The next afternoon, the new Mrs. Hitler swallowed a cyanide capsule and was dead within minutes. Adolph Hitler followed her in death after shooting himself in the mouth.

Their deaths also sounded the death knell for the Third Reich. At 2:41 AM on May 7, in a modest schoolhouse in Rheims, France, Field Marshall Alfred Gustav Jodl signed an unconditional surrender. The war in Europe was over.

18

THE DAWN OF A NEW WORLD

"LA GUERRE EST FINIE!" proclaimed the headlines of the May 7 edition of the French newspaper *Le Monde*. Virginia and Goillot had returned to Paris on that day to find a city mad with elation at the news that the war was over.

The two had speculated about a German capitulation. The cancellation of their mission into Austria because of rapid developments in the military situation was their first clue. And tidbits of information gleaned from the OSS contact in Zürich further supported their guess. Virginia had met with him to return the money and radios she'd been entrusted with for their aborted mission.

Sheer *joie de vivre* blossomed all around them in Paris, even more so than the last time they had been there. Goillot once again was able to spend time with his mother and sister. And for the first time in a long while, Virginia relaxed, allowing herself six weeks in Paris to unwind from the pressure of five years of war. Total unproductivity was out of the question, of course, so she devoted time each day to writing various reports to OSS headquarters in Washington. She detailed the HECKLER mission, not just for the sake of fully reporting her work, but because she wanted the American government to realize how much the French had assisted her. Compensation for them, she said, should be considered a priority.

Virginia's report cataloged all of her supporters: Farmer Lopinat in Crozant, Colonel and Mme Vessereau in Cosne, Estelle Bertrand in Sury-près-Léré; and in Le Chambon, Mme Lebrat, Edmund and Maurice Lebrat, Dédé, Lieutenant Bob, and the others. They had given up their homes, shared their scanty food stores, and risked capture and death without ever asking for, or even thinking of, recompense. Their generosity and bravery deserved the utmost attention from Washington.

On June 17, Virginia made good on her promise to herself when she and Goillot were finally able to head to Lyon. She had no idea of what and whom they would find. They went first to Dr. Rousset's office. He answered the door himself, looking thin and tired, but smiling broadly when he saw Virginia, and told her the story of what had happened in the months after she left. All of them had been visited by the Gestapo at one time or another. At this news, the guilt that Virginia had managed to keep at bay for nearly three years flooded her emotions. She felt she had deserted them just when they needed her the most.

But Pep waved her off kindly. She did what she had to do. She knew too much and was too valuable. They were well aware of the risks they were taking, and they took them nonetheless. After the Gestapo had questioned him in Lyon, he continued, they sent him to Fresnes and then on to Buchenwald late in 1943.

The Nazis allowed him to work as a doctor there, and he managed to hide away more than 150 medical files on English and American prisoners. The men had been brought to Buchenwald after the Germans had caught them trying to escape. They were eventually turned over to the Gestapo and never returned. Rousset said he knew they'd be liberated one day, and when the Americans finally arrived, he took the files with him as his part to prove what had taken place.

Virginia and Goillot next went to the home of the Catins, who welcomed them effusively and told their story. After the Gestapo had beaten Mme Catin while trying to extract information, they sent her, too, to Fresnes and then to Ravensbrück women's prison. Finally she was shipped to a concentration camp in Czechoslovakia. The Americans had liberated the camp and she had only been home a short while. M. Catin had managed to avoid capture, and continued working with the Resistance. But when he finally returned to his flat, it had been picked clean by the Germans. There was no furniture, no clothing, no pots and pans, not even any eating utensils.

A visit to the Joulians was next. They told Virginia the same story of torture for information about the "Limping Lady" and the Resistance. And they returned from prison to nothing but bare walls and floors in both their home and factory. All of the machinery was gone, and with it, their means of earning a living.

The Germans had been through Mme Guérin's beautiful home, too, she told Virginia and Goillot when they arrived. They sent her to a prison camp, then stole her artwork, antique rugs, draperies, even the plumbing. But at least she had survived, she said. Her dear friend, M. Genet, had not been so lucky. The Gestapo beat and tortured him, and when he wouldn't give up any information, they loaded him into a cattle car with 150 other prisoners. A Resistance friend had seen him manacled, "his wrists and arms in tatters." He suffocated on the way to Buchenwald.

With each visit, Virginia's emotions became more and more jumbled. On the one hand, she was relieved to see that most of her dear and faithful friends had survived. But on the other hand, it broke her heart to hear what they had been through to protect her and the Resistance. And seeing the abject poverty they now faced was almost unbearable.

Next they went to the Labouriers' home. Monsieur was wearing a suit loaned to him by a friend who was apparently much shorter than he was. Madame wore a tattered blouse and a skirt made from the ticking she had taken off her mattress in the concentration camp. Their fleet of trucks had disappeared long before and, like their friends, they didn't have the money to replace them.

When they left Lyon, Virginia and Goillot traveled cross-country, picking up radios Virginia knew had been stashed throughout France. This part of the trip was difficult, too. France was a burned-out shell of her former self, filled with people without home or hope. Mile upon mile of landscape had been ravaged by the war. What the Germans had not stolen or destroyed before the Allies' arrival had been laid to waste in the fight for freedom.

Virginia saw conflicting emotions on the faces of the people. Their country had been liberated from the evil it had struggled against, yet more than two million of their compatriots were still straggling home from German POW, labor, and concentration camps. And those were the lucky ones.

Poverty was everywhere. As in Lyon, homes had been stripped of all useful items. The food shortage, a way of life under the Nazis, showed no sign of being relieved any time soon. Displaced persons wandered the roads. And of course, there were many scores to be settled, both judicially and privately.

Virginia and Goillot returned to Paris on Saturday morning, June 23, having traveled about a thousand miles. Virginia realized that no matter how much she might want to, she couldn't single-handedly help the entire nation. But she could urge SOE headquarters in London to help those who had unselfishly assisted her. They needed compensation for their devastating losses, she wrote. They had sacrificed everything, and deserved not only the highest praise, but help in starting their lives over as well.

Virginia wrote a long report about Abbé Ackuin, too, based on information she had gleaned from her friends in Lyon. Her instincts had been right on the money about him and there was no question in her mind that his treachery had triggered their arrests. She would have loved to get her hands on him, and she would have had no compunction about shooting him. But she knew a far worse fate would be for him to fall into the hands of Resistance members.

AT THE TIME VIRGINIA WAS WRITING her memorandum in Paris, Robert Alesh, alias Abbé Ackuin, was already in custody. Although his experiences since leaving Lyon in 1942 had been difficult, it would soon get worse now that he was in Allied hands.

Germany had had a number of intelligence organizations during the war, including the Abwehr, which hated the Gestapo. The feeling was mutual and the two zealously competed with one another. Alesh had been employed by the Abwehr. At about the same time the Gestapo was arresting Virginia's circuit members in Lyon in 1943, it also picked up Alesh in Paris. The Abwehr was incensed. It had planned to use Virginia's group as a source of information about Allied plans. Alesh had ingratiated himself with the group's members and his espionage work might have proven invaluable.

Furthermore, Alesh had intercepted and decoded many of Virginia's messages. He knew she suspected him, but he also knew a great deal about her circuit and its operations. Finally securing Alesh's release, the Abwehr continued to pay him until June 1944. It was then that the Germans departed from Paris, leaving Alesh in an ugly predicament. He had been responsible for the arrests and deaths of many Resistance members there, as well as in Lyon, and he knew the consequences he faced if any of their families or friends should find him. His only recourse was to leave the city and head home to Luxembourg. He began his journey by bicycle, but was stranded in Brussels amid the liberating Allied forces.

Ever resourceful, Alesh forged a letter from the Archbishop of Paris to a Belgian priest, detailing alleged mistreatment at the hands of the Germans.

He used the letter as his entrée to secure a job as a chaplain for refugees at a center in Brussels. He worked there from November 1944 to May 1945 when he was finally arrested by the Allies. After they finished interrogating him, they turned him over to French authorities. Although there were never any official documents to support the conjecture, the rumor that traveled in the Resistance circles was that the abbé had gotten precisely what he deserved—execution.

A MONTH EARLIER, ON MAY 12, 1945, a note to President Truman's secretary, Miss Rose Conway, had been delivered to the White House from General Donovan. It read, "Will you please hand the attached memorandum to the President?"

The memorandum announced that Virginia Hall had been awarded the Distinguished Service Cross. The DSC is a military decoration of the United States Army, which is awarded for "extreme gallantry and risk of life in actual combat with an armed enemy force. Actions which merit the Distinguished Service Cross must be of such a high degree as to be above those required for all other U.S. combat decorations," with the exception of the Congressional Medal of Honor. Donovan's memorandum spared no accolades:

> Miss Virginia Hall, an American civilian working for this agency in the European Theater of Operations, has been awarded the Distinguished Service Cross for extraordinary heroism in connection with military operations against the enemy.
>
> We understand that Miss Hall is the first civilian woman in this war to receive the DSC.
>
> Despite the fact that she was well known to the Gestapo, Miss Hall voluntarily returned to France in March 1944 to assist in sabotage operations against the Germans. Through her courage and physical endurance, even though she had previously lost a leg in an accident, Miss Hall, with two American officers, succeded in organizing, arming and training three FFI Battalions which took part in many engagements with the enemy and a number of acts of sabotage. . . . In addition Miss Hall provided radio communication between London Headquarters and the Resistance Forces in the Haute Loire Department. . . . This is the most dangerous type of work as the enemy, whenever two or

more direction finders could be tuned in on a transmitter, were able to locate the transmittal point to within a couple of hundred yards. It was frequently necessary for Miss Hall to change her headquarters in order to avoid detection.

Inasmuch as an award of this kind has not been previously made during the present war, you may wish to make the presentation personally.

Signed, William J. Donovan, Director

General Donovan's office contacted Virginia upon her return to Paris, to let her know that she had been awarded the DSC and that the president was most anxious to make the presentation himself. Virginia certainly didn't want to insult the president, but she was not the least bit interested in fanfare. She had been sent to Europe to perform a job, which she had done. Bestowing an award on her simply for doing her work was as ludicrous as giving one to the horse that pulled a milk cart. And receiving it at a public ceremony in the White House was out of the question. She had witnessed the effectiveness of an intelligence organization and was sure it would be something the government would continue to support, even if it was in a different form. She had every intention of being a part of that nascent organization and any future in espionage would be ruined for her if her photo was splashed across newspapers from coast to coast.

The Paris OSS office cabled General Donovan that Miss Hall

> feels very strongly that she should not receive any publicity or any announcement as to her award. Understand that at her request the British government made no publicity of an award [Member of the British Empire] she received from them. She states that she is still operational and most anxious to get busy. Any publicity would preclude her from going on any operation.

It was well known at OSS headquarters that it was far easier to agree with Virginia Hall than to argue with her. The presentation was delayed until Virginia's return to Washington, DC, on September 23. It was made privately four days later, by General Donovan in his office, with only Mrs. Hall witnessing her daughter's honor.

Although accolades had certainly not been the impetus for her work, Virginia discovered she had also been awarded the French Croix de guerre avec palme. Like the Member of the British Empire, and the Distiguished Service Cross, the Croix de guerre had first been created during World War I for "those individuals who distinguish themselves by acts of heroism involving combat with enemy forces." Virginia was gracious in receiving that award as well, although it was in absentia. But the awards were far less important to her than what she had seen as the result of coordinated intelligence work.

Virginia's ceremony in General Donovan's office was overshadowed by an executive order President Truman had issued the week before. The Office of Strategic Services had been offically disbanded. While Donovan's idea of a peacetime intelligence agency had appealed to President Roosevelt, his successor had no intention of creating an "American Gestapo." Furthermore, J. Edgar Hoover's FBI had long been jealous of another intelligence agency treading on its turf. Hoover had exercised his considerable influence over the president to discourage any competition for valuable governmental resources.

Effective at the close of business on September 28, Virignia's resignation from the OSS was officially filed. She was not about to close the door on her future, however, and she added her thoughts in the second paragraph of her resignation letter. "I am deeply interested in the future of intelligence work and would like to be considered in the event that an intelligence organization is established."

Virginia's next stop was Box Horn Farm, where she settled in with her mother for a little R & R. As she had held privileged information throughout the war, she was very close-mouthed about her experiences in Europe, even with her family. The OSS had recently issued documents giving former agents guidelines on acceptable disclosures. But Virginia was of the opinion that secret work should remain secret.

Shortly after her arrival home, Goillot visited her at Box Horn. He had left Paris after Virginia and resettled in New York City. Mrs. Hall was not impressed with the Frenchman when she met him. While she thought he was pleasant enough, she found it shocking that Virginia and Goillot made no secret of the fact that they had lived together while they were in Europe. Virginia was now thirty-nine, and Mrs. Hall thought it was high time she think about finding a husband. Her opinion of Goillot, however, was that he was well beneath the standards of the husband she had envisioned for her daughter.

With the future of intellligence up in the air, Virginia turned her thoughts once again to her prewar goal: a position within the Foreign Service. Certainly after all the skills she had aquired with the OSS, the State Department would recognize her value. She applied by letter on March 1, 1946.

Sirs:

You will find enclosed my application for appointment to the Foreign Service Auxiliary. It was suggested that I make this application as I was with the Foreign Service from 1931 to spring 1939, and during three years and a half in Venice worked at practically everything that is done in a consulate. . . . I would be grateful if you could inform me at your early convenience whether this application can be taken under consideration or not.

A response arrived just two weeks later.

My dear Miss Hall,

With reference to your application for an appointment in the Foreign Service Auxiliary, I am very sorry to inform you that a recent budgetary curtailment has forced the Department to suspend recruitment for the Auxiliary. In view of these circumstances, the Department regrets that it will not be possible to offer you an appointment.

Incredibly, after all of her experiences, it was yet another dead end in a long series from the State Department. But down the street in the nation's capital, the intelligence pot was still being stirred. President Truman had reconsidered his hasty dissolution of the OSS, and in January of 1946, he created the Central Intelligence Group.

The CIG was the brainchild of Admiral Leahy, the American ambassador to Vichy, whom Virginia had numerous meetings with during her time in Lyon. The agency's missions were to provide strategic warning and conduct clandestine activities. It functioned under the direction of a National

Intelligence Authority, which was composed of a residential representative and the secretaries of state, war, and navy.

Virginia was elated when she heard the news. This was an organization that would suit not only her interests, but her skills as well. She applied for a position and given her many contacts from her OSS days, including Admiral Leahy, she was soon hired as a "field representative." The downside was that the job would require her to travel, just as her relationship with Goillot was continuing to blossom. But the good-natured Goillot supported Virginia completely. He would remain in the United States and they could write one another and reunite as time and resources allowed.

Virginia spent all of 1947 in Europe, traveling between Italy, Switzerland, and France. As she had when she worked for SOE, she used journalism as her cover. But her real work was to collect economic, financial, and political intelligence on postwar Europe. She also reported on the Communist movements growing in Italy and Yugoslavia.

Virginia returned briefly to the United States in early 1948. The previous December, the CIG had been dissolved and the National Security Council was established. Under its auspices, a new organization was created, called the Central Intelligence Agency. Its job was to coordinate the nation's intelligence activities, as well as correlate, evaluate, and disseminate intelligence that might affect national security. Virginia joined many of her fellow OSS veterans transferring to the new agency, making her one of the CIA's first female agents. During the course of her work over the next two years, she continued to travel between New York and Europe, still using journalism as her cover and still in love with Paul Goillot.

The CIA brought Virginia back to the United States late in 1948 for a new assignment with one of its front organizations called the National Committee for a Free Europe. The organization was linked to Radio Free Europe. Goillot was still living in New York, so Virginia moved in with him. Her job was to interview incoming refugees and prepare radio propaganda to counteract the new threat facing Europe: Communism.

CHANGES WERE OCCURRING in the world of intelligence. The United States had been keeping an ever-watchful eye on Soviet chief Joseph Stalin, who, one observer noted, "made Hitler look like a Boy Scout." A war with the Soviet Union was a frightening possibility, as Communism was spreading throughout Eastern Europe. It had already overtaken China and half of the Korean peninsula. The latter had been arbitrarily divided at the end of World War II, and the two halves were now at war with one another. And in Washington, Senator Joseph McCarthy, having ruined the careers of some and the morale of all at the State Department with his accusations of Communist affiliation, was now ready to rip into the CIA. It was a new day in espionage, and it was time to replace field-hardened World War II veterans like Virginia with younger agents equipped to handle the challenges.

The CIA assigned Virginia a corner desk back at headquarters in Washington. It wasn't that her work for the agency wasn't appreciated—it was. She prepared clandestine "hot and cold" war plans for the Southern European Division and a political action plan for South Asia. In 1956, she became the first woman on the CIA's Career Staff, and later set up political and psychological projects in South America.

But what Virginia really wanted was to be an operative again, working in the field. She knew that was where her real strengths lay, and she was convinced that, as she had during World War II, she could make a difference in this new postwar world. She would have gladly undergone any training necessary to bring her up to speed, convinced as always that she could be as good as anyone.

The CIA saw it differently. Her skills were outdated, her aggressiveness offensive to the younger men who were her supervisors. And while new agents delighted in Virginia's stories of the war years, her experience was dismissed as not pertinent to the new era in intelligence. As a young, enthusiastic woman, she had tried to follow her dream into Foreign Service, only to run into a roadblock. Now at the end of her career, a similar obstacle arose. Once again Virginia Hall didn't fit in.

EPILOGUE

THE CASUALTY FIGURES of the European theater of World War II were staggering. As Virginia Hall did more than her share to free France of the Nazi choke hold, 340,000 French soldiers and sailors died around her. The country's civilian casualties, including the deaths of Resistance members, were 470,000. Seventy-five thousand French Jews died, while hundreds of thousands of Jews who had sought refuge in France were deported to camps, where many died as well.

But Hitler's genocide stretched beyond the Jews, whose deaths totaled more than six million. Polish Catholics, Soviet prisoners of war, the handicapped, homosexuals, gypsies, and Jehovah's Witnesses were also targets. The Nazi inhumanity to man resulted in 13,114,500 deaths.

The war involved twenty-one countries that suffered a total loss of 20,494,000 military personnel. In addition, 21,073,000 civilians perished, either as a result of the fighting or as a part of Hitler's Final Solution. The final death toll for the war was 41,567,000, a figure that exceeds the combined populations of the states of New York and Texas, according to the U.S. Census Bureau's 2003 Current Population Survey.

The Special Operations Executive sent a total of 480 agents into France to help organize the fight against the Nazis. Forty of those agents were women. Exactly 25 percent never came home; 15 of the 120 deaths were female.

The Office of Strategic Services didn't keep such accurate statistics. Over the course of the war, about thirty thousand men and women were employed by the agency, including support people stateside as well as agents in the field. While there is no conclusive total number of agents that were sent to France, it is known that at least thirty-seven were there in the agency's service. And Virginia was the only woman to operate her own réseau.

JUSTICE WAS DUE THE MEN who had engineered the bloodiest conflict the world had ever known. To that end, the European war criminals were tried in Nuremberg, Germany, a city that had suffered massive bombing in the closing days of the war. During Hitler's glory years, the city had been the site of the annual Reichsparteitage, rallies celebrating the Nazi party. It was only fitting, then, that the party's demise should take place there as well.

On November 20, 1945, twenty-four former Nazis were brought to trial before an international tribunal. Their charges were crimes against humanity. The presiding tribunal handed down verdicts almost a year later, on October 1, 1946. Twelve men were sentenced to death, two of whom committed suicide before their executions. Three men received life sentences. Three more were mentally unfit, and the rest received prison sentences varying from ten to twenty years.

The French dealt with their traitors themselves. De Gaulle's new French government arrested Henri Pétain in April of 1945 and charged him with treason. He was sentenced to death, a sentence that was later commuted to life imprisonment, given his advanced age. He died behind bars on July 23, 1951, at the age of ninety-five. Pierre Laval, Vichy's premier, fled to Spain at the end of the war, only to be captured there in May 1945. After the French government got its hands on him on July 30, he was shot by a firing squad at Fresnes Prison outside Paris.

Tried as a collaborator in 1949, René Bousquet, Vichy's chief of police and the architect of the massive Jewish roundup at the Vélodrome d'Hiver, received a suspended sentence as a reward for alleged acts of resistance. An investigation of his wartime activities was resumed and a second trial was to begin in the fall of 1993. The trial never took place, as Bousquet was murdered in June of that year. His murderer claimed he was "the good" sent to destroy "the evil."

Joseph Darnand, leader of the deadly Milice, fled to Germany after the Allies landed in Normandy. Captured there at the end of the war and returned to France, he was tried and executed in 1945.

Postwar research attributes Klaus Barbie as being ultimately responsible for the arrest and torture of 14,311 Resistance members, the deportation of 7,500 people, and the murder of 4,342. At the war's end, however, the

American and British intelligence agencies protected and employed him. His police skills were of use in repressing the leftist resistance to the Allied occupation of Germany after the war.

No longer needed in 1955, he and his family escaped to Bolivia, where Nazi hunters found him in 1983 and had him extradited to France. Ironically, the same man who murdered Bousquet tried to kill Barbie before he could stand trial, but was unsuccessful. Barbie went to trial in Lyon for crimes against humanity and was found guilty in 1987. Sentenced to life imprisonment, the "Butcher of Lyon" died of leukemia in the prison hospital at Lyon on September 25, 1991.

IN LIGHT OF THEIR ACTS OF BRAVERY during the war, it is often difficult to imagine the mortality of the unique, and often mysterious, individuals Virginia met during her career with the SOE and the OSS. And while some were easier to get along with than others, they all made sacrifices in the name of freedom.

Tall, handsome, Cardiff-born Jacques de Guélis was thirty-four when he and Virginia first met in London in 1941. After his initial trip to France in advance of Virginia's arrival, de Guélis parachuted twice more into occupied Europe, landing in Corsica in 1942 and again in France after D-Day. He was still clearing Germany of Nazis on May 16, 1945, when he was involved in a motor accident. He died of his injuries three months later on August 7.

The de Vomécourt brothers willingly sacrificed a great deal for their homeland, as did many who Virginia came in contact with. While the youngest brother, Philippe, managed to escape capture, Pierre's imprisonment following his capture in 1942 continued until the war's end. He was liberated from Colditz in Germany in 1945 by the Americans. Their elder brother Jean was not as lucky. Also captured, he was sent via cattle car to a concentration camp in Germany. Like most prisoners, he was most probably kicked, beaten, starved, and tortured, all of which he survived. Even tuberculosis, which he contracted in camp, could not knock him down. Once recovered, he was made senior orderly at the camp hospital, a position he maintained until it became evident that the Russians' arrival was eminent in their sweep through Germany. The Nazis chose to liquidate all who had witnessed their brutality and Jean was executed along with the other prisoners.

Peter Churchill was thirty-three when he first landed on the shores of occupied France in 1942, just weeks before his first meeting with Virginia.

After his arrest by the Abwehr, and his imprisonment, along with that of his courier, Odette Sansom, in Fresnes Prison outside of Paris, he was sent to a German prison camp. He survived the ordeal, as did she, and they married in 1945, only to divorce in 1955. Churchill wrote four memoirs about his experiences during the war and died in 1972.

At the time of his death, Churchill was just one year older then Aramis was when he met Virginia in 1944. Aramis was sixty-two at the time, the oldest agent the OSS ever sent to the field. His real name was Henry Laussucq and he was a commercial artist from Pittsburgh. Laussucq's official debriefing is rather huffy in several spots. Regarding Virginia's move from Lopinat's farm to the town of Cosne, he says she "then went to a farm a few miles from there but *did not* disclose her address to me." Further in the report he states that she contacted him through their "cut out" (an intermediary) that she was moving again and that he would "surely hear from somebody somehow, *which I never did.*"

After the war ended, he gave an interview to a United Press writer, to whom he told that he "was accompanied into France by a young woman radio operator, still identified only as 'Diane' who later disappeared." He described a variety of adventures that culminated in his holding off the Germans in the Paris Hôtel de Ville, the city hall, along with three other Resistance members. They possessed stolen Vichy police files that ultimately helped in the liberation of Paris.

Laussucq returned to London on September 11, 1944, and from there, made his way to the United States. He died in Schenectady, New York, in 1975 at the age of ninety-three.

Lieutenant Bob was surprisingly young when he and Virginia met in Le Chambon in 1944. Bob was only twenty-four, yet his air of maturity enabled him to lead Maquis groups skillfully. He spoke glibly about the auto accident in May 1943 in Lyon, and of his hospitalization, near arrest, and escape. Bob's story lacked the fact that it was the second time he had suffered a head injury, the first coming as the result of parachute training prior to dropping into France. The final details are sketchy, but reports show that he checked into a Paris hospital on February 4, 1946, and died two weeks later at the age of twenty-five.

THE "LIMPING LADY" quietly became Virginia Hall Goillot in a judge's chambers in 1950. She was forty-four years old. Mrs. Hall had managed to overcome her image of Goillot as not worthy of her daughter, and when she was told about the marriage, offered the opinion that it was about time. It mattered little to the bride and groom, who were content in their lives. Virginia's mother died in 1956.

Shortly after their marriage, while Virginia was still employed by the CIA, Goillot tried his hand as a restaurateur. But when the business didn't go as planned, he happily settled in as a househusband.

When Virginia retired from the CIA in 1966, at the mandatory age of sixty, she and Goillot moved to a farm in Barnestown, Maryland, sharing their home with five French poodles. To keep herself busy, she gardened, worked on a hand loom, read avidly, was addicted to crossword puzzles, and even reprised her knack for making French cheese. They grew old together, in love until her death on July 12, 1982. Goillot died five years later.

Virginia was never bitter about the fact that her career hadn't begun or ended as she would have liked. Rather, she chose to remember the magnificent days in the middle, the days when her clever mind and brave heart helped defeat Fascists bent on world domination. It was the excitement of those days that she loved to recall, never alluding to the impressive list of accolades she had accumulated for her daring. Virginia had never developed a taste for them, making that very plain in her final report to the OSS. She was asked if she had been decorated in the field. Her answer, pragmatic as always, was, "No, nor was there any reason for me to be."

BIBLIOGRAPHY

BOOKS

Binney, Marcus. *The Women Who Lived for Danger: the Women Agents of SOE in the Second World War.* London: Hodder and Stoughton, 2002.

Bolle, Pierre. *Le Plateau Vivarais-Lignon; Accueil et Résistance, 1939–1944.* Le Chambon-sur-Lignon: Société d'Histoire de la Montagne, 1992.

Churchill, Peter. *Duel of Wits.* New York: G. P. Putnam's Sons, 1953.

Churchill, Peter. *Of Their Own Choice.* London: Hodder and Stoughton, 1952.

Dear, Ian. *Sabotage and Subversion: the SOE and OSS at War.* London: Cassell Military Paperbacks, 1999.

Défourneaux, Réné. *The Winking Fox: Twenty-two Years in Military Intelligence.* Indianapolis: Indiana Creative Arts, 1997.

De Vomécourt, Philippe. *Les Artisans de la Liberté.* Paris: Imprimerie Mordacq, 1975.

Fayol, Pierre. *Le Chambon-sur-Lignon sous l'occupation: les Résistance Locales, l'aide Interallié, l'action de Virginia Hall (OSS).* Paris: Edition l'Harmattan, 1990.

Fischer, Klaus P. *Nazi Germany.* New York: Barnes & Noble Books, 1995.

Foot, M.R.D. *SOE in France.* London: Her Majesty's Stationary Office, 1966.

Gildea, Robert. *Marianne in Chains: Daily Life in the Heart of France During the German Occupation.* Henry Holt & Company, 2003.

Haines, Gerald. "Virginia Hall Goillot: Career Intelligence Officer," *Prologue*, Winter 1994, pp. 249–260.

Jackson, Julian. *France: the Dark Years, 1940–1944*. Oxford: Oxford University Press, 2001.

Keegan, John, editor. *Atlas of the Second World War*. London: Harper Collins, 1998.

Landau, Elaine. *Nazi War Criminals*. New York: Franklin Watts, 1990.

Marino, Andy. *A Quiet American: The Secret War of Varian Fry*. New York: St. Martin's Press, 1999.

McCullough, David G., editor. *American Heritage Picture History of World War II*. New York: American Heritage Publishing Co., Inc., 1966.

McIntosh, Elizabeth P. *Sisterhood of Spies: the Women of the OSS*. New York: Dell Publishing, 1998.

Miller, Francis Trevelyan, editor. *The Complete History of World War II*. Chicago: Readers' Service Bureau, 1947.

Moon, Tom. *This Grim and Savage Game*. Philadelphia: DaCapo Press Edition, 1991.

Rossiter, Margaret. *Women in the Resistance*. New York: Praeger, 1991.

Ruby, Marcel. *F Section, SOE: the Buckmaster Networks*. London: Leo Cooper Ltd., 1988.

Ryan, Cornelius. *The Longest Day: the Classic Epic of D-Day*. New York: Touchstone, 1959.

Seaman, Mark. *Secret Agent's Handbook: the WWII Spy Manual of Devices, Disguises, Gadgets, and Concealed Weapons*. Guilford: The Lyons Press, 2001.

Smith, R. Harris. *OSS: the Secret History of America's First Central Intelligence Agency*. Berkeley: University of California Press, 1972.

FILMS

13 rue Madelaine. Twentieth Century Fox, 1947.

Charlotte Gray. Warner Brothers, 2001.

Conspiracy. HBO Films, 2004.

Eye of Vichy (L'Oeil de Vichy). Institut National de l'audiovisuel, TFI Films Production, 1993.

Is Paris Burning? (Paris, brulé-t-il?). Paramount Studios, 1966.

One Against the Wind. Republic Pictures, 1991.

Secrets of War. Image Entertainment Inc., 1998.

Sisters in the Resistance. Women Make Movies, 2000.

Spies: OSS Covert Action. Columbia House Company, 1992.

The Sorrow and the Pity. Milestone, 1969.

Weapons of the Spirit: the Astonishing Story of a Unique Conspiracy of Goodness. Chambon Foundation, 1989.

Wish Me Luck. BBC Television, 1988.

DOCUMENTS

All official reports, debriefings, radio transmissions and training information taken from declassified documents held by the following institutions:

National Archives and Records Administration
   College Park, MD
Imperial War Museum
   London, England
The Public Records Office,
   Kew, England
Centre de la Résistance et de la Déportation
   Lyon, France
Archives de France
   Paris, France

INDEX